Advanced Applications of Python Data Structures and Algorithms

Mohammad Gouse Galety
Department of Computer Science, Samarkand International University of Technology, Uzbekistan

Arul Kumar Natarajan
CHRIST University (Deemed), India

A. V. Sriharsha
MB University, India

A volume in the Advances in Systems Analysis, Software Engineering, and High Performance Computing (ASASEHPC) Book Series

Published in the United States of America by
  IGI Global
  Engineering Science Reference (an imprint of IGI Global)
  701 E. Chocolate Avenue
  Hershey PA, USA 17033
  Tel: 717-533-8845
  Fax: 717-533-8661
  E-mail: cust@igi-global.com
  Web site: http://www.igi-global.com

Library of Congress Cataloging-in-Publication Data

Names: Galety, Mohammad Gouse, 1976- editor. | Natarajan, Arulkumar, 1986-
    editor. | AV, Sriharsha, editor.
Title: Advanced applications of Python data structures and algorithms /
    edited by Mohammad Galety, Arulkumar Natarajan, Sriharsha AV.
Description: Hershey, PA : Engineering Science Reference, [2023] | Includes
    bibliographical references and index. | Summary: "Assist in
    understanding and applying the fundamentals of data structures and their
    many implementations. Data structures play a critical role in creating
    efficient applications. To improve one's ability to solve problems by
    utilizing proper data formats. Upon successful completion of reading
    this textbook, students will have gained the ability to: Recognize and
    use the most fundamental types of data structures and algorithms. Be
    familiar with the advantages and disadvantages of various data
    structures. Use the proper data structure in the given problem's
    solution context. Improve your ability to program to address a
    particular problem. To distinguish between programmers and
    non-programmers, it is necessary to know about Data Structures and
    Algorithms"-- Provided by publisher.
Identifiers: LCCN 2022050718 (print) | LCCN 2022050719 (ebook) | ISBN
    9781668471005 (h/c) | ISBN 9781668471012 (s/c) | ISBN 9781668471029
    (eISBN)
Subjects: LCSH: Python (Computer program language) | Data structures
    (Computer science) | Computer algorithms.
Classification: LCC QA76.73.P98 A37 2023 (print) | LCC QA76.73.P98
    (ebook) | DDC 005.13/3--dc23/eng/20230104
LC record available at https://lccn.loc.gov/2022050718
LC ebook record available at https://lccn.loc.gov/2022050719

This book is published in the IGI Global book series Advances in Systems Analysis, Software
Engineering, and High Performance Computing (ASASEHPC) (ISSN: 2327-3453; eISSN: 2327-
3461)

British Cataloguing in Publication Data
A Cataloguing in Publication record for this book is available from the British Library.

All work contributed to this book is new, previously-unpublished material.
The views expressed in this book are those of the authors, but not necessarily of the publisher.

For electronic access to this publication, please contact: eresources@igi-global.com.

Advances in Systems Analysis, Software Engineering, and High Performance Computing (ASASEHPC) Book Series

ISSN:2327-3453
EISSN:2327-3461

Editor-in-Chief: Vijayan Sugumaran Oakland University, USA

MISSION

The theory and practice of computing applications and distributed systems has emerged as one of the key areas of research driving innovations in business, engineering, and science. The fields of software engineering, systems analysis, and high performance computing offer a wide range of applications and solutions in solving computational problems for any modern organization.

The **Advances in Systems Analysis, Software Engineering, and High Performance Computing (ASASEHPC) Book Series** brings together research in the areas of distributed computing, systems and software engineering, high performance computing, and service science. This collection of publications is useful for academics, researchers, and practitioners seeking the latest practices and knowledge in this field.

COVERAGE

- Storage Systems
- Engineering Environments
- Computer System Analysis
- Distributed Cloud Computing
- Network Management
- Virtual Data Systems
- Software Engineering
- Enterprise Information Systems
- Performance Modelling
- Human-Computer Interaction

IGI Global is currently accepting manuscripts for publication within this series. To submit a proposal for a volume in this series, please contact our Acquisition Editors at Acquisitions@igi-global.com or visit: http://www.igi-global.com/publish/.

Titles in this Series

For a list of additional titles in this series, please visit:
www.igi-global.com/book-series/advances-systems-analysis-software-engineering/73689

Neuromorphic Computing Systems for Industry 4.0
S. Dhanasekar (Department of ECE, Sree Eshwar Engineering College, India) K. Martin Sagayam (Karunya Institute of Technology and Sciences, India) Surbhi Vijh (KIET Group of Institutions, India) Vipin Tyagi (Jaypee University of Engineering and Technology, India) and Alex Norta (Tallinn University of Technology, Estonia)
Engineering Science Reference • © 2023 • 300pp • H/C (ISBN: 9781668465967) • US $270.00

Business Models and Strategies for Open Source Projects
Francisco José Monaco (Universidade de São Paulo, Brazil)
Business Science Reference • © 2023 • 300pp • H/C (ISBN: 9781668447857) • US $270.00

Principles, Policies, and Applications of Kotlin Programming
Duy Thanh Tran (University of Economics and Law, Ho Chi Minh City, Vietnam & Vietnam National University, Ho Chi Minh City, Vietnam) and Jun-Ho Huh (Korea Maritime and Ocean University, South Korea)
Engineering Science Reference • © 2023 • 457pp • H/C (ISBN: 9781668466872) • US $215.00

Concepts and Techniques of Graph Neural Networks
Vinod Kumar (Koneru Lakshmaiah Education Foundation (Deemed), India) and Dharmendra Singh Rajput (VIT University, India)
Engineering Science Reference • © 2023 • 247pp • H/C (ISBN: 9781668469033) • US $270.00

Cyber-Physical System Solutions for Smart Cities
Vanamoorthy Muthumanikandan (Vellore Institute of Technology, Chennai, India) Anbalagan Bhuvaneswari (Vellore Institute of Technology, Chennai, India) Balamurugan Easwaran (University of Africa, Toru-Orua, Nigeria) and T. Sudarson Rama Perumal (ROHINI College of Engineering and Technology, India)
Engineering Science Reference • © 2023 • 300pp • H/C (ISBN: 9781668477564) • US $270.00

701 East Chocolate Avenue, Hershey, PA 17033, USA
Tel: 717-533-8845 x100 • Fax: 717-533-8661
E-Mail: cust@igi-global.com • www.igi-global.com

Table of Contents

Detailed Table of Contents

Chapter 1

D. Varshaa, Coimbatore Institute of Technology, India
A. Keerthana Devi, Coimbatore Institute of Technology, India
M. Sujithra, Coimbatore Institute of Technology, India

Computer science encompasses various subfields, with data structures and algorithms being important. This chapter aims to enhance proficiency in constructing and analyzing data structures effectively. Studying data structures equips students with the skills to solve real-world problems using suitable structures. The study of data structures offers diverse programming techniques for complex problems yet introduces challenges due to intricate complexities that reshape program architecture. Covering all aspects in a single semester is impractical, as data structures receive extensive attention in graduate, upper-division, and lower-division programs. This text is an introductory resource for the stack, queue, linked list, graph, trees, searching, and sorting algorithms. It also offers insights into their Python implementation and its complexities, applications, and sample code.

Chapter 2

Saleem Raja Abdul Samad, University of Technology and Applied
  Sciences, Shinas, Oman
N. Arulkumar, CHRIST University (Deemed), India
Justin Rajasekaran, University of Technology and Applied Sciences,
  Shinas, Oman
R. Vinodini, Little Angels Institute, Karur, India
Pradeepa Ganesan, University of Technology and Applied Sciences,
  Shinas, Oman

Computer programming aims to organize and process data to get the desired result. Software developer chooses a programming language for application development based on the data processing capabilities of the language. The list is one of the sequential data structures in Python. A list is limited to a particular data type, such as numbers or strings. Occasionally, a list may include data of mixed types, including numbers and strings. Elements in the list can be accessed by using the index. Usually, a list's elements are enclosed within square brackets and divided using commas. The list may be referred to as a dynamic-sized array, which denotes that its size increases as additional data is added and that its size is not predefined. List data structure allows repetition; hence, a single data item may appear several times in a list. The list assists us in solving several real-world problems. This chapter deals with the list's creation and manipulation, the complexity of processing the list, sorting, stack, and queue operations.

Chapter 3

Kavita Srivastava, Institute of Information Technology and Management, GGSIP University, India

In a linear data structure, the elements are arranged in a specific order. Each element on a linear data structure is connected to the elements that proceed it as well as the element that follows it. In other words, the elements are placed in sequential order. Hence, it is possible to traverse the elements in sequential order in a single pass. The objective of the chapter is to provide a basic understanding of linear data structures and their implementation in Python. The chapter is organized as follows. The chapter starts with an introduction to the linear data structure. The objective is to provide a basic understanding of linear data structures. A comparison of linear data structures and non-linear data structures is given next. Next, all of the above-mentioned data structures are explained in brief. The Python implementation of all of these data structures is provided. After that, their applications and their implementation in Python is discussed. The chapter concludes by highlighting the essential concepts.

Chapter 4

S. Rajasekaran, University of Technology and Applied Sciences, Ibri, Oman
Mastan Vali Shaik, University of Technology and Applied Sciences, Ibri, Oman

The chapter provides a comprehensive and in-depth exploration of two fundamental linear data structures in computer science: Stack and Queue. It begins with an introduction to these data structures, highlighting their key features and fundamental differences. It then explains various operations that can be performed on both data structures, such as push, pop, enqueue, and dequeue. These implementations are thoroughly compared and contrasted, highlighting their advantages and disadvantages. These applications arc discussed in detail, showcasing the versatility of Stack and Queue data structures in different scenarios. The chapter includes Python code snippets demonstrating Stack and Queue data structures further to aid the reader's understanding of the material. This chapter provides a comprehensive and practical guide to Stack and Queue data structures, making it a valuable resource for computer science students, researchers, and practitioners.

Chapter 5

Gurram Sunitha, School of Computing, Mohan Babu University,
Tirupati, India
Arman Abouali, Technical University Clausthal, Germany
Mohammad Gouse Galety, Samarkand International University of
Technology, Uzbekistan
A. V. Sriharsha, Mohan Babu University, India

Algorithms are at the heart of computer programming. They form the basis of all software applications and help to solve complex computational problems. Various problem-solving strategies involve divide and conquer, greedy, recursion, dynamic programming, backtracking, etc. This can be used to solve optimization problems that have overlapping subproblems. It aims to find an optimal solution by breaking down a problem into sub-problems in order to manage the complexity of the problem-solving and remembering their solutions in order to avoid repeating computation time in future steps. Mathematical optimization is a crucial component of dynamic programming, and it allows us to efficiently solve a wide range of problems that involve making decisions over time. This chapter discusses dynamic programming's relevance, mathematical optimization, ability to solve a wide range of issues, important qualities, and top-down and bottom-up problem-solving methodologies. Dynamic programming solves some typical computational problems effectively, and Python code is supplied for reference.

Chapter 6

R. Sruthi, Coimbatore Institute of Technology, India
G. B. Anuvarshini, Coimbatore Institute of Technology, India
M. Sujithra, Coimbatore Institute of Technology, India

Data science is extremely important because of the immense value of data. Python provides extensive library support for data science and analytics, which has functions, tools, and methods to manage and analyze data. Python Libraries are used for exploratory data analysis. Libraries in Python such as Numpy, Pandas, Matplotlib, SciPy, etc. are used for the same. Data visualization's major objective is to make it simpler to spot patterns, trends, and outliers in big data sets. One of the processes in the data science process is data visualization, which asserts that after data has been gathered, processed, and modelled, it must be represented to draw conclusions. As a result, it is crucial to have systems in place for managing and regulating the quality of corporate data, metadata, and data sources. So, this chapter focuses on the libraries used in Python, their properties, functions, how few data structures are related to them, and a detailed explanation about their purpose serving as a better foundation for learning them.

Chapter 7

Tesfaye Fufa Gedefa, Space Science and Geospatial Institute, Ethiopia
Galety Mohammed Gouse, Samarkand International University of
*   Technology, Uzbekistan*
Garamu Tilahun Iticha, Debre Markos University, Ethiopia

NumPy is a Python library for performing numerical data structures and specialized computing. It improves the components of N-dimensional arrays and provides operations and tools to interface with these arrays. NumPy implements the N-dimensional array, or ndarray, and provides Python-specific scientific methods for performing realistic array and matrix operations. When compared to array programming in other languages, it will allow us to do a wide range of mathematical operations and data manipulations. NumPy can be used with other Python packages and programming languages such as C and C++. NumPy now supports object-oriented programming as well. For example, a class called ndarray may be an N-dimensional array with multiple ways of performing various data structure operations and characteristics.

Chapter 8

Mastan Vali Shaik, University of Technology and Applied Sciences, Ibri,
*   Oman*
Rajasrkaran Selvaraju, University of Technology and Applied Sciences,
*   Ibri, Oman*

One of the powerful data types for programmers that a Python supports is a list. A list is a mutable data structure that holds an ordered collection of items. Lists are useful to work with related data. A tuple is an immutable data type that stores values in a sequence. Slicing can be used to get a range of items. In Python, a set is variable that can store a variety of data, and different data types perform different operations.

A set data type in Python is used to store multiple values in a single variable. In Python, dictionary is one of the built-in data types where elements are key: value pairs. In other programming languages, these are called associative memory or associative arrays. Dictionaries are faster in execution, provide easy lookups, and are implemented as hash tables. This chapter focuses on data collection in Python.

Chapter 9

    Gurram Sunitha, School of Computing, Mohan Babu University,
        Tirupati, India
    A. V. Sriharsha, Mohan Babu University, India
    Olimjon Yalgashev, Samarkand International University of Technology,
        Uzbekistan
    Islom Mamatov, Samarkand International University of Technology,
        Uzbekistan

Data visualisation is the process of visualizing data for the purpose of analyzing and correlating data to confirm complicated ideas and to spot visual patterns after an investigation. Data visualization allows data scientists to quickly identify visual patterns and trends that may not be immediately apparent from raw data. Visualization also enables us to build models that are easier for stakeholders to understand and apply. Data visualization is an essential tool for exploratory data analysis (EDA). Plotly Express is a terse, high-level Python visualization library. It is a wrapper module for Plotly library that provides simple interface for visualizing data in the form of various plots, maps, graph objects, layouts, traces, figures, etc. Plotly Express is a user-friendly, high-level interface to Plotly that generates easily styleable, interactive, beautiful, and informative figures visualizing various types of data. Plotly Express provides interactive visualizations.

Chapter 10

    P. Thamilselvan, Bishop Heber College, India

The advancement of technology has led to an exponential increase in the volume, velocity, and variety of data generated, necessitating the development of effective methods for analyzing and extracting valuable insights from large datasets. This research focuses on enhancing big data analytics and recommendation systems using Python, specifically employing hierarchical clustering and a filtering approach with the slicing technique. This study proposes a novel approach to leverage Python's capabilities in processing and analyzing big data. Hierarchical clustering algorithms organize and structure data into hierarchical groups, enabling efficient exploration and extraction of relevant information. Additionally, a filtering mechanism is integrated with the slicing technique, allowing for identifying and extracting specific subsets of data based on predefined criteria. Experiments are conducted using real-world datasets in the context of recommendation systems to evaluate the approach's effectiveness.

Chapter 11

Jency Jose, CHRIST University (Deemed), India
N. Arulkumar, CHRIST University (Deemed), India

Wireless sensor networks (WSNs) are widely utilized in various fields, including environmental monitoring, healthcare, and industrial automation. Optimizing energy consumption is one of the most challenging aspects of WSNs due to the limited capacity of the batteries that power the sensors. This chapter explores using Python libraries to optimize the energy consumption of WSNs. In WSNs, various nodes, including sensor, relay, and sink nodes, are introduced. How Python libraries such as NumPy, Pandas, Scikit-Learn, and Matplotlib can be used to optimize energy consumption is discussed. Techniques for optimizing energy consumption, such as data aggregation, duty cycling, and power management, are also presented. By employing these techniques and Python libraries, the energy consumption of WSNs can be drastically decreased, thereby extending battery life and boosting performance.

Chapter 12

Agrata Gupta, CHRIST University (Deemed), India
N. Arulkumar, CHRIST University (Deemed), India

Blockchain is the foundation of cryptocurrency and enables decentralized transactions through its immutable ledger. The technology uses hashing to ensure secure transactions and is becoming increasingly popular due to its wide range of applications. Python is a performant, secure, scalable language well-suited for blockchain applications. It provides developers free tools for faster code writing and simplifies crypto analysis. Python allows developers to code blockchains quickly and efficiently as it is a completely scripted language that does not require compilation. Different models such as SVR, ARIMA, and LSTM can be used to predict cryptocurrency prices, and many Python packages are available for seamlessly pulling cryptocurrency data. Python can also create one's cryptocurrency version, as seen with Facebook's proposed cryptocurrency, Libra. Finally, a versatile and speedy language is needed for blockchain applications that enable chain addition without parallel processing, so Python is a suitable choice.

#### Chapter 13

This chapter investigates Python's involvement in self-supervised contrastive learning (SSCL) for medical imagery with report generation. The research highlights the relevance of SSCL as a method for creating medical imaging reports and the benefits of implementing it using Python. The literature review gives a complete overview of SSCL approaches in medical imaging and shows the advantages of SSCL implementation using Python libraries such as PyTorch, TensorFlow, and Keras. The study's methodology describes the research topics, survey design, methods of data gathering, and analytic procedures. The study named SSCL-GMIR findings indicate that several practitioners utilize SSCL in medical imaging using Python modules. This study highlights Python's significance in implementing SSCL for creating medical imaging report documents, offering researchers and practitioners a more efficient and effective method for producing accurate and informative reports and diagnoses.

This chapter examines how Python can assist in predicting type 2 diabetes using insulin DNA sequences, given the substantial problem that biologists face in objectively evaluating diverse biological characteristics of DNA sequences. The chapter highlights Python's various libraries, such as NumPy, Pandas, and Scikit-learn, for data handling, analysis, and machine learning, as well as visualization tools, such as Matplotlib and Seaborn, to help researchers understand the relationship between different DNA sequences and type 2 diabetes. Additionally, Python's ease of integration with other bioinformatics tools, like BLAST, EMBOSS, and ClustalW, can help identify DNA markers that could aid in predicting type 2 diabetes. In addition, the initiative tries to identify unique gene variants of insulin protein that contribute to diabetes prognosis and investigates the risk factors connected with the discovered gene variants. In conclusion, Python's versatility and functionality make it a valuable tool for researchers studying insulin DNA sequences and type 2 diabetes prediction.

Preface

In today's rapidly evolving technological landscape, efficient data management and analysis are pivotal in numerous domains, ranging from scientific research and finance to healthcare and beyond. As the demand for sophisticated data processing and algorithmic solutions grows, Python has emerged as a powerful programming language, providing a rich ecosystem of data structures and algorithms. It is with great pleasure that we present *Advanced Applications of Python Data Structures and Algorithms*, a comprehensive compilation of cutting-edge techniques and practices that harness the full potential of Python to tackle complex data challenges.

This book delves into the depths of Python's data structures and algorithms, exploring their applications in diverse fields and showcasing the versatility of this language. It is designed for both seasoned professionals seeking to enhance their skills and beginners aspiring to master the art of data manipulation and algorithmic problem-solving.

Chapter 1, "Fundamentals of Data Structures: Stacks, Queues, Linked Lists, and Graphs," provides a solid foundation by introducing fundamental data structures and their applications.

Chapter 2, "Organizing Data Using List: A Sequential Data Structure," explores the intricacies of list data structures and their sequential nature, highlighting their significance in efficient data organization.

Chapter 3, "Linear Data Structures and Their Applications," takes a deeper dive into linear data structures such as arrays and explores their practical applications in various domains.

Chapter 4, "A Comprehensive Analysis of Stack and Queue Data Structures and Their Uses," delves into the nuances of stack and queue data structures, showcasing their importance and usage scenarios in different contexts.

Chapter 5, "Dynamic Programming With Python," offers an in-depth exploration of dynamic programming techniques, empowering readers to solve complex optimization problems efficiently.

Chapter 6, "Exploratory Data Analysis in Python," equips readers with essential skills to analyze and derive insights from complex datasets, employing Python's versatile libraries.

Chapter 7, "Empowering Scientific Computing and Data Manipulation With Numerical Python (NumPy)," emphasizes the role of NumPy in scientific computing, highlighting its powerful data manipulation and analysis capabilities.

Chapter 8, "Exploring Python's Powerful Data Collections," dives into Python's extensive collection of data structures, showcasing their applications and benefits in diverse scenarios.

Chapter 9, "Interactive Visualization With Plotly Express," introduces readers to the world of interactive data visualization using Plotly Express, enabling them to create captivating visual representations of their data.

Chapter 10, "Enhancing Big Data Analytics and Recommendation Systems With Python: Hierarchical Clustering and Filtering Using Slicing Technique," focuses on applying Python in advanced analytics, particularly hierarchical clustering and filtering techniques for big data and recommendation systems.

Chapter 11, "Optimizing Energy Consumption in Wireless Sensor Networks Using Python Libraries," explores how Python libraries can be leveraged to optimize energy consumption in wireless sensor networks, contributing to sustainable and efficient systems.

Chapter 12, "An Exploratory Study of Python's Role in the Advancement of Cryptocurrency and Blockchain Ecosystems," investigates Python's role in the evolution of cryptocurrency and blockchain technologies, shedding light on their potential applications and challenges.

Chapter 13, "Exploring the Role of Python in Self-Supervised Contrastive Learning for Generating Medical Imaging Reports," examines how Python facilitates self-supervised contrastive learning techniques in medical imaging, paving the way for automated report generation and improved healthcare diagnostics.

Chapter 14, "Python's Role in Predicting Type 2 Diabetes Using Insulin DNA Sequence," delves into the use of Python to predict and analyze type 2 diabetes using DNA sequence data, offering insights into the potential of Python in personalized medicine and healthcare.

This book aims to contribute to data structures and algorithms by exploring Python's capabilities and their applications in diverse domains. Delving into advanced topics and showcasing practical implementations equips readers with the tools to tackle complex data challenges and make informed decisions.

We hope that *Advanced Applications of Python Data Structures and Algorithm* serves as a valuable resource for researchers, data scientists, software engineers, and enthusiasts alike, empowering them to unlock the full potential of Python and revolutionize their approach to data management and algorithmic problem-solving.

We invite you to embark on this enlightening journey through the pages of this book and explore the endless possibilities that await you.

Mohammad Gouse Galety
Department of Computer Science, Samarkand International University of Technology, Uzbekistan

Arul Kumar Natarajan
CHRIST University (Deemed), India

A. V. Sriharsha
MB University, India

Acknowledgment

This book is based on the research conducted on Data Structures using Python programming. We are grateful to each other for encouraging us and starting the book editing, preserve with it, and finally publishing it.

We would not be able to get our work done without the continual support and vision of Elizabeth Barrantes, Assistant Development Editor; IGI Global is just incredible.

Finally, we would like to acknowledge with gratitude the support of (the editors) each other and the authors. This book would not have been possible without Dr Arul Kumar.

Introduction

This foreword serves as an introduction to *Advanced Applications of Python Data Structures and Algorithms*, an extensive guide that explores the vast capabilities of Python in the realm of data structures and algorithms. The book exemplifies Python's growing technological significance, presenting practical solutions to intricate problems.

Within the following pages, readers will embark on an engaging journey encompassing a diverse range of topics that vividly showcase the power and versatility of Python. The chapters cover various subjects, including Plotly Express for interactive visualization, utilizing lists for data organization, applying NumPy for scientific computing, and exploring Python's robust data collections. This well-structured progression of knowledge empowers readers with a profound understanding of the subject matter.

Advanced Applications of Python Data Structures and Algorithms effectively highlights Python's applicability in various domains, such as self-supervised contrastive learning, blockchain ecosystems, big data analytics, and medical imaging. Moreover, the book addresses critical concerns, including the prediction of type 2 diabetes and the optimization of energy consumption in wireless sensor networks, thus exemplifying Python's potential to tackle significant societal challenges.

The authors' meticulous crafting of each chapter seamlessly bridges theoretical foundations with practical applications. This collaborative endeavour presents readers with an invaluable resource to enhance their comprehension of Python, data structures, and algorithms. By delving into the depths of this book, readers will be inspired to unlock novel possibilities and achieve excellence in their pursuits. Unlock

Chapter 1
Fundamentals of Data Structures:
Stacks, Queues, Linked Lists, and Graphs

D. Varshaa
Coimbatore Institute of Technology, India

A. Keerthana Devi
Coimbatore Institute of Technology, India

M. Sujithra
Coimbatore Institute of Technology, India

ABSTRACT

Computer science encompasses various subfields, with data structures and algorithms being important. This chapter aims to enhance proficiency in constructing and analyzing data structures effectively. Studying data structures equips students with the skills to solve real-world problems using suitable structures. The study of data structures offers diverse programming techniques for complex problems yet introduces challenges due to intricate complexities that reshape program architecture. Covering all aspects in a single semester is impractical, as data structures receive extensive attention in graduate, upper-division, and lower-division programs. This text is an introductory resource for the stack, queue, linked list, graph, trees, searching, and sorting algorithms. It also offers insights into their Python implementation and its complexities, applications, and sample code.

DOI: 10.4018/978-1-6684-7100-5.ch001

INTRODUCTION

A data structure is a meticulously designed framework for organizing, manipulating, retrieving, and storing data. It encompasses a variety of simple and intricate forms, all devised to arrange data in a manner suited to specific use cases. Users can conveniently access and employ the required information using data structures. These structures facilitate data organization in a manner comprehensible to machines and individuals. A data structure can be either developed or selected to facilitate data storage for various operations. In certain instances, the core operations of an algorithm and the design of the data structure are closely intertwined. Each data structure incorporates details about the values and connections of the data, and in rare cases, it may include functions capable of modifying the data.

Conventional elementary data types, such as integers or floating-point numbers, often prove inadequate for effectively expressing the logical intent underlying data processing and application. However, programs involved in receiving, manipulating, and outputting information must be aware of how data should be organized to streamline the processing tasks. Data structures facilitate efficient utilization, persistence, and sharing by logically amalgamating individual data elements. They provide a formal model that delineates the arrangement of data elements. Data structures serve as the foundation for increasingly complex applications. These structures are constructed by aggregating data elements into logical units that represent abstract data types relevant to the algorithm or application at hand, thereby enabling the development of sophisticated systems.

STACK

A stack is a linear data structure that embodies the Last-In-First-Out (LIFO) principle (Carullo, 2020). Under this principle, the item most recently added to the stack is the first to be removed. The stack can be likened to a collection of plates, wherein the plate most recently placed on top is the one to be taken when selecting. Moreover, accessing the plate at the bottom necessitates removing all the plates above it. The stack data structure operates similarly, adhering to this analogy.

Operations On Stack

The following are vital operations associated with a stack data structure:

- **Push:** This operation involves adding an element to the top of the stack.
- **Pop:** This operation entails removing an element from the top of the stack.

- **IsEmpty:** This operation allows checking whether the stack is empty or not.
- **IsFull:** This operation verifies whether the stack has reached its maximum capacity.
- **Peek:** This operation permits retrieving the value of the top element without removing it.

Stack Implementation Using Python's Built-in List

Python's inherent data structure, the list, can be employed as a stack by utilizing specific methods. In place of the conventional "push()" operation, the "append()" method is utilized to add elements to the top of the stack, ensuring adherence to the Last-In-First-Out (LIFO) principle. Similarly, the "pop()" method facilitates the removal of elements from the stack in the prescribed LIFO order. The stack implementation using Python is given in Figure 1.

QUEUE

A queue is defined as a linear data structure characterized by open ends and the execution of operations according to the First In, First Out (FIFO) principle (Alcoz et al., 2020). Within this definition, a queue is a list where all additions occur at one end, and all deletions occur at the other. The operation is initiated on the element first pushed into the Queue. The general representation of Queue operations is given in Figure 2.

FIFO Principle of Queue

A queue exhibits similarities to a line of individuals awaiting ticket purchase, where the individual at the front of the line is the first to receive service, adhering to the "first come, first served" principle. The front of the Queue, also known as the head, represents the position of the entry prepared to be served, while the rear, referred to as the tail, denotes the position of the most recently added entry. The First-In-First-Out (FIFO) characteristic of a queue is visually illustrated in Figure 3.

Characteristics of Queue

The characteristics of a queue data structure encompass the following key aspects:

- **Versatility:** Queues can handle a wide range of data types.

Figure 1. Stack Implementation using Python

```python
# Creating an empty stack
def check_empty(stack):
    return len(stack) == 0

# Adding items into the stack
def push(stack, item):
    stack.append(item)
    print("pushed item: " + item)

# Removing an element from the stack
def pop(stack):
    if (check_empty(stack)):
        return "stack is empty"

    return stack.pop()

stack = create_stack()
push(stack, str(1))
push(stack, str(2))
push(stack, str(3))
push(stack, str(4))
print("popped item: " + pop(stack))
print("stack after popping an element: " + str(stack))
```

Figure 2. Queue: Operations

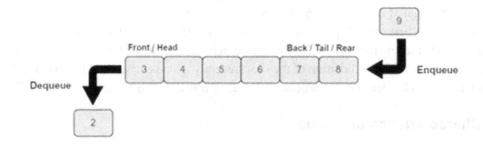

Figure 3. FIFO property of Queue

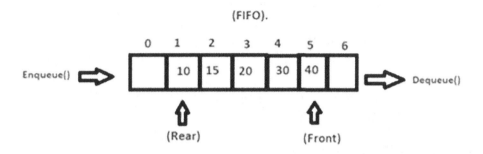

- **Accessibility:** Both ends of the Queue, the front, and the rear, are easily accessible for efficient operations.
- **Efficiency:** Queues demonstrate swift and smooth movement, facilitating effective data management.

Queue Representation Using Array

Queues can be represented using an array, similar to how stacks are implemented (Streib et al., 2017) (Patel, 2018). In this particular representation, the following variables are employed:

- **Queue:** This is the name assigned to the array that holds the elements of the Queue.
- **Front:** This variable indicates the index in the array where the first element of the Queue is stored.
- **Rear:** This variable denotes the index in the array where the last element of the Queue is stored.

LINKED LIST

A linked list comprises a sequence of interconnected data structures (Karimov, 2020) (Wiener, 2022). It is a collection of links with associated data referred to as elements. The relationship between one link and another is established through a connection known as "Next," whereby each link references the following link in the list. The linked list represents the second most commonly utilized data structure, surpassed only by the array. To comprehend the concept of a linked list, it is essential to familiarize oneself with the following key terms:

- **Link:** Each link within the linked list can store data elements.
- **Next:** This attribute of each link denotes the reference to the following link in the list, referred to as "Next."
- **LinkedList:** A Linked List encompasses the connection link to the initial link in the sequence, designated as "First."

Linked List Representation

The linked list can be perceived as a succession of nodes, wherein each node is connected to the next node. This visual representation of the linked list is illustrated in Figure 4, showcasing the overall structure.

Figure 4. Linked list representation

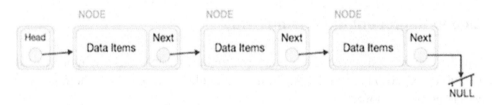

The linked list representation is given in Figure 4. Here, the primary constituent of Linked Lists is the initial link element, denoted as "first." Each link within the Linked List encompasses a data field or fields, and a link field is known as "next." Every link establishes a connection with the subsequent link in the sequence by utilizing its following link. To signify the termination point of the list, the final link is endowed with a null link.

Types of Linked Lists (Medjedovic & Tahirovic, 2022):

- **Simple Linked List:** Only forward item navigation is feasible in this type of linked list. It allows traversal in a single direction.
- **Doubly Linked List:** Unlike a simple linked list, a doubly linked list enables movement in both forward and backward directions. Each item within the list links to the next and previous elements.
- **Circular Linked List:** In a circular linked list, the first element is connected to the last element as its predecessor, while the last element is linked to the

first element as its successor. This circular arrangement allows for seamless cyclic traversal of the list.

Figure 5. Singly linked list: Insertion operation

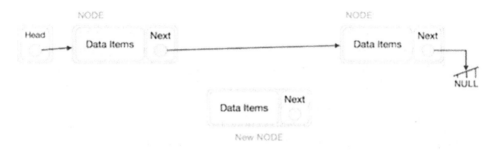

Linked List: Fundamental Operations

The following are the essential operations supported by a linked list:

- **Insertion:** This operation involves adding a new element to the beginning of the list, effectively updating the list's starting position.
- **Deletion:** The deletion operation removes the first member from the list, resulting in the adjustment of the list's structure.
- **Display:** The display operation presents the complete contents of the list, enabling comprehensive visualization of its elements.
- **Search:** By utilizing a specified key, the search operation aims to locate a particular element within the list.
- **Delete:** This operation involves the removal of an element from the list using a specified key, thereby eliminating the corresponding entry from the list's structure.

SINGLY LINKED LIST

Insertion Operation

Adding a new node to a linked list necessitates multiple steps. In this context, the process will be examined through diagrams (Almadhoun & Parham-Mocello, 2023). A node is to be created employing the identical structure, followed by identifying

7

the appropriate position for its placement. The procedure for inserting a node in a singly linked list is illustrated in Figure 5.

Deletion Operation

The deletion operation involves a sequence of steps that will be explained through visual representations. Initially, search algorithms are utilized to locate the target node within the linked list for removal. Subsequently, the necessary adjustments to the list's links are made. The node preceding the target node, commonly called the "left" node, is redirected to the node succeeding the target node. This ensures the continuity of the list's connectivity. Furthermore, the link associated with the target node is eradicated, eliminating the target node from the list. It becomes inaccessible via the preceding or succeeding nodes. The subsequent consideration pertains to the object stored within the target node. Based on the requirements, appropriate measures, such as memory deallocation, can be undertaken to remove the target node altogether. Lastly, after the deletion process, the removed node no longer exists within the linked list, and its memory allocation can be managed accordingly. Figure 6 illustrates the deletion operation in the singly linked list.

Figure 6. Singly linked list: Deletion operation

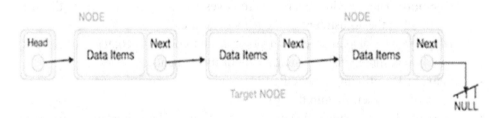

Reverse Operation

Reversing the linked list is executed with meticulous attention to detail, ensuring a complete reversal of the elements' order. To accomplish this, the last node in the list is modified to point back to the head node, effectively reversing the direction of the linked list. To commence the reverse operation, the traversal begins at the head and continues until the list ends. At this point, the pointer of the last node is adjusted to reference its preceding node, facilitating the reversal. Verifying that the last node is not the final node in the original list is imperative. To ensure this, a temporary node is introduced, resembling the head node and pointing to the last node. Subsequently, all nodes on the left side of the list are iteratively adjusted to point to their preceding nodes, sequentially reversing the pointers.

Except for the first node adjacent to the head node, all subsequent nodes are modified to point to their predecessor, effectively updating their successor. Consequently, the first node is assigned a NULL pointer. To complete the reversal process, the head node is updated to point to the new first node, utilizing the temporary node to facilitate this adjustment. As a result of these particular operations, the linked list undergoes a complete reversal, with the elements appearing in the reverse order compared to their original configuration. Figure 7 demonstrates the reverse operation in the linked list.

Figure 7. Singly linked list: Reverse operation

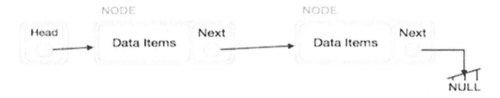

DOUBLY LINKED LIST

A variant of a linked list, known as a doubly linked list, provides enhanced navigation capabilities in both forward and backward directions compared to a single linked list (Besta et al., 2019). The fundamental terminology associated with the concept of a doubly linked list is outlined below.

- **Link:** Each link is a container for storing data elements within a linked list.
  - ○ **Next Link:** Every link in a linked list references the following link.
  - ○ **Prev Link:** Each link in a linked list references the preceding link.
- **LinkedList:** A LinkedList comprises a connecting link to the First and Last links, representing the initial and final links in the list, respectively.

Doubly Linked List: Representation

The doubly linked list representation is given in Figure 8. The following are the essential considerations:

- The doubly linked list consists of the first and last link elements.

- Each link encompasses one or more data fields beside the next and prev link fields.
- Each link establishes a connection with the following link through its next link.
- Each link establishes a connection with the preceding link through its prev link.
- The concluding link in the list is indicated by a null link, denoting the end of the list.

Figure 8. Doubly linked list representation

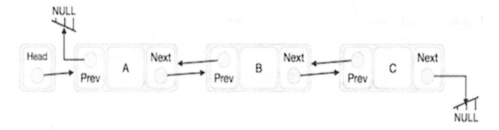

CIRCULAR LINKED LIST

A circular linked list is a variation of a linked list in which the first element points to the last element, and the last element points back to the first element. This circular structure can be formed from a singly linked or doubly linked list (Yang & Li, 2020; Sher, 2004).

Figure 9. Singly linked list as circular

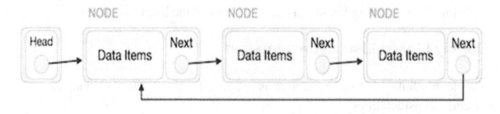

Singly Linked List as Circular

In the context of a singly linked list, it is noteworthy that the next pointer of the final node is directed toward the initial node. Figure 9 depicts the Singly Linked List represented as a circular structure.

Doubly Linked List as Circular

Within a doubly linked list, the establishment of a circular direction is achieved through the assignment of the previous pointer of the initial node to the last node, and correspondingly, the next pointer of the last node is directed towards the first node. Figure 10 showcases the Doubly Linked List represented as a circular structure.

The following are the key points to consider based on the given an example:

- In both a singly linked list and a doubly linked list, the "next" pointer of the last link points to the first link in the list.
- In the case of a doubly linked list, the "previous" pointer of the first link points to the last item.

Figure 10. Doubly linked list as circular

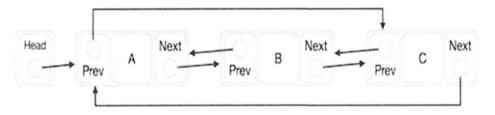

Fundamental Operations of a Circular List

A circular list supports the following significant operations:

- **Insertion:** This operation adds a new element to the beginning of the list.
- **Removal:** This operation removes an element from the beginning of the list.
- **Display:** This operation displays the contents of the list when selected.

Figure 11. Example of graph data structure

GRAPH

A group of nodes with data and connections to other nodes makes up a graph data structure (Chen et al., 2020). Let us use an illustration to try to comprehend this. Everything on Facebook is a node. Everything with data is a node, including User, Photo, Album, Event, Group, Page, Comment, Story, Video, Link, and Note. Every connection between two nodes is an edge. If you share a photo, join a group, "like" a page, etc., that relationship gains a new edge.

An example of graph data structure is given in Figure 11. The entirety of Facebook is represented by the collection of nodes and edges, constituting a graph data structure utilized for data storage (Souravlas et al., 2021). A graph (V, E) is a data structure comprising the following components:

- A collection of vertices denoted as V.
- A collection of edges is denoted as E, wherein each edge is represented as an ordered pair of vertices (u, v).

Terms in Graph data structure

- **Adjacent:** If there is an edge between two vertices, they are said to be adjacent.
- **Path:** A path is a sequence of edges that allows us to move from vertex A to vertex B.
- **Directed Graph:** A graph in which an edge (u,v) does not always imply the presence of an edge (v, u). Arrows represent edges in such a graph to indicate their direction.

Graph Representation

Graphs can be represented in two ways:

1. **Adjacency Matrix:** An adjacency matrix is a two-dimensional array of size V x V, where V represents the number of vertices in the graph. Each row and column within the matrix correspond to a vertex in the graph. If the value of any element a[i][j] is 1, it signifies the existence of an edge between vertex i and vertex j.
2. **Adjacency List:** An adjacency list is an array of linked lists representing a graph. The index of the array corresponds to a vertex, and each element within the linked list associated with that index represents the other vertices connected to the corresponding vertex by an edge.

Graph Operations

Graph operations encompass the following functionalities:

- **Element Existence Check:** This operation verifies the presence of an element within the graph.
- **Graph Traversal:** This operation involves traversing the graph to visit and explore its vertices and edges.
- **Element Addition:** This operation facilitates the addition of elements, including vertices and edges, to the graph.
- **Path Finding:** This operation determines the path between two specified vertices within the graph.

TREE

A tree is a nonlinear hierarchical data structure comprising nodes linked together by edges (Dutta, 2020) (Piatkowski, 2020). An example of tree data structure is given in Figure 12.

Figure 12. A tree data structure

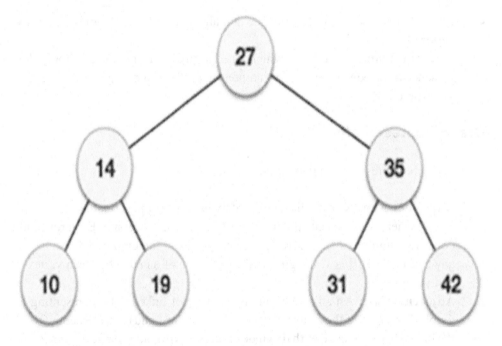

Binary Tree

A binary tree is a tree data structure in which each parent node has no more than two children. A binary tree node comprises three components: data item, address of the left child, and address of the right child.

Full Binary Tree

A full Binary tree is a binary tree in which each parent node/internal node has two or no children. Figure 13 displays a full binary tree.

Figure 13. Full binary tree

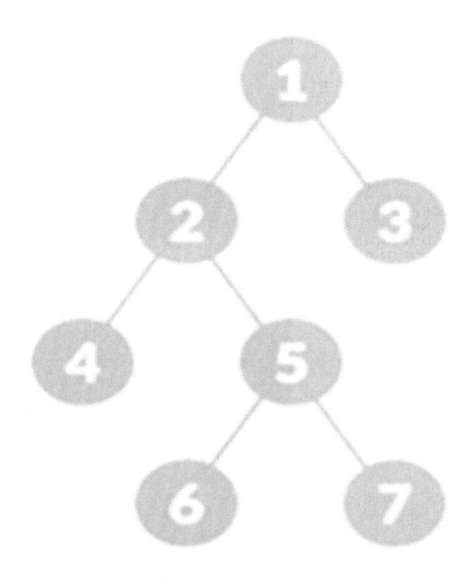

Python Implementation

Figure 14 showcases the Python implementation of a full binary tree.

Figure 14. Python implementation of full binary tree

```
class Node:
    def __init__(self, item):
        self.item = item
        self.leftChild = None
        self.rightChild = None
def isFull_bin_Tree(root):
    if root is None:
        return True
    if root.leftChild is None and root.rightChild is None:
        return True
    if root.leftChild is not None and root.rightChild is not None:
        return (isFullTree(root.leftChild) and isFullTree(root.rightChild))
    return False
root = Node(1)
root.rightChild = Node(3)
root.leftChild = Node(2)
root.leftChild.leftChild = Node(4)
root.leftChild.rightChild = Node(5)
root.leftChild.rightChild.leftChild = Node(6)
root.leftChild.rightChild.rightChild = Node(7)
if isFull_binTree(root):
    print("The tree is a full binary tree")
else:
    print("The tree is not a full binary tree")
```

Figure 15. Perfect binary tree

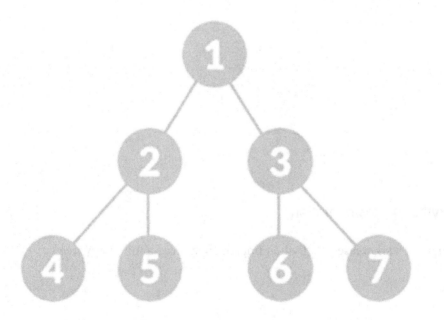

Figure 16. Python implementation of perfect binary tree

```python
class newNode:
    def __init__(self, k):
        self.key = k
        self.right = self.left = None
def calculateDepth(node):
    d = 0
    while (node is not None):
        d += 1
        node = node.left
    return d
def is_perfect(root, d, level=0):
    if (root is None):
        return True
    if (root.left is None and root.right is None):
        return (d == level + 1)
    if (root.left is None or root.right is None):
        return False
    return (is_perfect(root.left, d, level + 1) and
            is_perfect(root.right, d, level + 1))
root = None
root = newNode(1)
root.left = newNode(2)
root.right = newNode(3)
    print("The tree is a perfect binary tree")
else:
    print("The tree is not a perfect binary tree")
```

Perfect Binary Tree

A perfect binary tree is one in which each internal node has exactly two child nodes, and all leaf nodes are on the same level. An example of perfect binary tree is given in Figure 15.

Python Implementation

The Python implementation of a perfect binary tree is presented in Figure 16.

Figure 17. Complete binary tree

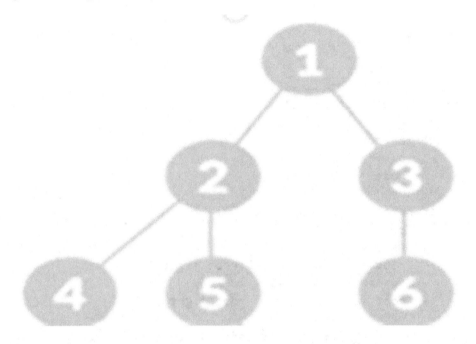

Complete Binary Tree

In contrast to a full binary tree, a complete binary tree exhibits two significant distinctions. Firstly, a complete binary tree mandates that each level be filled, necessitating the presence of all nodes at each respective level. Secondly, each leaf component of a complete binary tree must lean towards the left, signifying that the left subtree of every node is populated before the right subtree. It is crucial to acknowledge that while a complete binary tree satisfies the conditions above, it does not invariably qualify as a full binary tree. The absence of a right sibling for the last leaf element in a complete binary tree indicates the potential absence of a right-sided child node. Figure 17 displays the complete binary tree.

Python Implementation

Figure 18 presents the Python implementation of a complete binary tree.

Balanced Binary Tree

It is a binary tree in which each node's left and right subtree height differences are either 0 or 1. Balanced binary tree is given in Figure 19.

Figure 18. Python implementation of complete binary tree

```python
class Node:
    def __init__(self, item):
        self.item = item
        self.left = None
        self.right = None
def count_nodes(root):
    if root is None:
        return 0
    return (1 + count_nodes(root.left) + count_nodes(root.right))
def is_complete(root, index, numberNodes):
    if root is None:
        return True
    if index >= numberNodes:
        return False
    return (is_complete(root.left, 2 * index + 1, numberNodes)
            and is_complete(root.right, 2 * index + 2, numberNodes))
root = Node(1)
root.left = Node(2)
root.right = Node(3)
root.left.left = Node(4)
root.left.right = Node(5)
root.right.left = Node(6)
node_count = count_nodes(root)
index = 0
if is_complete(root, index, node_count):
    print("The tree is a complete binary tree")
else:
    print("The tree is not a complete binary tree")
```

Figure 19. Balanced binary tree with depth represented by df

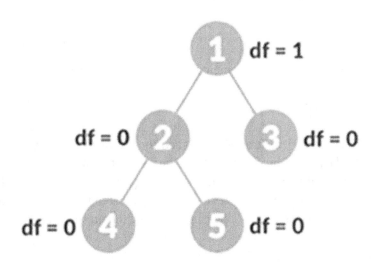

Figure 20. Python implementation of balanced binary tree

```python
class Node:
    def __init__(self, data):
        self.data = data
        self.left = self.right = None
class Height:
    def __init__(self):
        self.height = 0
def isHeightBalanced(root, height):
    left_height = Height()
    right_height = Height()
    if root is None:
        return True
    l = isHeightBalanced(root.left, left_height)
    r = isHeightBalanced(root.right, right_height)
    height.height = max(left_height.height, right_height.height) + 1
    if abs(left_height.height - right_height.height) <= 1:
        return l and r
    return False
height = Height()
root = Node(1)
root.left = Node(2)
root.right = Node(3)
root.left.left = Node(4)
root.left.right = Node(5)
if isHeightBalanced(root, height):
    print('The tree is balanced')
else:
    print('The tree is not balanced')
```

Python Implementation

Figure 20 describes the Python implementation of a Balanced Binary Tree.

Binary Search Tree

Binary search trees are a data structure designed for efficiently managing sorted lists of numbers. The term "binary" stems from the fact that each tree node can have a maximum of two children. This structure enables quick searching of numbers, with a time complexity of O(log(n)), hence the name "search tree." By leveraging the properties of binary search trees, one can determine the presence or absence of a number with significant efficiency.

The following are the properties of the Binary Search Tree:

Figure 21. AVL tree

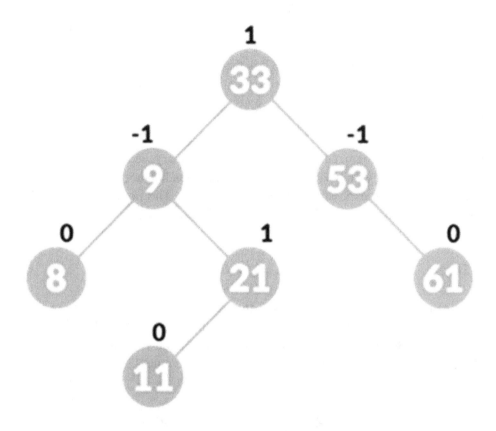

Figure 22. B-tree

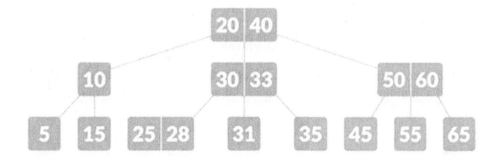

- The first characteristic of a binary search tree (BST) is that the root node is greater than all nodes of the left subtree.
- The second characteristic states that every node in the right subtree of a BST exceeds the root node in value.
- The third characteristic of a BST is that each node's two subtrees are also BSTs, meaning they possess the first two characteristics.

AVL Tree

The AVL tree, recognized as a self-balancing binary search tree, includes supplementary data within each node, referred to as the balance factor. This factor assumes one of three possible values: -1, 0, or +1. The nomenclature "AVL" originates from its creators, Georgy Adelson-Velsky and Landis. The AVL tree is depicted in Figure 21.

B-Tree

A distinctive type of self-balancing search tree, referred to as a "B-tree," incorporates the capability for each node to accommodate multiple keys and children. It is also recognized by the term "height-balanced m-way tree" as an alternative designation. The graphical depiction of the B-Tree is presented in Figure 22.

Properties:

- For every node x, the keys are stored in ascending order.
- A Boolean value x. The leaf is present within each node, representing its status as a leaf node when set to true.
- In the case of a tree with an order of n, an internal node can hold a maximum of n - 1 keys, accompanied by a pointer to each child.
- Each node can possess a minimum of n/2 children and a maximum of n children except for the root.
- All leaves share an equal depth, also known as the height (h) of the tree.
- The root must have at least two children and contain one key.
- If n is greater than or equal to 1, then for any B-tree with n keys, a height (h) and a minimum degree (t) of at least 2, the inequality $h \geq \log t(n+1)/2$ holds true.

B+Tree

A B+ tree constitutes an advanced variant of a self-balancing tree structure wherein all the values reside within the leaf level.

Properties:

1.   All leaves are at the same level.
2.   The root has at least two children.
3.   Each node except the root can have a maximum of m children and at least m/2 children.
4.   Each node can contain a maximum of m - 1 key and a minimum of $\lceil m/2 \rceil$ - 1 key.

Red-Black Tree

The Red-Black tree is a self-balancing binary search tree that incorporates an additional bit within each node to indicate its color, either red or black.
     Properties:

•   The Red/Black Property states that each node is assigned a red or black color.
•   According to the Root Property, the tree's root node is always black.
•   The Leaf Property specifies that all leaf nodes (NIL nodes) in the tree are black.
•   As per the Red Property, if a node is colored red, all its children must be colored black.
•   The Depth Property asserts that for any given node, every direct path from that node to any of its descendant leaves contains an equal number of black nodes.

SEARCHING

Searching is finding a specific element within a data collection (Mehlhorn, 2013; Kochenderfer & Wheeler, 2019).

Linear Search

In a sequential search technique such as linear search, the search process initiates from one end of the list and progressively examines each element until the target element is encountered. Linear search is recognized as the most elementary and direct search algorithm.

Figure 23. Binary search

```python
def binarySearch(array, x, low, high):
    while low <= high:
        mid = low + (high - low)//2
        if array[mid] == x:
            return mid
        elif array[mid] < x:
            low = mid + 1
        else:
            high = mid - 1
    return -1
```

Binary Search

The process of determining the position of an element within a sorted array can be accomplished by utilizing a search technique known as binary search. This approach involves consistently searching the middle element of the array for the desired element. The binary search algorithm can be implemented through two distinct methods, elucidated as follows:

- Iterative Method
- Recursive Method

Python Implementation

The Python implementation of the Binary Search using the iterative method is illustrated in Figure 23.

Figure 24. Bubble sort

```python
def bubbleSort(array):
    for i in range(len(array)):
        for j in range(0, len(array) - i - 1):
            if array[j] > array[j + 1]:
                temp = array[j]
                array[j] = array[j+1]
                array[j+1] = temp
```

SORTING

Sorting is arranging elements in a specific order within a data collection. Various sorting algorithms are available to achieve this task efficiently.

Bubble Sort

Bubble Sort is a sorting algorithm that analyzes adjacent elements and swaps them iteratively until the desired order is achieved (Inayat, 2021).

Python Implementation

Figure 24 provides the Python implementation of the bubble sort algorithm.

Figure 25. Selection sort

```python
def selectionSort(array, size):
    for step in range(size):
        min_idx = step
        for i in range(step + 1, size):
            if array[i] < array[min_idx]:
                min_idx = i
        (array[step], array[min_idx]) = (array[min_idx], array[step])
```

Figure 26. Insertion sort

```python
def insertionSort(array):
    for step in range(1, len(array)):
        key = array[step]
        j = step - 1
        while j >= 0 and key < array[j]:
            array[j + 1] = array[j]
            j = j - 1
        array[j + 1] = key
```

Selection Sort

The selection sort, a well-known sorting algorithm, follows a procedure where the smallest element from an unsorted list is chosen during each iteration and subsequently inserted at the beginning of the list (Salihu et al., 2022).

Python Implementation

Figure 25 presents the Python implementation of the Selection sort algorithm.

Insertion Sort

Insertion sort is an efficient sorting algorithm that, following each iteration, strategically inserts an unsorted element into its correct position within the sorted portion of the array (Arslan, 2022).

Python Implementation

The Python implementation of the Insertion sort algorithm can be found in Figure 26.

Merge Sort

Merge sort is a highly utilized sorting algorithm that is founded upon the fundamental concept of the Divide and Conquer algorithm. It involves decomposing a complex

Figure 27. Merge sort

```
void merge(int arr[], int p, int q, int r) {
    int n1 = q - p + 1;
    int n2 = r - q;
    int L[n1], M[n2];
    for (int i = 0; i < n1; i++)
        L[i] = arr[p + i];
    for (int j = 0; j < n2; j++)
        M[j] = arr[q + 1 + j];
    int i, j, k;
    i = 0;
    j = 0;
    k = p;
    while (i < n1 && j < n2) {
        if (L[i] <= M[j]) {
            arr[k] = L[i];
            i++;
        } else {
            arr[k] = M[j];
            j++;
        }
        k++;
    }
    while (i < n1) {
        arr[k] = L[i];
        i++;
        k++;
    }
    while (j < n2) {
        arr[k] = M[j];
        j++;
        k++;
    }
}
```

problem into multiple smaller subproblems, individually resolving each subproblem and subsequently integrating the sub-solutions to obtain the final complete solution.

Python Implementation

Figure 27 presents the Python implementation of the Merge sort algorithm.

Figure 28. Quick sort

```python
def partition(array, low, high):
    pivot = array[high]
    i = low - 1
    for j in range(low, high):
        if array[j] <= pivot:
            i = i + 1
            (array[i], array[j]) = (array[j], array[i])
    (array[i + 1], array[high]) = (array[high], array[i + 1])
    return i + 1
def quickSort(array, low, high):
    if low < high:
        pi = partition(array, low, high)
        quickSort(array, low, pi - 1)
        quickSort(array, pi + 1, high)
data = [8, 7, 2, 1, 0, 9, 6]
print("Unsorted Array")
print(data)
size = len(data)
quickSort(data, 0, size - 1)
print('Sorted Array in Ascending Order:')
print(data)
```

Quick Sort

Quicksort is a divide-and-conquer sorting algorithm that selects a pivot element from the array to divide it into subarrays. During the partitioning process, the pivot element is positioned such that elements greater than the pivot are placed on the right side, while elements smaller than the pivot are placed on the left side. The same partitioning method is applied recursively to the left and right subarrays until each subarray contains only one element. At this stage, the individual elements are sorted, and combining them results in a sorted array.

Python Implementation

Figure 28 presents the Python implementation of the Quick Sort algorithm.

Figure 29. Counting sort

```python
def countingSort(array):
    size = len(array)
    output = [0] * size
    count = [0] * 10
    for i in range(0, size):
        count[array[i]] += 1
    for i in range(1, 10):
        count[i] += count[i - 1]
    i = size - 1
    while i >= 0:
        output[count[array[i]] - 1] = array[i]
        count[array[i]] -= 1
        i -= 1
    for i in range(0, size):
        array[i] = output[i]
```

Counting Sort

Counting Sort is a sorting technique that organizes the elements of an array based on the frequency of each distinct element. The sorting process is facilitated by mapping the count of each element to an index in an auxiliary array, which serves as a container for the counts.

Python Implementation

The Python implementation of the Counting Sort algorithm is illustrated in Figure 29.

Radix Sort

Radix Sort is a sorting technique that involves grouping the individual digits of the same place value before sorting the elements. Subsequently, the components are arranged in either ascending or descending order.

Figure 30. Radix sort

```python
def countingSort(array, place):
    size = len(array)
    output = [0] * size
    count = [0] * 10
    for i in range(0, size):
        index = array[i] // place
        count[index % 10] += 1
    for i in range(1, 10):
        count[i] += count[i - 1]
    i = size - 1
    while i >= 0:
        index = array[i] // place
        output[count[index % 10] - 1] = array[i]
        count[index % 10] -= 1
        i -= 1
    for i in range(0, size):
        array[i] = output[i]
def radixSort(array):
    max_element = max(array)
    place = 1
    while max_element // place > 0:
        countingSort(array, place)
        place *= 10
```

Python Implementation

Figure 30 showcases the Python implementation of the Radix Sort algorithm.

Bucket Sort

The bucket sort technique involves partitioning the elements of an unsorted array into multiple buckets. Subsequently, each bucket is sorted either by employing the recursive application of the bucket algorithm or by utilizing any suitable sorting algorithm.

Figure 31. Bucket sort

```python
def bucketSort(array):
    bucket = []
    for i in range(len(array)):
        bucket.append([])
    for j in array:
        index_b = int(10 * j)
        bucket[index_b].append(j)
    for i in range(len(array)):
        bucket[i] = sorted(bucket[i])
    k = 0
    for i in range(len(array)):
        for j in range(len(bucket[i])):
            array[k] = bucket[i][j]
            k += 1
    return array
```

Python Implementation

The Python implementation of the Bucket Sort algorithm is presented in Figure 31.

Figure 32. Heap sort

```python
def heapSort(arr):
    n = len(arr)
    for i in range(n//2, -1, -1):
        heapify(arr, n, i)
    for i in range(n-1, 0, -1):
        # Swap
        arr[i], arr[0] = arr[0], arr[i]
        heapify(arr, i, 0)
```

Heap Sort

The heap sort algorithm is prominent in computer programming due to its popularity and efficiency. This sorting technique necessitates comprehending two distinct data structures: arrays and trees.

Python Implementation

Figure 32 provides the Python implementation of the Heap Sort algorithm.

Shell Sort

Shell Sort is a well-known sorting algorithm that can be considered a generalized version of the insertion sort algorithm. It operates by sorting elements that are initially far apart from each other, gradually decreasing the interval between the components to be sorted.

Python Implementation

The Python implementation of the Shell Sort algorithm is illustrated in Figure 33.

Figure 33. Shell sort

```python
def shellSort(array, n):
    interval = n // 2
    while interval > 0:
        for i in range(interval, n):
            temp = array[i]
            j = i
            while j >= interval and array[j - interval] > temp:
                array[j] = array[j - interval]
                j -= interval
            array[j] = temp
        interval //= 2
```

CONCLUSION

The chapter introduces the concept of data structures, which are frameworks used for organizing, manipulating, retrieving, and storing data. Data structures facilitate efficient access and utilization of data by machines and individuals. The chapter focuses on three types of data structures: stacks, queues, and linked lists. A stack is a last-in-first-out (LIFO) data structure with operations like push, pop, isEmpty, isFull, and peek. A queue is a first-in-first-out (FIFO) data structure with similar operations. Linked lists consist of interconnected nodes, and there are different types like singly linked lists, doubly linked lists, and circular linked lists. The chapter also briefly mentions the graph data structure, consisting of nodes and edges representing relationships between data elements.

REFERENCES

Alcoz, A. G., Dietmüller, A., & Vanbever, L. (2020, February). SP-PIFO: Approximating Push-In First-Out Behaviors using Strict-Priority Queues. In NSDI (pp. 59-76). Academic Press.

Almadhoun, E., & Parham-Mocello, J. (2023). Students' difficulties with inserting and deleting nodes in a singly linked list in the C programming language. *Journal of Computer Languages*, *74*, 101184. doi:10.1016/j.cola.2022.101184

Arslan, B. (2022). *Search and Sort Algorithms for Big Data Structures*. Academic Press.

Besta, M., Peter, E., Gerstenberger, R., Fischer, M., Podstawski, M., Barthels, C., .. . Hoefler, T. (2019). *Demystifying graph databases: Analysis and taxonomy of data organization, system designs, and graph queries*. arXiv preprint arXiv:1910.09017.

Carullo, G. (2020). Data Structures. *Implementing Effective Code Reviews: How to Build and Maintain Clean Code*, 27-42.

Chen, Z., Wang, Y., Zhao, B., Cheng, J., Zhao, X., & Duan, Z. (2020). Knowledge graph completion: A review. *IEEE Access : Practical Innovations, Open Solutions*, *8*, 192435–192456. doi:10.1109/ACCESS.2020.3030076

Dutta, S., Chowdhury, A., Debnath, I., Sarkar, R., Dey, H., & Dutta, A. (2020). The role of data structures in different fields of computer-science: A review. *Journal of Mathematical Sciences & Computational Mathematics*, *1*(3), 363–373. doi:10.15864/jmscm.1310

Inayat, Z., Sajjad, R., Anam, M., Younas, A., & Hussain, M. (2021, November). Analysis of Comparison-Based Sorting Algorithms. In *2021 International Conference on Innovative Computing (ICIC)* (pp. 1-8). IEEE.

Karimov, E. (2020). Linked Lists. *Data Structures and Algorithms in Swift: Implement Stacks, Queues, Dictionaries, and Lists in Your Apps*, 41-54.

Kochenderfer, M. J., & Wheeler, T. A. (2019). *Algorithms for optimization*. MIT Press.

Medjedovic, D., & Tahirovic, E. (2022). *Algorithms and data structures for massive datasets*. Simon and Schuster.

Mehlhorn, K. (2013). *Data structures and algorithms 1: Sorting and searching* (Vol. 1). Springer Science & Business Media.

Patel, M. (2018). *Data Structure and Algorithm With C*. Educreation Publishing.

Piatkowski, J. (2020). The Conditional Multiway Mapped Tree: Modeling and Analysis of Hierarchical Data Dependencies. *IEEE Access : Practical Innovations, Open Solutions*, 8; 74083–74092. doi:10.1109/ACCESS.2020.2988358

Salihu, A., Hoti, M., & Hoti, A. (2022, December). A Review of Performance and Complexity on Sorting Algorithms. In *2022 International Conference on Computing, Networking, Telecommunications & Engineering Sciences Applications (CoNTESA)* (pp. 45-50). IEEE. 10.1109/CoNTESA57046.2022.10011382

Sher, D. B. (2004). A simple implementation of a queue with a circularly linked list. *SIGCSE Bulletin*, *36*(3), 274–274. doi:10.1145/1026487.1008112

Souravlas, S., Anastasiadou, S., & Katsavounis, S. (2021). A survey on the recent advances of deep community detection. *Applied Sciences (Basel, Switzerland)*, *11*(16), 7179. doi:10.3390/app11167179

Streib, J. T., Soma, T., Streib, J. T., & Soma, T. (2017). Stacks and Queues Using References. *Guide to Data Structures: A Concise Introduction Using Java*, 173-198.

Wiener, R. (2022). Queues and Lists. In *Generic Data Structures and Algorithms in Go: An Applied Approach Using Concurrency, Genericity and Heuristics* (pp. 187–236). Apress. doi:10.1007/978-1-4842-8191-8_6

Yang, Y., & Li, X. (2020, October). Design and Implementation of Sliding Window with Circular Linked List for Dynamic Data Flow. In *Proceedings of the 4th International Conference on Computer Science and Application Engineering* (pp. 1-5). 10.1145/3424978.3425152

Chapter 2
Organizing Data Using Lists:
A Sequential Data Structure

Saleem Raja Abdul Samad
University of Technology and Applied Sciences, Shinas, Oman

N. Arulkumar
CHRIST University (Deemed), India

Justin Rajasekaran
University of Technology and Applied Sciences, Shinas, Oman

R. Vinodini
Little Angels Institute, Karur, India

Pradeepa Ganesan
University of Technology and Applied Sciences, Shinas, Oman

ABSTRACT

Computer programming aims to organize and process data to get the desired result. Software developer chooses a programming language for application development based on the data processing capabilities of the language. The list is one of the sequential data structures in Python. A list is limited to a particular data type, such as numbers or strings. Occasionally, a list may include data of mixed types, including numbers and strings. Elements in the list can be accessed by using the index. Usually, a list's elements are enclosed within square brackets and divided using commas. The list may be referred to as a dynamic-sized array, which denotes that its size increases as additional data is added and that its size is not predefined. List data structure allows repetition; hence, a single data item may appear several times in a list. The list assists us in solving several real-world problems. This chapter deals with the list's creation and manipulation, the complexity of processing the list, sorting, stack, and queue operations.

DOI: 10.4018/978-1-6684-7100-5.ch002

Figure 1. Three items list

```
country=['india','oman','dubai']
```

THE BASICS OF LIST

Python has a sequence data type called List. It can ably hold multiple elements of different data types. However, it may have multiple elements of the same data type in practice. The elements in a list are separated by commas (Erciyes, 2021). All the elements in a list must be placed inside the square bracket [], as shown in Figure 1.

Accessing an Item in the List

A list is an ordered sequence of items, and each element is accessed by its index, as shown in Figure 2. The index must be an integer. The first item is indexed with [0], the second with [1], and so on.

Figure 2. Accessing an item in the list using an index

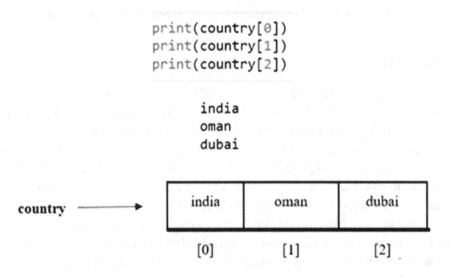

```
print(country[0])
print(country[1])
print(country[2])


india
oman
dubai
```

Python allows negative indexing for its sequences, as shown in Figure 3. The last item is represented by the index of -1, the second last by -2, and so on.

Figure 3. Accessing an item in the list using a negative index

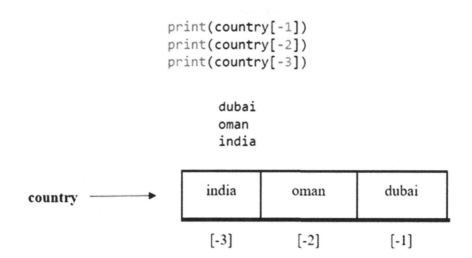

Changing an Item in the List

The List is mutable (Oliphant, 2007). That is, items in the List can be modified even after the creation of the List. After creating a list, objects may be added, removed, shifted, and moved about at will. Python provides several methods for modifying lists. To change an item or set of items in a list, we can use an assignment operation on the specific index or range of index positions (Schwarz et al., 2020). Figure 4 illustrates modifying an item or a set of items within a list by employing an index. This visualization showcases the steps involved in altering the content of the List, providing valuable insights into the manipulation of data using indexing techniques.

Adding Items to the List

The append() method is a popular option for adding a single item to an existing list. Using the append() function, adding an item to the end of a list is straightforward. This procedure is efficient and uncomplicated, preserving the original List's order. Attach() is particularly useful when adding a single element without modifying the existing objects.

In situations where multiple items are added to a list, the extend() method is applicable. extend(), unlike append(), permits the addition of numerous items to a list, effectively expanding its size. With the extend() function, it is possible to append multiple elements in a single operation, providing flexibility and efficiency. This

Figure 4. Changing an item/set of items in a list using an index

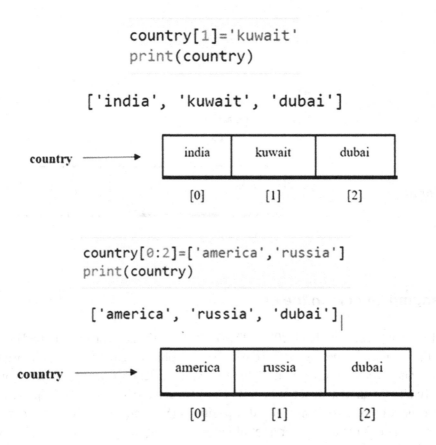

```
country[1]='kuwait'
print(country)
```

`['india', 'kuwait', 'dubai']`

country ⟶

india	kuwait	dubai
[0]	[1]	[2]

```
country[0:2]=['america','russia']
print(country)
```

`['america', 'russia', 'dubai']`

country ⟶

america	russia	dubai
[0]	[1]	[2]

method is advantageous when sequentially adding multiple items or combining two listings into one.

Although both methods can add items to a list, their functionality and application are distinct. The append() method excels at adding a single item to the end of a list, making the operation straightforward and concise. On the other hand, the extend() method is more versatile because it permits adding multiple elements at once. It is especially advantageous when multiple items or merge lists must be appended (Martelli, 2006).

In Figure 5, the item 'srilanka' is appended to the end of list 'country'. The extend() adds a specified set of items at the end of the existing List, as given in Figure 6.

Here the list "country_2" items are added to the end of the existing list 'country'. Table 1 showcases the Membership Operator in Python, illustrating its functionality and usage in different scenarios.

Figure 5. Adding an item to a list using the append() method

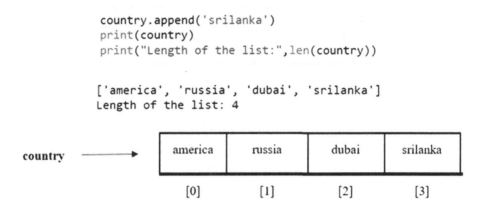

```
country.append('srilanka')
print(country)
print("Length of the list:",len(country))


['america', 'russia', 'dubai', 'srilanka']
Length of the list: 4
```

country ⟶	america	russia	dubai	srilanka
	[0]	[1]	[2]	[3]

Searching and Sorting the Items

Python's membership operator can be used to find the item in the List, as shown in Figure 7. Python has two membership operators (Dubois et al., 1996).

Figure 8 illustrates how the default ordering of the List's contents by Python's built-in sort() method is alphanumerical and ascending (Lutz Mark, 2013).

Figure 6. Adding a set of items into an existing list using extend() method

```
country_2=['india','england','canada']
country.extend(country_2)
print(country)
print("Length of the list:",len(country))

['america', 'russia', 'dubai', 'srilanka', 'india', 'england', 'canada']
Length of the list: 7
```

country ⟶	america	russia	dubai	srilanka	india	england	canada
	[0]	[1]	[2]	[3]	[4]	[5]	[6]

Table 1. Membership operator in Python

in	Returns True if the specified value is found in the List.
not in	Returns True if the specified value is not found in the List.

Figure 7. Searching an item in a list

```
if 'india' in country:
    print('The keyword india is present the country list')
    print('Its Index is :', country.index('india'))
if 'india' not in country:
    print('The keyword india is NOT present the country list')
```

```
The keyword india is present the country list
Its Index is : 3
```

Figure 8. Sorting the items in a list

```
print ("Before sorting the list:", country)
country.sort()
print("After sorting the list:", country)
```

```
Before sorting the list: ['america', 'russia', 'dubai', 'srilanka', 'india', 'england', 'canada']
After sorting the list: ['america', 'canada', 'dubai', 'england', 'india', 'russia', 'srilanka']
```

Time Complexity

Index lookup and assignment require a constant amount of time regardless of how long the List is; hence they are $O(1)$. Append has constant time complexity, i.e., $O(1)$. Extend has a time complexity of $O(k)$. Here, k is the list length that needs to be increased. $O(n \log n)$ time complexity is required for sorting (Navghare et al., 2020).

STACK

A fundamental data structure for effective data organization is the Stack. It is an ordered collection of items (data) that are accessed on a LAST IN FIRST OUT (LIFO) basis (Saabith et al., 2019). The end of the Stack, where items are added or removed, is considered the TOP of the Stack. The other end of the Stack is known as the BASE or BOTTOM. The most recently inserted item is always on top of the

Figure 9. PUSH and POP operation in stack

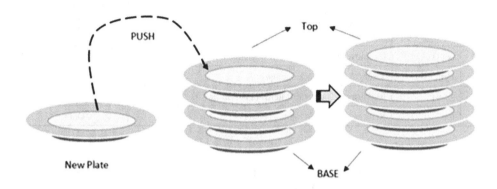

PUSH operation

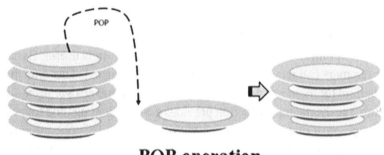

POP operation

Stack and can be removed first. Push and Pop are the terms for adding items to stacks and removing them from stacks.

The operations PUSH and POP in the Stack are shown in Figure 9 (Hetland, 2017). The top of the plate rack is for adding the new plates. Plates are removed from the bottom of the plate rack. Table 2 contains the most fundamental operations for a Stack.

The push(n) operation is an essential list function, as it permits the insertion of an item on top of the stack. The argument 'n' when utilizing push(n) represents the item to be added to the list. This operation guarantees that the new item is placed at the top of the array, where it can be accessed or modified as necessary. The pop() operation, on the other hand, functions to remove the uppermost element from the stack. This operation is beneficial when it is necessary to extract or delete a list item.

Table 2. Stack operations

No	Operation	Description	Time Complexity
1	push(n)	To insert an item on top of the Stack. The argument 'n' is an item to push.	O(1)
2	pop()	It removes the Stack's topmost element of the Stack.	O(1)
3	isempty()	To check if the Stack is empty.	O(1)
4	size()	It returns the number of items in the Stack.	O(1)
5	top()	Returns the Stack's topmost element.	O(1)

The prior element at the top of the list is removed when pop() is executed, making the element below it the new element at the top.

The isempty() function is utilized to determine whether a stack is empty or not. This operation determines whether or not the array contains elements. If the array is empty, this function returns true to indicate that no items are present. In contrast, if the stack is not empty, the function returns false, indicating the presence of list elements. When working with collections, it is frequently necessary to know how many items they comprise. This is where the size() function is useful. By utilizing size(), programmers can retrieve the number of stack elements. This information is especially helpful for memory management and determining the overall extent of the data structure. Lastly, the top() function provides a convenient method for accessing the stack's uppermost element without modifying the list. This operation retrieves the value of the item at the top of the stack, allowing developers to investigate or use it without modifying the structure of the list.

Code for stack operations using the List

```
# Empty List
country=[]
# Add an item on top of the Stack.
def push(x):
    country.append(x)
    print("push operation result:", country)
# Remove an item from the top of the Stack.
def pop():
    if (len(country)>0):
        x=country.pop()
        print("removed element:", x)
        print("pop operation result:", country)
# Check whether or not the Stack is empty.
```

```
def empty():
    if (len(country)==0):
        print("Stack is empty")
    else:
        print("Stack is NOT empty")
# Find the number of items in the Stack.
def size():
    print("size() operation result:", len(country))
# Find the top item in the Stack
def top():
    if (len(country)>0):
        x=country[-1]
        print("top of the stack is:", x)
while(1):
        print ("Stack Operations")
        print ("****************")
        print ("1. PUSH")
        print ("2. POP")
        print ("3. IS EMPTY")
        print ("4. SIZE")
        print ("5. TOP")
        print ("6. EXIT")
        inp=int(input("Enter your choice number"))
        if(inp > 6 | inp < 1):
            print("Wrong choice so try again ")
        else:
            if(inp == 1):
                name=input("Enter the country name to added in
the stack:")
                push(name)
            if(inp == 2):
                pop()
            if(inp == 3):
                empty()
            if(inp == 4):
                size()
            if(inp == 5):
                top()
            if (inp == 6):
```

Figure 10. ENQUEUE operation

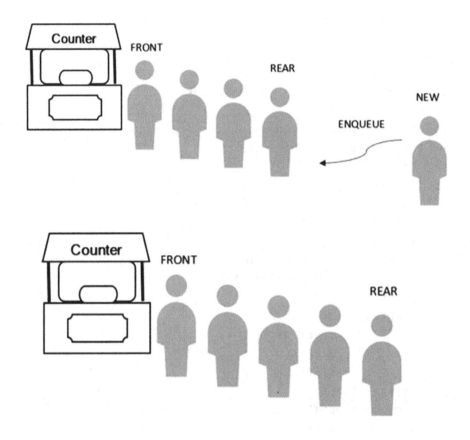

```
                    break
print("Completed >>>>")
```

QUEUE

A queue is a sequential data structure that stores items (data) in an order where new items are added at one end, generally called the "rear." The removal of an existing item occurs at the other end, commonly called the "front.". A newly added item to a queue will be at the rear of that queue. The first item added to the queue will be at the front. This concept is FIFO, which stands for "first in, first out" (Popescu & Bîră, 2022). ENQUEUE and DEQUEUE are used to add and delete items from the queue (Kobbaey et al., 2022) (Hunt, 2019).

Figure 11. DEQUEUE operation

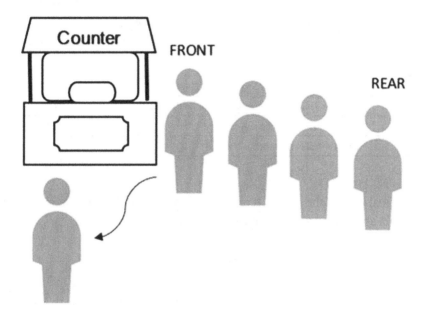

Figure 10 depicts the queue's ENQUEUE, and Figure 11 presents the DEQUEUE operations. At a ticket counter, people are standing in a queue. The first person to join the queue will also be the first to depart it. Table 3 lists the most frequent queue operations.

Enqueue(n), dequeue(), isempty(), size(), front(), and rear() are the operations conducted on a queue utilizing a list. The enqueue(n) operation appends a new item to the end of the queue, as indicated by the 'n' operand. It ensures that the newly added item is placed at the end of the sequence, preserving the order in which elements were added.

The dequeue() operation, on the other hand, removes the first item from the queue. By eliminating the item from the front of the queue, the FIFO principle is maintained by promoting the next item to the front. To determine whether the queue is vacant, we can use the isempty() function. It returns a Boolean value signifying whether the queue is vacant or contains elements. The size() function returns the quantity of elements presently in the queue. It provides valuable information regarding the queue's size and capacity, allowing us to manage and optimize the storage accordingly.

Moreover, the front() function permits access to the first item in the queue. It returns the element without removing it, which is beneficial when we need a sneak look at the subsequent item to be processed. Similarly, the rear() operation permits

Table 3. The most common queue operations

No	Operation	Description	Time Complexity
1	enqueue(n)	It adds a new item to the queue's end. Its 'n' argument denotes an item for addition.	O(1)
2	dequeue()	It removes the first item from the queue. It takes no parameters and returns the item.	O(1)
3	isempty()	To check if the queue is empty.	O(1)
4	size()	It has the details of the number of items in the queue.	O(1)
5	front()	The first item in the queue is returned.	O(1)
6	rear()	The last item in the queue is returned.	O(1)

access to the final item in the queue. It returns the element without removing it and provides details about the most recently inserted item.

Code for Queue operations using the List

```
# Empty List
country=[]
# Add an item on rear of the queue.
def enqueue(x):
    country.append(x)
    print("Enqueue operation result:", country)
# Remove an item from the front of the queue.
def dequeue():
    if (len(country)>0):
        x=country.pop(0)
        print("removed element:", x)
        print("Dequeue operation result:", country)
# Check whether or not the queue is empty.
def empty():
    if (len(country)==0):
        print("Queue is empty")
    else:
        print("Queue is NOT empty")
# Find the number of items in the queue.
def size():
    print("size() operation result:", len(country))
```

```
# Find the top item in the Stack
def front():
    if (len(country)>0):
        x=country[0]
        print("Front item in the queue is:", x)
def rear():
    if (len(country)>0):
        y=country[-1]
        print("Rear item in the queue is:", y)
while(1):
        print ("Queue Operations")
        print ("****************")
        print ("1. ENQUEUE")
        print ("2. DEQUEUE")
        print ("3. IS EMPTY")
        print ("4. SIZE")
        print ("5. FRONT")
        print ("6. RARE")
        print ("7. EXIT")
        inp=int(input("Enter your choice number"))
        if(inp > 7 | inp < 1):
            print("Wrong choice so try again ")
        else:
            if(inp == 1):
                name=input("Enter the country name to added in
the queue:")
                enqueue(name)
            if(inp == 2):
                pop()
            if(inp == 3):
                empty()
            if(inp == 4):
                size()
            if(inp == 5):
                front()
            if(inp == 6):
                rear()
            if (inp == 7):
                break
print("Completed >>>>")
```

RESEARCH DIRECTIONS AND CHALLENGES

These research challenges serve as a springboard for exploring advanced topics and stretching the limits of data organization with Python lists. Researchers can delve deeper into these areas to advance list-based data administration and propose novel solutions to the challenges below.

Develop and investigate efficient collection management algorithms. Consider scenarios in which the size of the List exceeds the quantity of available memory, and study Lists optimization techniques such as disk-based storage, cache, and parallel processing. Examine optimization techniques such as appending, extending, and modifying list items. Analyze techniques such as algorithmic enhancements, memory management strategies, and specialized data structures created for specific use cases.

Explore and develop advanced list indexing and searching techniques. Consider instances in which the List contains intricate data structures or nested lists. Explore techniques such as multidimensional indexing, indexing based on particular properties or attributes, and the implementation of effective search algorithms for diverse data patterns. List Compression and Encoding Techniques: Analyze techniques for compressing and encoding lists to reduce storage requirements and improve data transfer efficiency. Explore list-specific compression algorithms, encoding schemes, and data representations. Consider the tradeoffs between compression ratios, encoding/decoding rates, and memory consumption.

List Visualization and Interactive Exploration: An investigation into techniques for effectively visualizing large lists. Create interactive frameworks or tools that enable users to investigate and analyze lists efficiently. Consider using data visualizations like heat maps, scatter graphs, and hierarchical representations to identify patterns, relationships, and outliers. Security and Privacy of Lists: Examine methods for ensuring the security and privacy of lists, particularly in scenarios involving sensitive or confidential data. Examine techniques such as data anonymization, secure storage, access control mechanisms, and encryption algorithms to safeguard list data's confidentiality and integrity.

Examine approaches for integrating and interoperating lists with other data structures and systems. Analyze techniques for data exchange between databases and Lists, cloud storage, and distributed computing frameworks. Consider obstacles such as data consistency, synchronization, and the maintenance of efficient data flow between systems. Examine List data structures for tasks involving machine learning and data extraction. Develop techniques and algorithms for data analysis and extraction from collections. Examine obstacles associated with list data, such as feature extraction, dimensionality reduction, outlier detection, and pattern recognition.

Preprocessing and Cleaning of List-Based Data: Examine inventory preprocessing and cleansing techniques to ensure data quality and dependability. Formulate algorithms for absent values, outliers, duplicate entries, and inconsistent data management in Lists. Explore list-specific techniques for data imputation, outlier detection, and data validation. Examine methods for collaborating and sharing listings in a decentralized or distributed environment. In collaborative list editing scenarios, investigate techniques for versioning, conflict resolution, access control, and data consistency. Consider obstacles such as efficient synchronization, change merging, and data integrity maintenance in distributed list environments.

CONCLUSION

In this chapter, the organization of data using the list was explored, a sequential data structure in Python. The basics of lists and their ability to hold multiple elements of different data types were learned. The access of elements in a list using indices was discovered, allowing retrieval of specific items based on their position. Python's support for negative indexing provided a convenient way to access items from the end of the list. Furthermore, the mutability of lists was discussed, enabling modification of their content even after creation. Various methods for modifying lists were explored, including changing items at specific indices or ranges of indices. Additionally, the append() and extend() methods were examined for adding items to lists, understanding their differences and use cases.

The chapter also covered searching and sorting operations on lists. The use of Python's membership operator to find items in a list and the sorting of a list using the built-in sort() method were learned. Furthermore, the time complexity of different list operations, including index lookup, assignment, append, extend, and sorting, was discussed. Next, the stack data structure was introduced as a fundamental tool for effective data organization. The concept of a stack as a Last-In-First-Out (LIFO) structure was understood, and essential operations such as push and pop were learned. The implementation of a stack using a list in Python was explored, and code examples for stack operations were provided.

Lastly, the queue data structure, which follows the First-In-First-Out (FIFO) principle, was discussed. The enqueue and dequeue operations for adding and removing items from a queue were examined. Similar to the stack, code examples for queue operations implemented using a list were presented. Throughout this chapter, various research directions and challenges for further exploration were identified. These include the development of efficient collection management algorithms, investigation of advanced list indexing and searching techniques, exploration of optimization techniques for large lists, and consideration of scenarios with complex data structures or nested lists.

In conclusion, this chapter has provided a comprehensive overview of organizing data using lists as a sequential data structure in Python. By understanding the fundamentals, operations, and time complexity of lists, as well as exploring the stack and queue data structures implemented with lists, readers are equipped with valuable knowledge for effective data organization and manipulation. The presented research directions and challenges serve as an invitation for researchers to delve deeper into advanced topics and propose innovative solutions to enhance list-based data administration

REFERENCES

Dubois, P. F., Hinsen, K., & Hugunin, J. (1996). Numerical Python. *Computers in Physics*, *10*(3), 262–267. doi:10.1063/1.4822400

Erciyes, K. (2021). *A Short Review of Python. In Algebraic Graph Algorithms.* Springer. doi:10.1007/978-3-030-87886-3

Hetland, M. L. (2017). *Beginning Python: From novice to professional.* Apress. doi:10.1007/978-1-4842-0028-5

Hunt, J. (2019). ADTs, Queues and Stacks. In *A Beginners Guide to Python 3 Programming* (pp. 407–414). Springer. doi:10.1007/978-3-030-25943-3_34

Kobbaey, T., Xanthidis, D., & Bilquise, G. (2022). Data Structures and Algorithms with Python. In Handbook of Computer Programming with Python (pp. 207-272). Chapman and Hall/CRC. doi:10.1201/9781003139010-6

Lutz, M. (2013). *Learning Python: Powerful object-oriented programming.* O'Reilly Media, Inc.

Martelli, A. (2006). *Python in a Nutshell.* O'Reilly Media, Inc.

Navghare, N., Kedar, P., Sangamkar, P., & Mahajan, M. (2020). Python and OpenCV in automation of live Surveillance. In *Machine Learning and Information Processing* (pp. 235–243). Springer. doi:10.1007/978-981-15-1884-3_22

Oliphant, T. E. (2007). Python for scientific computing. *Computing in Science & Engineering*, *9*(3), 10–20. doi:10.1109/MCSE.2007.58

Popescu, G. V., & Bîră, C. (2022, June). Python-Based Programming Framework for a Heterogeneous MapReduce Architecture. In *2022 14th International Conference on Communications (COMM)* (pp. 1-6). IEEE. 10.1109/COMM54429.2022.9817183

Saabith, A. S., Fareez, M. M. M., & Vinothraj, T. (2019). Python current trend applications-an overview. *International Journal of Advance Engineering and Research Development*, 6(10).

Schwarz, J. S., Chapman, C., & Feit, E. M. (2020). *An Overview of Python. Python for Marketing Research and Analytics*. Springer. doi:10.1007/978-3-030-49720-0

Chapter 3
Linear Data Structures and Their Applications

Kavita Srivastava
Institute of Information Technology and Management, GGSIP University, India

ABSTRACT

In a linear data structure, the elements are arranged in a specific order. Each element on a linear data structure is connected to the elements that proceed it as well as the element that follows it. In other words, the elements are placed in sequential order. Hence, it is possible to traverse the elements in sequential order in a single pass. The objective of the chapter is to provide a basic understanding of linear data structures and their implementation in Python. The chapter is organized as follows. The chapter starts with an introduction to the linear data structure. The objective is to provide a basic understanding of linear data structures. A comparison of linear data structures and non-linear data structures is given next. Next, all of the above-mentioned data structures are explained in brief. The Python implementation of all of these data structures is provided. After that, their applications and their implementation in Python is discussed. The chapter concludes by highlighting the essential concepts.

INTRODUCTION

In the realm of data organization and efficient data processing, data structures play a vital role. They enable us to arrange and manage data effectively, allowing for the seamless execution of related operations. Data structures can be broadly categorized into Linear Data Structures and Non-Linear Data Structures. The linear arrangement facilitates sequential traversal in a single pass, distinguishing them from non-linear

DOI: 10.4018/978-1-6684-7100-5.ch003

systems. Common examples of linear data structures include arrays, linked lists, stacks, and queues (Domkin, 2021). Let's explore these data structures in detail, along with their applications.

Arrays

An array is a collection of elements identified by an index or a key. Details in an array are stored contiguously in memory, allowing random access. Furthermore, all elements in an array must belong to the same data type. Arrays find applications in various software systems that require storing similar records, such as employee management systems, library management systems, flight booking systems, and video rental applications (McKinney, 2010). They are also extensively used in image processing, where two-dimensional arrays represent image pixels.

Linked Lists

A linked list consists of interconnected nodes. Each node contains a data value and a pointer to the next node. Linked lists can be either singly linked or doubly linked. In a singly linked list, each node has a pointer to the next node, while in a doubly linked list, nodes have pointers to both the next and previous nodes, enabling bidirectional traversal. Circular linked lists, a variant of singly linked lists, have the last node pointing back to the first node. Linked lists are employed when storing records in non-contiguous memory locations and when dynamic memory allocation is required (Boockmann & Lüttgen, 2020). Applications of linked lists include web page navigation through hyperlinks, organization of social media content and feeds, symbol table management in IDEs and compilers, multiplayer games, and the implementation of various operating system algorithms.

Stacks

A stack follows the Last-In-First-Out (LIFO) principle, where elements are added and removed from the top of the Stack. The push() operation adds an element to the top, while the pop() function removes the topmost element. Stacks find numerous applications, such as evaluating postfix expressions, maintaining history and logs, creating playlists, and implementing recursion (Buckley & Buckley, 2017).

Queues

A queue operates on the First-In-First-Out (FIFO) principle, where elements are added at the back and removed from the front. The primary application of queues lies in CPU scheduling. Queue data structures are employed whenever maintaining records in a FIFO order is crucial. They are also used in communication networks for message sending, email systems, congestion control, data packet forwarding, and more. Additionally, queues play a role in request and response systems, printer queues, multiplayer games, and other scenarios requiring the maintenance of a queue-like structure (Zhang, 2013).

Linear data structures offer various ways to manipulate and organize data, including sorting, searching, and traversing elements. The choice of a data structure depends on specific requirements, such as the need for fast random access or efficient insertion and deletion operations. Implementing linear data structures is straightforward, resembling the arrangement of memory cells, and they efficiently utilize memory resources. Primarily employed in software application development, these structures play a pivotal role. In the following sections, we will delve into a comparison between linear and non-linear data structures.

How Do Linear Data Structures Differ From Other Data Structures?

Linear data structures, as compared to other data structures, exhibit distinct characteristics and play a vital role in various applications. The dissimilarities between linear data structures and other data structures are noteworthy. Here are some key differences:

- **Accessing Elements:** Linear data structures enforce a sequential order for elements, necessitating specific access patterns. For instance, a stack follows the LIFO (Last-In-First-Out) order, while a queue adheres to the FIFO (First-In-First-Out) order. In contrast, data structures like trees and graphs allow random access to elements.
- **Storage and Manipulation:** Linear data structures store elements in a contiguous memory block, enabling straightforward traversal and manipulation. On the other hand, data structures such as trees and graphs involve intricate relationships between elements, demanding more sophisticated algorithms for manipulation.
- **Memory Usage:** Linear data structures exhibit linear memory usage, meaning that memory consumption increases proportionally with the number of elements stored. Conversely, data structures like trees and graphs can have non-linear memory usage patterns.
- **Performance:** Linear data structures offer rapid access and manipulation times for specific operations, like popping an element from a stack or inserting

an element into a queue. However, certain operations, such as searching for an element, might be slower than data structures like trees and hash tables.

When selecting a data structure, the choice depends on the specific requirements of the problem. Factors like the necessity for fast random access or efficient insertion and deletion operations come into play. Linear data structures are beneficial for simple problems with direct element relationships. However, data structures such as trees and graphs may prove more suitable for more complex situations. The following section will detail the characteristics of Linear Data Structures.

CHARACTERISTICS OF LINEAR DATA STRUCTURES

Linear data structures possess distinctive features that make them versatile tools in programming (Millman & Aivazis, 2011):

- **Sequential Access:** Elements within linear data structures are accessed in a specific order, following a Last-In-First-Out (LIFO) pattern like in a stack or a First-In-First-Out (FIFO) pattern like in a queue.
- **Linear Memory Usage:** As the data size increases, linear data structures consume memory proportionally, maintaining a linear relationship between data and memory usage.
- **Straightforward Manipulation:** Elements are stored in contiguous memory locations, enabling effortless traversal and manipulation.
- **Swift Operations for Specific Tasks:** Linear data structures offer rapid access and manipulation times for specialized operations such as element popping from a stack or element insertion into a queue.
- **Restricted Element Access:** Due to the enforced order, accessing elements randomly becomes more challenging than other data structures like trees and hash tables.
- **Efficient Insertion and Deletion:** Linear data structures provide efficient insertion and deletion times for specific operations like popping an element from a stack or inserting a part into a queue.

These characteristics bestow linear data structures with the ability to solve straightforward problems efficiently. However, alternative data structures such as trees and graphs might prove more suitable for more complex issues. In the subsequent section, we delve into significant applications where linear data structures find practical use.

APPLICATIONS OF LINEAR DATA STRUCTURES

Linear data structures offer many practical applications, showcasing their versatility and usefulness in various domains. Here are some special applications (Gibbons & Matias, 1999):

- **Storing and Retrieving Data:** Linear data structures efficiently store and retrieve information. Numerous storage systems leverage these structures to ensure swift access to data whenever needed.
- **Dynamic Memory Allocation:** Linked lists provide an effective means of implementing dynamic memory allocation. This feature is precious when allocating memory for objects on the heap.
- **Stack-Based Algorithms:** Stack data structures prove invaluable in implementing stack-based algorithms. These structures can efficiently accomplish tasks such as expression evaluation and maze traversal.
- **Queue-Based Algorithms:** Queue-based algorithms are highly efficient for tasks like breadth-first search and simulating real-life queues. Queues are a fundamental component for implementing such algorithms.
- **History Management:** Linear data structures, like stacks and queues, find practical use in applications such as web browsers and text editors. They enable tracking recent actions, facilitating the essential undo and redo functionalities.
- **Computer Networks:** Queues, as linear data structures, are crucial in managing communication within computer networks. They ensure the orderly transmission of data between devices.
- **Data Compression:** Linear data structures, such as stacks, prove valuable in data compression algorithms. These structures enable efficient data encoding and decoding, contributing to effective compression techniques.

These examples provide a glimpse into the vast realm of applications for linear data structures. When selecting a data structure, specific problem requirements, such as the need for rapid random access or efficient insertion and deletion operations, guide the decision-making process. The following section will delve into the advantages of employing linear data structures.

ADVANTAGES OF LINEAR DATA STRUCTURES

In the realm of Python programming, linear data structures serve many purposes and offer numerous benefits. Here, we delve into the advantages that make them invaluable tools (Goodrich et al., 2013):

- **Simplicity at Its Core:** Linear data structures possess an innate simplicity that renders them easily understandable and implementable. Consequently, they are optimal for introductory computer science courses, providing a smooth learning curve.
- **Swift and Targeted Operations:** With linear data structures, specific operations are executed remarkably quickly and efficiently. Whether it involves extracting an element from a stack or inserting an element into a queue, these structures excel at rapid access and manipulation.
- **Efficiency in Insertion and Deletion:** Seamlessly accommodating insertion and deletion operations, linear data structures facilitate optimal efficiency. These structures offer streamlined performance, whether it entails popping an element from a stack or inserting an element into a queue.
- **Seamless Sequential Access:** Applications that require sequential access to elements find an ideal ally in linear data structures. Whether storing and retrieving data, managing historical records, or navigating computer networks, these structures exhibit exceptional suitability.
- **Minimal Resource Overhead:** Linear data structures boast a remarkable advantage in terms of resource utilization. The overhead they impose remains minimal, sparing unnecessary memory consumption and computational burden associated with maintaining relationships between elements.
- **Dynamic Memory Allocation Possibilities:** The prowess of dynamic memory allocation finds a proper implementation through linked lists, a type of linear data structure. This allows efficient memory allocation for objects on the heap, further expanding the capabilities of these structures.

The advantages above position linear data structures as a powerful solution for tackling simpler problems with direct element relationships. However, alternative data structures such as trees and graphs may be more adept for complex challenges. It is essential to recognize the drawbacks associated with linear data structures, which we will explore in the subsequent discussion.

DRAWBACKS OF LINEAR DATA STRUCTURES

Linear data structures, while immensely useful, do come with certain limitations. These limitations include the following (Othman, 2023):

- **Limited Access to Elements:** One drawback of linear data structures is that elements can only be accessed in a specific order. This makes it more challenging to access elements randomly compared to other data structures like trees and hash tables.
- **Slow Random Access:** Accessing elements randomly in linear data structures can be slow. Each element must be traversed sequentially to reach a specific location, hindering efficiency.
- **Fixed-Size:** Linear data structures like arrays have a predetermined size. They cannot dynamically grow or shrink to accommodate changes, which may pose constraints in flexible storage scenarios.
- **Memory Usage:** Linear data structures exhibit linear memory usage. This means that memory consumption increases linearly with data size. While this can be advantageous for smaller datasets, it becomes a drawback when dealing with applications that demand extensive data storage.
- **Complexity:** Managing large-sized data and complex relationships between elements can introduce complexity in implementing and maintaining linear data structures. As the data grows in size and complexity, handling and organizing it becomes more challenging.
- **Inefficiency for Complex Operations:** Linear data structures can prove inefficient for operations involving intricate relationships between elements. Tasks like finding the shortest path between two nodes in a graph may require more optimized data structures. Considering these drawbacks when selecting a data structure for a specific problem is crucial. Complex problems may be better suited to alternative data structures that provide more efficient and effective solutions.

ARRAYS

In linear data structures, arrays are a powerful tool, enabling us to refer to multiple elements by a single name and significantly reducing the amount of code required. Each piece within an array possesses a unique index that facilitates easy access. It's important to note that Python arrays should not be confused with lists or numpy arrays, as they are distinct entities. While Python lists also store values akin to arrays, they possess the flexibility of accommodating elements of different types, unlike arrays which mandate uniformity.

The following example demonstrates using Python lists and arrays for storing values.

```
mylist=[1,2,3,'A',"some text", True, [11,12,13], 'X', 3.5]
print(mylist)
```

Output

Figure 1. Python list

```
[1, 2, 3, 'A', 'some text', True, [11, 12, 13], 'X', 3.5]
```

In the context of linear data structures and their practical applications, it becomes evident that a list in Python can store a diverse range of values, including integers, characters, strings, Booleans, floating-point numbers, and even other lists. On the other hand, when working with arrays, all elements need to share the same data type. Fortunately, Python's array module facilitates the creation of arrays of values belonging to basic types. This functionality allows for the creation of arrays with integers ranging from one to eight bytes in size, floating-point values with sizes of four and eight bytes, and arrays containing Unicode characters with a size of two bytes. When using the array() function, the first parameter represents a code that specifies the desired type. To illustrate the practical usage of arrays in Python, consider the following program demonstration.

```
import array as my_array
a1=my_array.array('i', [10, 20, 30])
print('An Integer Array: ')
for i in range (0, 3):
    print (a1[i], end =" ")
print()
a2=my_array.array('d', [2.99, 1.34377, 12.70, 0.125])
print('An Floating Point Array: ')
for i in range (0, 4):
```

```
        print (a2[i], end =" ")
print()
```

Output

Figure 2. Python arrays

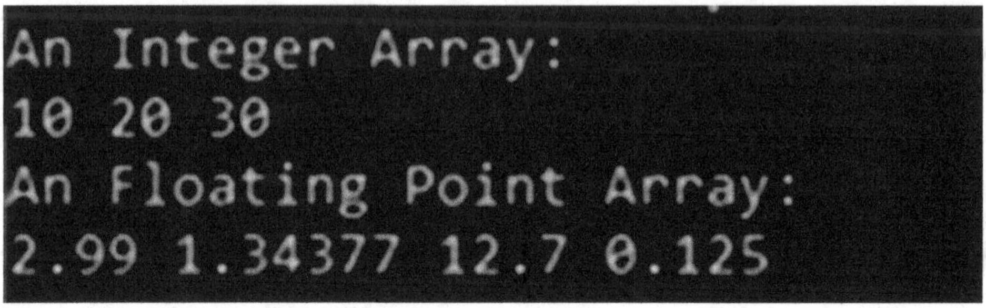

```
An Integer Array:
10 20 30
An Floating Point Array:
2.99 1.34377 12.7 0.125
```

When to mix the values belonging to different data types, Python doesn't allow it, as shown in the following code.

```
import array as my_array
a1=my_array.array('i', [10, 20, 3.5, 'ABC', 30])
print('An Integer Array: ')
for i in range (0, 3):
    print (a1[i], end =" ")
print()
```

Output

Figure 3. Creating Python arrays with different types

```
Traceback (most recent call last):
  File "D:\KavitaSrivastava\PythonBook\code\Arrays\array2.py", line
2, in <module>
    a1=my_array.array('i', [10, 20, 3.5, 'ABC', 30])
TypeError: 'float' object cannot be interpreted as an integer
```

SINGLY-LINKED LIST

Linear data structures, an essential concept in programming, resemble arrays as they consist of a collection of elements. However, unlike arrays, linked lists dynamically generate elements. Consequently, linked lists allocate only the necessary elements at a given moment, preventing memory wastage encountered with arrays. The advantage lies in the fact that linked lists eliminate the need for pre-allocated memory and allow non-contiguous locations for data storage. In a linked list, nodes store elements and are interconnected, with each node linked to the next one. Specifically, a singly linked list comprises nodes with a data field and a pointer called "next," which points to the subsequent node. The last node in the List points to a null value, indicating the end. The initial node, the head node (refer to Figure 4), marks the beginning of the linked List (Baka, 2017).

Figure 4. Nodes in linked list

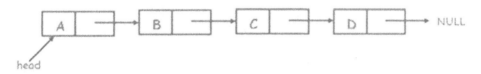

The process of traversing a linear data structure is simple. It begins by starting at the head node and then scanning each subsequent node through the next pointer until a null value is encountered. When creating a new list, two classes are required: "node" and "linked_list." The "node" class represents an individual node in the List and contains two essential members: "info" and "next." "info" stores the data value of the node, while "next" holds the reference to the next node in the List. In Python, the keyword "None" is used to indicate a null value, so the constructor assigns "None" to the "next" member. The data for a node is passed as a parameter to the constructor and then transferred to the "info" field. In the "linked_list" class, the single data member required is "head," which is initialized as "None" in the constructor. The code snippet below demonstrates the usage of the "create_list()" function for list creation and the "traverse_list()" function for list traversal. The Python code for creating a singly linked list is given below.

```python
class node:
        def __init__(self, info):
                self.info=info
                self.next=None
class linked_list:
        def __init__(self):
                self.head=None
        def create_list(self, info):
                if self.head is None:
                        self.head=node(info)
                        self.head.next=None
                else:
                        p=node(info)
                        q=self.head
                        while q.next is not None:
                                q=q.next
                        q.next=p
                        p.next=None
        def traverse_list(self):
                p=self.head
                while p is not None:
                        print(p.info, end=' ')
                        p=p.next
mylist=linked_list()
n=int(input('How many elements you want to enter in the list? '))
for i in range(n):
        info=int(input('Enter value: '))
        mylist.create_list(info)
print('The Elements in the Linked List are....', end=' ')
mylist.traverse_list()
```

Output

Figure 5. Elements in the linked list

```
How many elements you want to enter in the list? 7
Enter value: 12
Enter value: 84
Enter value: 568
Enter value: 33
Enter value: 91
Enter value: 3
Enter value: 49
The Elements in the Linked List are.... 12 84 568 33 91 3 49
```

create_list() Method

This method demonstrates its proficiency when provided with a parameter named "info," housing the cherished value of a data element. Its initial undertaking involves scrutinizing whether the List is devoid of any content, accomplished by assessing the status of the head node. Should an absence be detected, a node is promptly forged, launched as the head node, and bestowed with the virtue of having its next pointer set to None. Conversely, if the List possesses prior occupants, a deliberate traversal commences, tracing the path from the head node until the very last node. Herein lies the pivotal moment wherein the new value is warmly embraced by appending it to the List, as the previous node's next pointer seamlessly interlocks with the newly minted node. Alas, to maintain the structure, the following field of the new node graciously assumes the value of None, signifying the end of this union.

traverse_list() Method

the traverse_list() method displays all the nodes in the List, starting from the head and following the subsequent nodes' next field until the List ends.

Insertion

There are three situations for insertion in the List.

- Insertion at the first position
- Insertion at the last position

- Insertion at any Valid Position in the List

Deleting a Node

Like insertion, there are three situations for deletion.

- Deletion at the Beginning
- Deletion at the End
- Deletion at any Valid Position

DOUBLY LINKED LIST

A doubly linked list is an essential linear data structure incorporating an information field and two pointers - next and previous. This fundamental difference from a singly linked list enables seamless traversal in both the forward and reverse directions. By maintaining two-pointers, a doubly linked list provides increased flexibility. Using the diagram below, let's visualize a doubly linked list (Bandopadhyay & Shang, 2022).

Figure 6. Doubly linked list

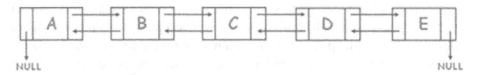

NULL   NULL

To implement linear data structures, we create a class called "node" to represent a node within the List. The "node" class consists of three members: "info", "next", and "previous". The "info" field stores the data value of the node, while the "next" and "previous" pointers are used to navigate between nodes. Additionally, the "doubly_linked_list" class contains a " head " field," which refers to the first node in the doubly-linked List. This class also defines two methods: "create_list()" and "traverse_list()." These methods are responsible for creating a new list and traversing through the existing List.

Furthermore, the "doubly_linked_list" class will later include node insertion and deletion methods. When adding a node to the List, we must ensure that the "next" and "previous" pointers are set correctly. If the List is empty, the new node becomes the head, so we assign the "head" field to the new node, and both the "previous" and "next" fields are set to None. However, if the List is not empty, adding a node involves traversing to the end of the List and making the last node point to the new node. This is achieved by assigning the "next" pointer of the last node to the new node, while the "previous" field of the new node should point to the node at the end of the existing List. The Python code for the Doubly Linked List is given below.

```python
class node:
        def __init__(self, info):
                self.info=info
                self.next=None
                self.previous=None
class doubly_linked_list:
        def __init__(self):
                self.head=None
        def create_list(self, info):
                p=node(info)
                if self.head is None:
                        self.head=p
                        self.head.next=None
                        self.head.previous=None
                else:
                        q=self.head
                        while q.next is not None:
                                q=q.next
                        p.previous=q
                        p.next=None
                        q.next=p
        def traverse_list(self):
                p=self.head
                while p is not None:
                        print(p.info, end=' ')
                        p=p.next
mylist=doubly_linked_list()
n=int(input('How many elements you want to enter in the list? '))
for i in range(n):
        info=int(input('Enter value: '))
        mylist.create_list(info)
print('\nThe Elements in the Linked List are (Traversing Forward)....', end=' ')
mylist.traverse_list()
```

Output

Figure 7. Elements in the doubly linked list

```
How many elements you want to enter in the list? 10
Enter value: 1
Enter value: 2
Enter value: 3
Enter value: 4
Enter value: 5
Enter value: 6
Enter value: 7
Enter value: 8
Enter value: 9
Enter value: 10

The Elements in the Linked List are (Traversing Forward).... 1 2 3 4 5 6 7 8 9 10
```

CIRCULAR LINKED LIST

This List also maintains a single pointer and each node's data field. However, the last node points to the head node (Guzdial & Ericson, 2012). The Python code for the Circular linked list is given below.

```python
class node:
        def __init__(self, info):
                self.info=info
                self.next=None
class circular_linked_list:
        def __init__(self):
                self.head=None
                self.last=None
        def append(self, info):
                p=node(info)
                if self.head is None:
                        self.head=p
                        self.last=p
                        self.last.next=self.head
                else:
                        self.last.next=p
                        self.last=p
                        self.last.next=self.head
```

```
        def display_circular(self):
                p=self.head
                print(p.info, end=' ')
                while p.next is not self.head:
                        p=p.next
                        print(p.info, end=' ')
                print('\nThe Next Element in the Circular
Linked List...', end=' ')
                print(p.next.info, end=' ')
circularlist=circular_linked_list()
n=int(input('How many elements you want to enter in the list?
'))
for i in range(n):
        info=int(input('Enter value: '))
        circularlist.append(info)
print('\nThe Elements in the Circular Linked List are....',
end=' ')
circularlist.display_circular()
```

STACK

The Stack stands out as it adheres to a Last In First Out (LIFO) order. This implies that elements are added and removed from the last position. Adding an element is known as the push() operation, while the removal is called the pop() operation. Moreover, the Stack includes a peek() operation that retrieves the topmost element from the Stack without deleting it. Presented below is the Python code for executing stack operations.

```
class node:
        def __init__(self, info):
                self.info=info
                self.next=None
class Stack:
        def __init__(self):
                self.head=None
                self.top=None
        def push(self, info):
                p=node(info)
```

67

```
            if self.isEmpty():
                    self.head=p
                    self.top=p
                    self.head.next=None
                    self.top.next=None
            else:
                    self.top.next=p
                    p.next=None
                    self.top=p
    def pop(self):
            if self.isEmpty():
                    print("\nStack is Empty!!!\nStack
Underflow!!!\n");
                    return -9999
            else:
                    n=self.top.info
                    if self.top==self.head:
                            self.top=None
                            self.head=None
                    else:
                            p=self.head
                            while p.next is not self.top:
                                    p=p.next
                            p.next=None
                            self.top=p
                    return n
    def peek(self):
            if self.isEmpty():
                    print("\nStack is Empty!!!\nStack
Underflow!!!\n");
                    return -9999
            else:
                    n=self.top.info
                    return n
    def stack_traversal(self):
            if not self.isEmpty():
                    p=self.head
                    while p is not None:
                            print(p.info, end=' ')
                            p=p.next
```

```
                    else:
                            print("\nStack is Empty!!!\n");
        def isEmpty(self):
                if self.top is not None:
                        return False
                else:
                        return True
mystack=Stack()
n=int(input('How many elements you want to enter in the stack?
'))
for i in range(n):
        info=int(input('Enter value: '))
        mystack.push(info)
print('\nStack Traversal\n')
mystack.stack_traversal()
print('\nElement at the top of stack: ')
print(mystack.peek())
print('\nAdding an element: ')
info=int(input('Enter value: '))
mystack.push(info)
print('\nElement at the top of stack: ')
print(mystack.peek())
print('\nRetrieving the elements of Stack...', end=' ')
while not mystack.isEmpty():
        x=mystack.pop()
        print(x, end=' ')
print('\nStack Traversal\n')
mystack.stack_traversal()
```

Output

Figure 8. Stack operations

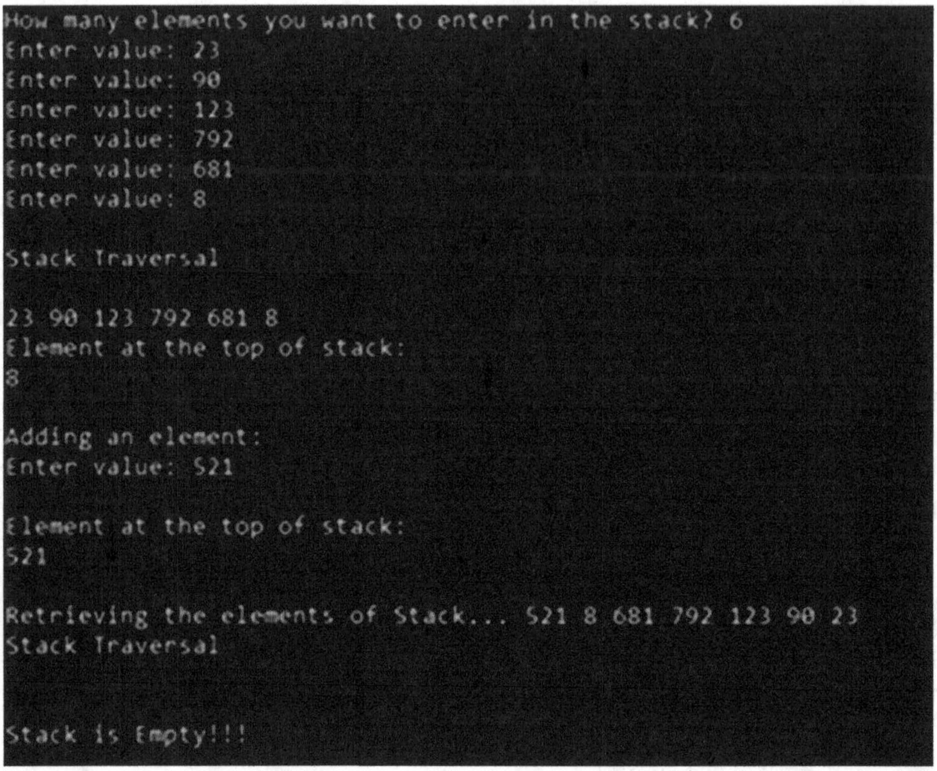

```
How many elements you want to enter in the stack? 6
Enter value: 23
Enter value: 90
Enter value: 123
Enter value: 792
Enter value: 681
Enter value: 8

Stack Traversal

23 90 123 792 681 8
Element at the top of stack:
8

Adding an element:
Enter value: 521

Element at the top of stack:
521

Retrieving the elements of Stack... 521 8 681 792 123 90 23
Stack Traversal

Stack is Empty!!!
```

QUEUE

A queue data structure follows the FIFO (First-In-First-Out) principle. This means elements are added to the queue from the last position and removed from the front. The two ends of a queue are the front and rear. Elements are removed from the front end and inserted at the rear end of the queue. The queue supports two essential operations: enqueue() and dequeue(). The enqueue() process adds an element to the queue, while the dequeue() operation removes an element from the queue. Additionally, the queue provides other functions such as isEmpty() and isFull().

In implementing a queue, the isEmpty() operation determines whether the queue contains any elements. It returns a valid Boolean value when the queue is empty. Similarly, the isFull() operation indicates whether the queue has reached its maximum capacity and produces an excellent Boolean value in such cases. However, if the queue is implemented using a linked list, the isFull() operation is unnecessary. Below is an example of implementing a Queue using a linked list in Python programming.

```python
class node:
        def __init__(self, info):
                self.info=info
                self.next=None
class Queue:
        def __init__(self):
                self.front=None
                self.rear=None
        def enqueue(self, info):
                my_node=node(info)
                if self.front is None:
                        self.front=my_node
                        self.rear=my_node
                        self.front.next=None
                        self.rear.next=None
                else:
                        if self.front==self.rear:
                                self.rear.next=my_node
                                self.rear=self.rear.next
                                self.rear.next=None
                                self.front.next=self.rear
                        else:
                                this_node=self.rear
                                self.rear.next=my_node
                                self.rear=my_node
                                self.rear.next=None
        def dequeue(self):
                if self.front is None and self.rear is None:
                        print('\nQueue is Empty!!!\n');
                else:
                        if self.front==self.rear:
                                self.front=None
                                self.rear=None
                        else:
                                this_node=self.front
                                self.front=this_node.next
                                this_node=None
```

```
        def isEmpty(self):
                if self.front is None and self.rear is None:
                        return True
                else:
                        return False
        def traverse_queue(self):
                if self.front is None and self.rear is None:
                        print('\nQueue is Empty!!!\n');
                else:
                        this_node=self.front
                        while this_node is not None:
                                print(this_node.info, end='
')
                                this_node=this_node.next
new_queue=Queue()
n=int(input('What is the size of the Queue?'))
for i in range(n):
        info=int(input('Enter value: '))
        new_queue.enqueue(info)
print('\nQueue Elements....\n', end=' ')
new_queue.traverse_queue()
print('\nRemoving element from queue....\n', end=' ')
new_queue.dequeue();
print('\nQueue Elements....\n', end=' ')
new_queue.traverse_queue()
print('\nRemoving element from queue....\n', end=' ')
new_queue.dequeue();
print('\nQueue Elements....\n', end=' ')
new_queue.traverse_queue()
print('\nAdding an element in queue....\n', end=' ')
new_queue.enqueue(int(input('Enter value: ')));
print('\nQueue Elements....\n', end=' ')
new_queue.traverse_queue()
```

Output

Figure 9. Operations on queue

```
What is the size of the Queue?5
Enter value: 1
Enter value: 2
Enter value: 3
Enter value: 4
Enter value: 5

Queue Elements....
 1 2 3 4 5
Removing element from queue....

Queue Elements....
 2 3 4 5
Removing element from queue....

Queue Elements....
 3 4 5
Adding an element in queue....
 Enter value: 78

Queue Elements....
 3 4 5 78
```

PRIORITY QUEUE

Each node is assigned a priority in a priority queue, and the nodes are organized based on their priority. The node with the highest priority is placed at the front, while the node with the lowest priority is at the rear. Consequently, the node with the highest priority is permanently removed when performing the Dequeue operation. Priority queues find practical use in various real-life scenarios (Üçoluk et al., 2012). For instance, in CPU job scheduling, jobs are arranged according to their priority, and higher-priority jobs are executed before lower-priority jobs. It is important to note that the node class includes an additional attribute called "priority." During the Enqueue operation, the program determines the element with a higher priority than the new node and inserts the new node before it. In this context, priority is represented as an integer ranging from 1 to 10, where 1 signifies the highest priority, and 10 describes the lowest.

CONCLUSION

In conclusion, this research work has comprehensively explored linear data structures and their applications, with a specific focus on arrays, linked lists, stacks, and queues. These data structures offer efficient ways to organize and manipulate data, making them invaluable tools in software development. The advantages of using linear data structures in Python programming have been highlighted, including their simplicity, swift and targeted operations, efficient insertion and deletion, seamless sequential access, minimal resource overhead, and dynamic memory allocation possibilities. It is important to note that this research has specifically emphasized implementing linear data structures using the Python programming language. Python offers a user-friendly and versatile environment for working with these data structures, enabling programmers to leverage Python's built-in features and libraries for efficient data processing.

The drawbacks of linear data structures have also been discussed, such as limited access to elements, slow random access, fixed size, memory usage, complexity, and inefficiency for complex operations. Considering these limitations when selecting a data structure for a specific problem is essential, especially when dealing with complex scenarios that may require alternative data structures like trees and graphs. Overall, the research has shed light on linear data structures' characteristics, applications, advantages, and drawbacks, emphasizing their significance in solving more straightforward problems and their limitations in more complex scenarios. By implementing these data structures using Python programming, developers can harness the power of these structures to efficiently organize and process data in various domains, ranging from storage systems and dynamic memory allocation to stack-based and queue-based algorithms, history management, computer networks, and data compression. The knowledge gained from this research work can serve as a solid foundation for further exploration and application of linear data structures in Python programming, enabling developers to make informed decisions when choosing the most appropriate data structure for a given problem.

REFERENCES

Baka, B. (2017). *Python Data Structures and Algorithms*. Packt Publishing Ltd.

Bandopadhyay, S., & Shang, H. (2022). SADHANA: A Doubly Linked List-based Multidimensional Adaptive Mesh Refinement Framework for Solving Hyperbolic Conservation Laws with Application to Astrophysical Hydrodynamics and Magnetohydrodynamics. *The Astrophysical Journal. Supplement Series, 263*(2), 32. doi:10.3847/1538-4365/ac9279

Boockmann, J. H., & Lüttgen, G. (2020, May). Learning Data Structure Shapes from Memory Graphs. LPAR.

Buckley, I. A., & Buckley, W. S. (2017). Teaching software testing using data structures. *International Journal of Advanced Computer Science and Applications, 8*(4).

Domkin, V. (2021). Linked Lists. *Programming Algorithms in Lisp: Writing Efficient Programs with Examples in ANSI Common Lisp*, 75-99.

Gibbons, P. B., & Matias, Y. (1999, January). Synopsis Data Structures for Massive Data Sets. In SODA (Vol. 10, pp. 909-910). doi:10.1090/dimacs/050/02

Goodrich, M. T., Tamassia, R., & Goldwasser, M. H. (2013). *Data structures and algorithms in Python*. John Wiley & Sons Ltd.

Guzdial, M., & Ericson, B. (2012, February). Listening to linked lists: Using multimedia to learn data structures. In *Proceedings of the 43rd ACM technical symposium on Computer Science Education* (pp. 663-663). 10.1145/2157136.2157358

McKinney, W. (2010, June). Data structures for statistical computing in Python. In *Proceedings of the 9th Python in Science Conference* (Vol. 445, No. 1, pp. 51-56). 10.25080/Majora-92bf1922-00a

Millman, K. J., & Aivazis, M. (2011). Python for scientists and engineers. *Computing in Science & Engineering, 13*(2), 9–12. doi:10.1109/MCSE.2011.36

Othman, J. (2023). Data structure uniqueness in Python programming language. *Enhancing Innovations in E-Learning for Future Preparation*, 68.

Üçoluk, G., Kalkan, S., Üçoluk, G., & Kalkan, S. (2012). Organizing Data. *Introduction to Programming Concepts with Case Studies in Python*, 165-194.

Zhang, H. L., Han, B. T., Xu, J. C., & Feng, Y. (2013). Preparation of the public bus schedule based on fcfs. In *Proceedings of 20th International Conference on Industrial Engineering and Engineering Management: Theory and Apply of Industrial Engineering* (pp. 1021-1029). Springer Berlin Heidelberg. 10.1007/978-3-642-40063-6_100

Chapter 4

A Comprehensive Analysis of Stack and Queue Data Structures and Their Uses

S. Rajasekaran

ⓘD https://orcid.org/0000-0002-7893-9072

University of Technology and Applied Sciences, Ibri, Oman

Mastan Vali Shaik

ⓘD https://orcid.org/0000-0002-0068-5519

University of Technology and Applied Sciences, Ibri, Oman

ABSTRACT

The chapter provides a comprehensive and in-depth exploration of two fundamental linear data structures in computer science: Stack and Queue. It begins with an introduction to these data structures, highlighting their key features and fundamental differences. It then explains various operations that can be performed on both data structures, such as push, pop, enqueue, and dequeue. These implementations are thoroughly compared and contrasted, highlighting their advantages and disadvantages. These applications are discussed in detail, showcasing the versatility of Stack and Queue data structures in different scenarios. The chapter includes Python code snippets demonstrating Stack and Queue data structures further to aid the reader's understanding of the material. This chapter provides a comprehensive and practical guide to Stack and Queue data structures, making it a valuable resource for computer science students, researchers, and practitioners.

DOI: 10.4018/978-1-6684-7100-5.ch004

INTRODUCTION TO STACK

A stack is a simple linear abstract data structure with finite (predefined) capacity that follows the Last In First Out (LIFO) principle. That means the element inserted last into the Stack will be removed first. Conversely, it can say that First In Last Out (FILO). That means the element inserted first into the Stack will be removed last. Both insert and delete operations are performed only on the Top of the Stack. TOP is a marker pointing to the current position in the Stack (Goodrich et al., 2013; Vasudevan et al., 2021). The initial value of Top is -1. Figure 1 provides examples of stack data structure.

Figure 1. Examples of stack data structure

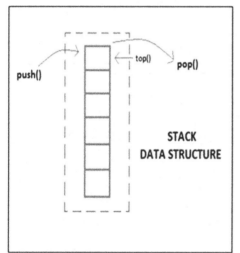

FEATURES OF STACK

The following features characterize the Stack.

1. A Stack consists of an ordered collection of homogeneous (same type) data elements.
2. The Stack accesses its data in LIFO or FILO order.
3. The push() method inserts new items into the Stack, while the drop() function removes components from the Stack. Only at one end of the Stack, termed the Top, are insert and delete operations done.

4. When a stack is filled, and no additional components can be added, it is in the Overflow state. Underflow describes a situation with no items, and the collection is empty.

STACK OPERATIONS

Table 1 provides details on different stack operations and their descriptions. (Dhruv et al., 2021)

Table 1. Stack operations

Basic Operations	Description
push()	Adds a new element at the Top of the Stack.
pop()	Deletes an existing element from the Top of the Stack.
Additional Operations	Description
top()	It just returns the top element of the Stack without removing it.
is_empty()	It returns true if the Stack is empty; otherwise, false.
is_full()	It returns true if the Stack is full; otherwise, false.
search(data)	It searches whether the particular element available in the Stack or not.
display()	It displays the stack contents.
len()	It returns the total number of elements available in the Stack.

PUSH Operation-Algorithm

1. First, check whether the Stack is full or has space to insert more elements.
2. Print the message "Stack Full" and exit if the Stack is full.
3. Increase the top value and add the new element if the Stack is incomplete.

POP Operation-Algorithm

1. The pop operation will check whether the Stack has data or is empty.
2. Displays "Stack underflow" and exits the application if the Stack is empty or contains no data.
3. Returns the element at the Top of the Stack and decreases the Top of the Stack containing data or is not empty.

Figure 2. Array implementation of Stack

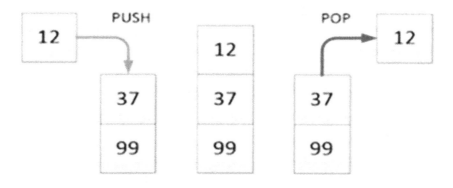

STACK IMPLEMENTATION

Two different methods are used to implement the stack operations. A Stack implementation using arrays is called a static implementation (Harris et al., 2020). The array implementation of the Stack is illustrated in Figure 2. Stack implementation using a linked list is called a dynamic implementation. Figure 3 outlines the Linked List implementation of Stack.

Figure 3. Linked List implementation of Stack

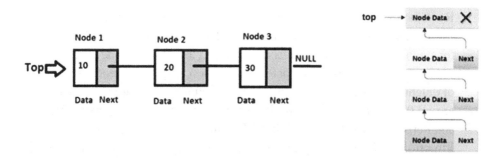

Table 2. Sample Stack for exercise

Element	H	@	M	#	C	T	%	P	D	$
Index	0	1	2	3	4	5	6	7	8	9

Exercise: Use the below Stack to find the answer to the following questions.

- The number of elements present in the Stack?
- What will Stack's content be after executing the algorithm below on the above Stack?

The algorithm for the Stack exercise is presented in Table 3.

Table 3. Stack exercise algorithm

1. Start
2. Push("^")
3. y=4
4. While y!=0 then
5. Pop()
6. y=y-1
7. Push("&")
8. End

APPLICATIONS OF STACK

Stacks are used for several purposes (Lambert, 2019).

1. **Reverse a String:** A given string can be reversed using Stack.
2. **Balancing Symbols in an Expression:** The compiler checks your program for syntax errors, but often a missing symbol (such as a missing parenthesis or a missing comment start character) causes the compiler to generate hundreds of diagnostic lines without identifying the actual error. Output is possible. To ensure that each right parenthesis, braces, and brackets must match their left counterparts, e.g., [()] is legal, but [(]) is illegal.
3. **Function Calls:** Most programming tool runtime systems use stacks to follow the chain of active functions. The runtime system pushes a frame onto the Stack with the following information whenever the process is called:
   ◦ Local variables and return values.
   ◦ A program counter that monitors instructions performed.
   ◦ After the function has finished executing, its frame will be taken off the Stack, and the method at the Top of the Stack will assume control.

4. **Web Browsers:** Stack can store the addresses of recently visited sites in Web browsers. Every time a user visits a new website, the website address is "pushed" onto the address stack. Browsers allow users to return to previously visited pages using the back button.

5. **Text Editors:** Text editors often have a "undo" function to undo recent changes and restore the document to its former state. This "undo" action may be accomplished by storing text modifications in batch.

6. **Recursion:** Recursion is another use case of stack solutions often preferred and implemented using stacks.

7. **Backtracking (Game Playing, Discovering Pathways, Exhaustive Searching):** The Backtracking approach is employed in algorithms when there are steps along a path (state) from a starting point to a goal.
   ◦ Go through the maze
   ◦ Find the path from one point to another on a diagram (roadmap)
   ◦ Play games with movement (chess, checkers)

In all of these scenarios, multiple options necessitate a system to recall decision points if a choice must be attempted. For example, in navigating through a maze, there comes a juncture where a decision needs to be made, and it is possible to discover that the chosen path leads to a dead-end. The objective is to return to the decision point and pursue the next alternative. Stacks serve as a viable component in the solution.

8. **Evaluation of Postfix Expressions:** Converting expressions from infix to postfix notation is another issue with expression manipulation. The operations of an expression are put between the operands in infix notation.

The algorithm to evaluate postfix expression is depicted in Figure 4.
Evaluate a postfix expression 3 6 4 * + 5 - using Stack (Table 4).

9. **Expression Transformations (Postfix to Prefix, Infix to Postfix, etc.):** The Stack transforms infix expressions into postfix expressions and postfix expressions into prefix expressions.

The algorithm to convert the infix to a postfix expression is given in Figure 5.
Using Stack, convert the following infix expression into its corresponding postfix expression.

P / (R + S) – N * M

Figure 4. Evaluate postfix expression: Algorithm

Algorithm to evaluate Postfix expression

Input: X and Output: Y

1. Add) to postfix expression X. [this step is optional]
2. Scan X from left to right and repeat Step 3 to 6 for each element of X until ")".
3. If an operand is encountered, PUSH it into the stack.
4. If an operator is encountered, then:
   - POP the stack and assign it to A. [A = POP( )]
   - POP the stack again and assign it to B. [B = POP( )]
   - Perform the operation C = B operator A. [Ex: if the operator is / then C = B / A]
   - PUSH C to stack
5. If a right parenthesis is encountered, then POP the stack and display the value as result.
6. END.

Table 5 outlines the infix to postfix expression.

Table 4. Evaluate postfix expression: Example

Symbol/Token	Operation	Stack Content	Calculation
3	PUSH(3)	3	
6	PUSH(6)	3 6	
4	PUSH(4)	3 6 4	
*	A = POP() B = POP() C = B * A PUSH(C)	3 24	A = 4 B = 6 C = 6 * 4 = 24
+	A = POP() B = POP() C = B + A PUSH(C)	27	A = 24 B = 3 C = 3 + 24 = 27
5	PUSH(5)	27 5	
-	A = POP() B = POP() C = B - A PUSH(C)	22	A = 5 B = 27 C = 27 - 5 = 22
)	POP()		**Result = 22**

Figure 5. Convert infix expression to postfix expression: Algorithm

---

Algorithm to Convert infix expression into postfix expression

Input: X and Output: Y

1. Push "("onto Stack, and add ")" to the end of X. (this step is optional)

2. Scan X from left to right and repeat Step 3 to 6 for each element of X until the Stack is empty.

3. If an operand is encountered, add it to Y.

4. If a left parenthesis is encountered, push it onto Stack.

5. If an operator is encountered, then:

   - Repeatedly pop from Stack and add to Y each operator (on the top of Stack) which has the same precedence as or higher precedence than operator.

   - Add this operator into Stack.

6. If a right parenthesis is encountered, then:

   - Repeatedly pop from Stack and add to Y each operator (on the top of Stack) until a left parenthesis is encountered.

   - Remove the left Parenthesis.

7. END.

Python Code for Stack Operations

The Stack data structure helps solve various computer science problems, and having a good understanding of its operations is crucial for any software developer. The following is the Python code for stack operations in Figures 6 and 7.

QUEUE: INTRODUCTION

A queue is a simple linear abstract data structure with a bounded (predefined) capacity that follows the First In First Out (FIFO) principle. This means the first element inserted into the Queue will be removed first. In reverse, it can be written as Last In Last Out (LILO). That means the last element inserted into the Queue will be removed last. Front and Rear are the two markers used to perform the queue operations. All the insertions will be done at the Rear, and the deletions at the Front. The initial value of both Front and Rear are -1, and both the values are reset to 0 when

Table 5. Convert infix expression to postfix expression: Example

Symbol/Token	Stack Content	Output
	(	
P	(	P
/	(/	P
(	(/ (	P
R	(/ (	P R
+	(/ (+	P R
S	(/ (+	P R S
)	(/	P R S +
-	(-	P R S + /
N	(-	P R S + / N
*	(- *	P R S + / N
M	(- *	P R S + / N M
)		**P R S + / N M * -**

the first data item is inserted into the Queue. Only the rear value will be increased for the subsequent insertion, and only the rear value will be raised for the deletions (Thomas, 2021). The examples of Queue data structure are given in Figure 8.

FEATURES OF QUEUE

The Queue has the following features.

1. A Queue consists of an ordered collection of homogeneous (same type) data elements.
2. The Queue accesses its data in FIFO or LILO order.
3. To insert new elements into the Queue enqueue() function and to delete an element from the queue dequeue() function is used. All the insertions will be done at the Rear, and the deletions will be done at the Front.
4. The Front refers to the first element of the Queue, and the Rear refers to the last element of the Queue.
5. The overflow condition occurs when the Queue is complete, and the underflow condition is when it is empty.

Figure 6. Stack data structure Python implementation Part 1

```python
# Stack Operations in python using classes and objects

# Create a stack class
class Stack:
  # class constructor to define empty stack
  def __init__(self):
    self.stack = []

  # Chech the empty stack
  def is_empty(self):
    return len(self.stack) == 0

  # Add data item into the stack
  def push(self, data):
    self.stack.append(data)
    print("Data item pushed into the stack : " + data)

  # Remove top data item from the stack
  def pop(self):
    if (self.is_empty()):
        return "Stack Underflow"
    return self.stack.pop()

  # Print top element from the stack
  def top(self):
    return self.stack[len(self.stack)-1]

  # Print stack content
  def disp(self):
    print("Stack Contents are : " + str(self.stack))

  # Find size of the stack
  def size(self):
    return len(self.stack)

  # Search a data item from the stack
  def search(self, sdata):
    if (is_empty(self.stack)):
        print("Stack Underflow")
    elif sdata in self.stack:
        print('Data item ',sdata, ' present in the stack')
    else:
        print('Data item ',sdata, ' not present in the stack')
```

QUEUE OPERATIONS

Table 6 provides the various queue operations.

Figure 7. Stack data structure Python implementation Part 2

```python
print("STACK OPERATIONS")
print('#'*20)
print('1. Push an element')
print('2. Pop an element')
print('3. Get top element')
print('4. Search an element')
print('5. Display Stack contents')
print('6. No. of elements in Stack')
print('7. Exit')

st = Stack()

while True:
    print("\n")
    ch=int(input('Enter your choice : '))
    print("\n")

    if ch==1:
        d=input('Enter the data item to be inserted : ')
        st.push(d)

    elif ch==2:
        print("Data item Popped from the stack: " + st.pop())

    elif ch==3:
        print("Data item at the top of the stack: " + st.top())

    elif ch==4:
        s=input('Enter the data item to be searched : ')
        st.search(s)

    elif ch==5:
        st.disp()

    elif ch==6:
        print("Number of elements in the Stack : ", st.size())

    elif ch==7:
        print("End Program")
        break
    else:
        print ("Wrong choice, Try again with correct choice " )
```

Figure 8. Examples of Queue data structure

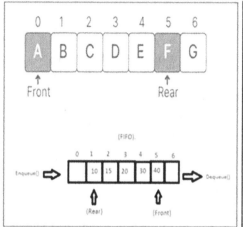

Table 6. Queue operations

Basic Operations	Description
Enqueue()	It will add an element at the Rear of the Queue.
Dequeue()	It will delete an element from the Front of the Queue.
Additional Operations	**Description**
Front()	It will return the front element of the Queue without removing it.
Rear()	It will return the rear element of the Queue without removing it.
Is_empty()	It returns true if the Queue is empty; otherwise false.
Is_full()	It returns true if the Queue is full; otherwise false.
Search(data item)	It will search whether the particular data item exists in the Queue.
Display()	Displays the queue contents.
len()	It returns the total number of elements present in the Queue.

Algorithm for Creating and Initializing Queue

The algorithm for creating and initializing a Queue is presented below.

1. Create an empty Queue.
2. Initialize two Front and Rear pointers with 0 [Front=rear=0].

Enqueue Operation

The following is the algorithm for Enqueue operation

1. First, check whether the Queue is complete or if there is a place to insert more items.
2. Print the message "Queue is full" and exit if the Queue is complete.
3. If the Queue is incomplete, set the Front and rear values to 0 when inserting the first item into the Queue. Only increase the rear value when enqueuing other items.

Dequeue Operation: Algorithm

The Queue operations are given in Figure 9. The following is the algorithm for Dequeue.

1. First, determine if the Queue is vacant or if items must be deleted.
2. If the Queue is empty, print the message "Queue is vacant" and terminate the program.
3. If the Queue is not empty, return the front element and increment its front value by 1.

Example: Queue operations and their effects are explained in Table 7. Consider an empty at the beginning and do the operations (Karumanchi, 2015).

QUEUE IMPLEMENTATION

Queues can be implemented in two different ways (Cutler et al., 2020). A queue implementation using arrays is called a static implementation. The array implementation of Queue is represented in Figure 10.

Queue implementation using a linked list is called a dynamic implementation. The linked list implementation of Queue is shown in Figure 11.

TYPES OF QUEUES

Queues are classified into four different types, which are mentioned below.

- Linear Queue/Simple Queue

Figure 9. Queue operations

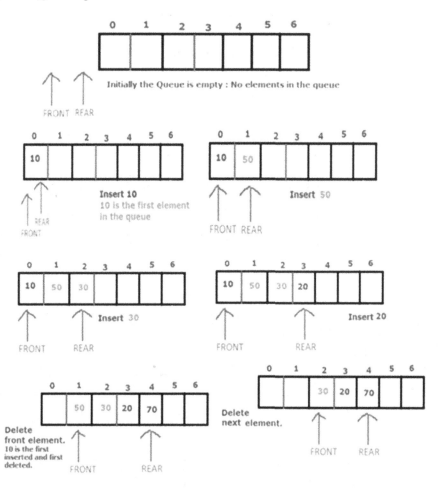

- Circular Queue
- Double Ended Queue
- Priority Queue

Simple/Linear Queue

The Simple/Linear Queue possesses the following features.

- Linear queues are the most basic types of queue data structure.
- Insert (Enqueue) operation is performed at REAR.
- Delete (Dequeue) operation is performed at FRONT.

Table 7. Queue operations: Example

Operations	Output Value	Queue Elements
Dequeue()	Error	[ ]
Enqueue(8)	-	[8]
Enqueue(3)	-	[8, 3]
Enqueue(5)	-	[8, 3, 5]
Enqueue(2)	-	[8, 3, 5, 2]
Empty()	False	
Len()	4	[8, 3, 5, 2]
Dequeue()	8	[3, 5, 2]
Dequeue()	3	[5, 2]
Enqueue(7)	-	[5, 2, 7]
Dequeue()	5	[5, 2, 7]
Len()	2	[2, 7]
Empty()	False	
Front()	2	[2, 7]
Rear()	7	[2, 7]
Dequeue()	2	[7]
Dequeue()	7	{]
Dequeue()	Error	[ ]
Empty()	True	[ ]
Len()	0	[ ]

- FRONT and REAR will point to -1 when Queue is empty.
- FRONT and REAR will be the same when a single element exists.
- A queue will be full when the REAR reaches the last index of the array.
- Always FRONT <= REAR.

Figure 10. Array implementation of Queue

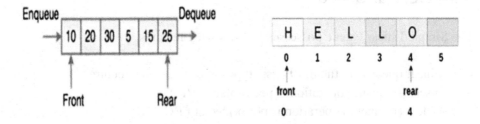

Figure 11. Linked list implementation of Queue

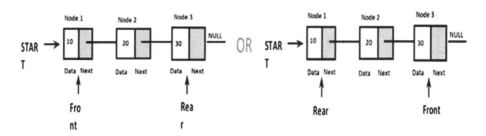

Figure 12. Linear Queue operations

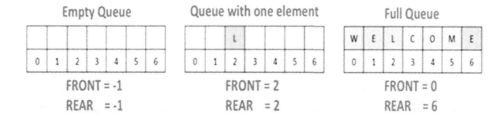

The linear queue operations are given in Figure 12.

Circular Queue

Figure 13 displays the Linear Queue along with its disadvantage.

Figure 13. Linear Queue with its disadvantage

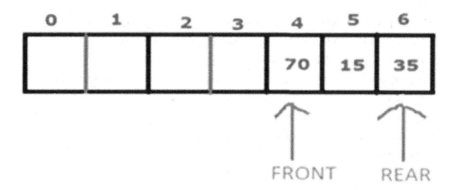

Figure 14. Circular Queue

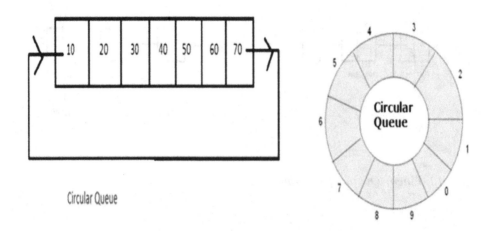

Circular Queue

Disadvantages of this linear Queue are enqueuer operation in the above Queue will generate an error message "Queue is full." However, the Queue has empty spots and cannot be used to save the element. To resolve this disadvantage, a circular Queue can be introduced (Charatan & Kans, 2022).

Features of Circular Queue

The following features are associated with the Circular Queue.

- The last node of the Queue will be connected to the first node of the Queue to form a circle shape, which is known as a circular Queue.
- It is more efficient than the linear queue data structure.
- Circular Queue accesses its data in the principle of First In First Out.
- Insert (Enqueue) operation is performed at FRONT at REAR & Delete (Dequeue) operation.
- FRONT and REAR will point to -1 when Queue is empty.
- FRONT and REAR will be the same when a single element exists.
- FRONT can be > REAR, unlike the Linear Queue.
- Full only when either FRONT = 0 and REAR = last index or FRONT = REAR+1.

The Circular Queue is specified in Figure 14, and the circular queue examples are presented in Figure 15.

Figure 15. Circular Queue examples

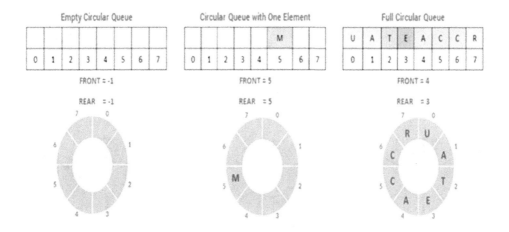

Sample Operations

Figure 16 provides a set of sample circular queue operations. These operations are used to manipulate a circular queue data structure, a linear data structure in which the first and last elements are connected to form a circle. These operations are essential for implementing and working with a circular queue data structure. By using these operations, we can add, remove, and manipulate elements in a circular queue. They also enable us to check the status of the circular Queue, such as if it is full or empty, and access the Front and Rear elements of the Queue (Aggarwal, 2021).

Double Ended Queue

A double-ended queue, a deque, is an ordered collection of queue-like items. It has two ends, Front and Rear, so the item stays in the collection, and the operations can be done at both ends.

Features of Double-Ended Queue

Here are the features that define the Double-Ended Queue.

- Double-ended Queue is also known as Deque (Not to be confused with Dequeue).
- FRONT and REAR will point to -1 when Queue is empty.
- FRONT and REAR will be the same when there exists a single element.

Figure 16. Circular Queue operations

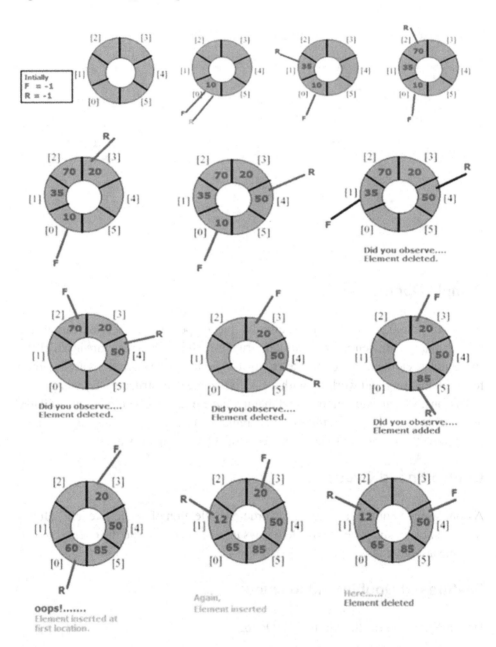

- Insert and delete can be performed on both ends (FRONT and REAR)

Figure 17. Double-ended Queue operations

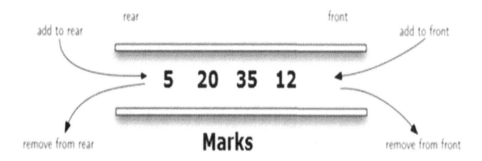

- EnqueFront will perform insert at FRONT, and EnqueueRear will perform insert at REAR.
- DequeueFront will perform delete at FRONT, and DequeRear will perform delete at REAR.

The Double-ended Queue operations are represented in Figure 17.

Priority Queue

A priority queue is an abstract data type resembling a simple queue data structure, with the addition of a "priority" value for each constituent of the Queue. Priority channels provide service to elements with a higher priority before those with a lower priority (Baka, 2017).

Features of Double-Ended Queue

The following features can describe the Double-Ended Queue.

- A priority queue is a type of Queue in which each data item is assigned an extra priority value, and items are accessed according to their priority.
- Data elements with a higher priority are accessed antecedent to those with a lower priority.
- If more than one data items have a similar priority value, it can be accessed in the order they were inserted into the priority queue.

Figure 18 depicts an example of a priority queue.

Figure 18. Priority Queue example

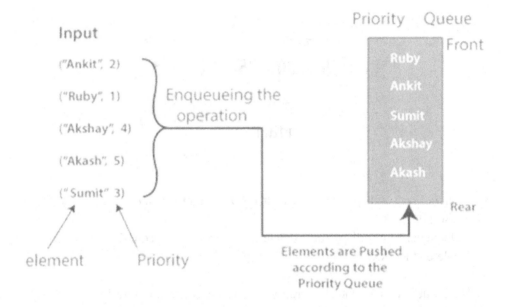

Python Code for Queue Operations

The Python code featured in Figure 19 and 20 is used for Queue operations.

APPLICATIONS OF QUEUE

Queue finds its applications in various domains, and some of them are listed below.

1. Service requests from a single shared resource (CPU, Disk, Printer, etc.) can be handled with the help of the Queue.

Figure 19. Queue data structure Python implementation Part 1

```python
# Queue Operations in python using classes and objects

# Create a Queue class
class Queue:
  # create constructor to define empty Queue
  def __init__(self):
    self.queue = []

  # Check the empty queue
  def is_empty(self):
    return len(self.queue) == 0

  # Add data item into the queue
  def enqueue(self, data):
    self.queue.append(data)
    print("Data item pushed into the queue : " + data)

  # Remove data item from the queue
  def dequeue(self):
    if (self.is_empty()):
        return "Queue Underflow"
    return self.queue.pop(0)

  # Print rear element from the queue
  def front(self):
    return self.queue[0]

  # Print front element from the queue
  def rear(self):
    return self.queue[len(self.queue)-1]

  # Print queue content
  def disp(self):
    print("Queue Contents are : " + str(self.queue))

  # Find size of the queue
  def size(self):
    return len(self.queue)

  # Search a data item from the queue
  def search(self, sdata):
    if (is_empty(self.queue)):
        print("Stack Underflow")
```

Figure 20. Queue data structure Python implementation Part 2

```
    elif sdata in self.queue:
        print('Data item ',sdata, ' is present in the queue')
    else:
        print('Data item ',sdata, ' is not present in the queue'
)

print("QUEUE OPERATIONS")
print('#'*20)
print('1. Enqueue an element')
print('2. Dequeue an element')
print('3. Get front element')
print('4. Get rear element')
print('5. Search an element')
print('6. Display Queue contents')
print('7. No. of elements in Queue')
print('8. Exit')

q = Queue()
while True:
    print("\n")
    ch=int(input('Enter your choice : '))
    print("\n")
    if ch==1:
        d=input('Enter the data item to be enqueued : ')
        q.enqueue(d)
    elif ch==2:
        print("Data item dequeued from the queue: " + q.dequeue(
))
    elif ch==3:
        print("Data item at the front of the queue: " + q.front(
))
    elif ch==4:
        print("Data item at the rear of the queue: " + q.rear())
    elif ch==5:
        s=input('Enter the data item to be searched : ')
        q.search(s)
    elif ch==6:
        q.disp()
    elif ch==7:
        print("Number of elements in the Stack : ", q.size())
    elif ch==8:
        print("End Program")
        break
    else:
        print ("Wrong choice, Try again with correct choice " )
```

2. Queues are used for asynchronous data transfer between two processes. Examples: File I/O, Pipes, and Sockets.
3. A call center phone system that uses queues to wait for a service agent to become available.
4. Frequently, computer systems must "hold" messages between two processes, programs, or even systems. This holding area is commonly known as a "buffer." It is implementable with a queue data structure.
5. The Round-robin processor scheduling algorithm is implemented using queues.

To discover the shortest path between two vertices in a weighted graph using search algorithms, artificial intelligence first attempts the most probable paths. A priority queue keeps track of undiscovered routes, prioritizing those with the minimum total path length.

DIFFERENCES BETWEEN STACK AND QUEUE DATA STRUCTURES

A few differences between Stack and Queue are discussed below for better understanding. The characteristics that distinguish Stack and Queue data structures are outlined in Table 8.

Table 8. Differences between Stack and Queue data structures

S.No.	Stack	Queue
1.	Data items can be accessed in a Last In First Out manner.	Data items can be accessed in a First In First Out manner.
2.	Only one marker is used [Top].	Two markers are used [Front and Rear].
3.	The Top is the only marker that helps do insertion and deletion operations.	The Rear helps to insert data items, and the Front helps to delete data items.
4.	Insert operation done through push().	Insert operation done through Enqueue().
5.	Delete operation done through pop().	Delete operation done through Dequeue().
6.	There is no memory wastage.	There is a chance for memory wastage.

CONCLUSION

The chapter thoroughly explained two essential linear data structures in computer science, namely Stack and Queue, by demonstrating their key features, operations, and implementation methods. Additionally, it has showcased the versatility of

Stack and Queue data structures by discussing their real-world applications, such as infix to postfix conversion, postfix expression evaluation, and finding the shortest path in a graph. The chapter has included clear and concise Python code snippets to make it easier for readers to comprehend and implement Stack and Queue data structures. This chapter has been an excellent resource for computer science students, researchers, and practitioners, providing a practical guide to understanding and utilizing these data structures. By exploring the different implementations and applications of Stack and Queue data structures, this chapter has offered readers a comprehensive understanding of how to apply them in various scenarios. Moreover, it has emphasized the critical differences between Stack and Queue data structures, enabling readers to choose the most appropriate structure for their needs. Overall, this chapter has provided a valuable resource for anyone looking to deepen their knowledge of Stack and Queue data structures.

REFERENCES

Aggarwal, S., & Kumar, N. (2021). Data structures. *Advances in Computers*, *121*, 43–81. doi:10.1016/bs.adcom.2020.08.002

Baka, B. (2017). *Python Data Structures and Algorithms*. Packt Publishing Ltd.

Charatan, Q., & Kans, A. (2022). Python Collections: Lists and Tuples. In *Programming in Two Semesters: Using Python and Java* (pp. 105–128). Springer International Publishing. doi:10.1007/978-3-031-01326-3_6

Cutler, J., Dickenson, M., Cutler, J., & Dickenson, M. (2020). Introduction to Data Structures. *Computational Frameworks for Political and Social Research with Python*, 59-71.

Dhruv, A. J., Patel, R., & Doshi, N. (2021). Python: the most advanced programming language for computer science applications. In *Proceedings of the international conference on culture heritage, education, sustainable tourism, and innovation technologies (CESIT 2020)* (pp. 292-299). Academic Press.

Goodrich, M. T., Tamassia, I. R., & Goldwasser, M. H. (2013). *Data Structures and Algorithms in Python*. John Wiley & Sons.

Harris, C. R., Millman, K. J., Van Der Walt, S. J., Gommers, R., Virtanen, P., Cournapeau, D., Wieser, E., Taylor, J., Berg, S., Smith, N. J., Kern, R., Picus, M., Hoyer, S., van Kerkwijk, M. H., Brett, M., Haldane, A., del Río, J. F., Wiebe, M., Peterson, P., ... Oliphant, T. E. (2020). Array programming with NumPy. *Nature*, *585*(7825), 357–362. doi:10.103841586-020-2649-2 PMID:32939066

Lambert, K. (2019). *Fundamentals of Python: Data Structures*. Cengage Learning.

Mailund, T. (2021). *Stacks and Queues. Introduction to Computational Thinking: Problem Solving, Algorithms, Data Structures, and More, 547-582*.

Vasudevan, S. K., Nagarajan, A. S., & Nanmaran, K. (2021). *Data Structures using Python*. Oxford University Press.

Chapter 5
Dynamic Programming With Python

Gurram Sunitha
School of Computing, Mohan Babu University, Tirupati, India

Arman Abouali
Technical University Clausthal, Germany

Mohammad Gouse Galety
ⓘD https://orcid.org/0000-0003-1666-2001
Samarkand International University of Technology, Uzbekistan

A. V. Sriharsha
Mohan Babu University, India

ABSTRACT

Algorithms are at the heart of computer programming. They form the basis of all software applications and help to solve complex computational problems. Various problem-solving strategies involve divide and conquer, greedy, recursion, dynamic programming, backtracking, etc. This can be used to solve optimization problems that have overlapping subproblems. It aims to find an optimal solution by breaking down a problem into sub-problems in order to manage the complexity of the problem-solving and remembering their solutions in order to avoid repeating computation time in future steps. Mathematical optimization is a crucial component of dynamic programming, and it allows us to efficiently solve a wide range of problems that involve making decisions over time. This chapter discusses dynamic programming's relevance, mathematical optimization, ability to solve a wide range of issues, important qualities, and top-down and bottom-up problem-solving methodologies. Dynamic programming solves some typical computational problems effectively, and Python code is supplied for reference.

DOI: 10.4018/978-1-6684-7100-5.ch005

INTRODUCTION

Algorithms are at the heart of computer programming. They form the basis of all software applications and help to solve complex computational problems. Various problem-solving strategies involve divide & conquer, greedy, recursion, dynamic programming, backtracking, etc. In optimization problems, greedy algorithms shall be used to find the best outcome given a set of conditions. The backtracking algorithm is used for problems that require exploring multiple solutions before finding the best one. The divide & conquer technique breaks a problem into smaller parts so that each part can be solved separately before being combined for a final solution. Finally, dynamic programming aims to find an optimal solution by breaking down a problem into sub-problems to manage the complexity of the problem-solving and remembering their answers to avoid repeating computation time in future steps. This chapter explores the fundamentals of dynamic programming and presents a detailed discussion of various computational problems solved using dynamic programming. Also, Python code is provided for reference.

DYNAMIC PROGRAMMING

Dynamic Programming is an essential algorithmic technique used to solve complex problems efficiently. It is widely used in various fields, such as computer science, operations research, and economics. Dynamic programming can solve optimization problems with overlapping subproblems by breaking them down into smaller subproblems and storing their solutions in a table for later use. This technique helps reduce the time complexity of these problems and makes them easier to solve (Kool et al., 2022). Dynamic programming is beneficial when dealing with issues that depend on previously calculated solutions or where multiple decisions must be made simultaneously (Şenaras, et al., 2021).

"Dynamic Programming" makes sense as dynamic means' changing' and programming means 'the set of instructions to be executed.' This was introduced by "Richard Bellman" in the 1950s, which is a mathematical optimization and a computer programming technique. This has been used in various disciplines, from economics to aeronautical engineering. Let us imagine what happens if a non-optimized code consumes much memory and computing time. Consequently, the processor may need help allocating resources for other services. Most of these problems can be controlled by using dynamic programming (Bertsekas, 2022).

Expressed, this is a technique for resolving complex problems by breaking them down into smaller, more manageable sub-problems and archiving the solutions for use when the smaller sub-problems come up later. The subproblems are computed to find the optimal solution to the complex problem. In brief words, this is an optimization technique over plain recursion.

Mathematical Optimization in Dynamic Programming

Mathematical optimization plays a significant role in dynamic programming, a powerful technique for solving problems involving making decisions over time. In dynamic programming, a problem is typically broken down into smaller sub-problems that can be solved recursively. The optimization part of dynamic programming involves finding the best decision at each sequence step to maximize some objective function. The objective function being maximized could be anything, depending on the problem (Taylor, 2019). For instance, the goal of a scheduling task can be to reduce the overall time complexity of the execution of a batch of jobs. Minimizing the overall cost of retaining inventory over time may be the goal function in an inventory management problem.

Optimization in dynamic programming can be done in several ways, depending on the problem being solved. One common technique is using a dynamic programming algorithm such as the Bellman-Ford or Dijkstra algorithms. These algorithms work by recursively computing the optimal decisions at each step in the sequence and using these decisions to build up a solution to the overall problem. Another technique for optimization in dynamic programming is to use linear programming. Linear programming is an essential problem-solving technique with applications in various fields. It can maximize or minimize operational resources, allocate resources efficiently, develop production and distribution plans, and solve optimization problems. Through linear programming, organizations can make more informed decisions that result in improved profits and outcomes. This technique is beneficial when there are multiple possible solutions with uncertain variables, as it enables organizations to make data-driven decisions based on strict parameters. Overall, mathematical optimization is a crucial component of dynamic programming, and it allows us to efficiently solve a wide range of problems that involve making decisions over time (Liu et al., 2020).

Key Attributes of Dynamic Programming

Dynamic programming is an algorithm-based approach to finding a problem's optimal solution. It involves breaking down a complex problem into smaller subproblems and solving each separately. With dynamic programming, reducing the time needed to solve a problem significantly by storing intermediate results in memory is possible. It can be applied to various issues, from optimization and planning to game theory and machine learning. It should be emphasized that the best solution to each subproblem affects the overall situation. The critical component of the optimization process in dynamic programming is the multistage aspect of problem-solving (Cooper, 2016). Dynamic programming offers a more all-encompassing framework for problem analysis than the other optimization methods.

Ingenuity is usually required before a particular challenge can be effectively comprehended as a dynamic programme. Delicate insights are frequently needed to reconstruct the formulation to solve it successfully. The steps in solving a problem using dynamic programming are as follows (Kennedy, 2012):

- **Define the Problem and Identify the Subproblems:** Dynamic programming is often used to solve problems that can be broken down into smaller subproblems. Define the problem you want to solve and identify the subproblems that will help you reach the solution.
- **Formulate a Recursive Relation:** Once you have identified the subproblems, you can formulate a recursive relation that describes the solution to each subproblem in terms of the solutions to smaller subproblems. This is often called the "optimal substructure" property.
- **Create a Memoization Table:** To avoid redundant computations, create a table to store the solutions to the subproblems as you compute them. This is called memoization, a key feature of dynamic programming.
- **Compute the Solutions to the Subproblems:** Starting with the smallest subproblems, use the recursive relation to compute the solutions to larger subproblems, filling in the memoization table as you go.
- **Build the Solution to the Original Problem:** Once you have computed the solutions to all of the subproblems, you can use them to build the solution to the actual problem.
- **Analyze the Time and Space Complexity:** As with any algorithm, it is essential to analyze your dynamic programming solution's time and space complexity to ensure it is efficient enough for your needs.

Its subproblem should possess the following key attributes to solve any problem using dynamic programming. They include:

- **Overlapping Subproblems:** Subproblems are said to be overlapping in nature if the subproblems are calculated multiple times to compute the original solution of the problem.
- **Optimal Substructure:** Any problem is said to have an optimal substructure if the complex problem's optimal solution is obtained by recursively solving the subproblem.

To solve a problem using a dynamic programming technique, it must have both overlapping subproblems and optimal substructure properties.

Other key attributes of Dynamic Programming include:

- Memoization stores the solutions to subproblems in a table or array for future reference. Memoization is used to avoid the repeated computation of subproblems and speed up the overall problem-solving process.
- **Computational Complexity:** Dynamic Programming can solve problems that would otherwise be computationally infeasible. By breaking the problem down into smaller subproblems and storing the solutions to these subproblems, Dynamic Programming can reduce the computational complexity of a problem from exponential to polynomial.
- **Greedy Approach:** In some cases, Dynamic Programming can be used to solve problems using a Greedy method. This involves making locally optimal choices at each step of the problem, which leads to a globally optimal solution. However, not all problems can be solved using a greedy approach, and in these cases, Dynamic Programming can provide an alternative solution.

Top-Down Approach of Dynamic Programming

Bottom-up dynamic programming is an efficient and effective way to solve programming problems. It is based on breaking down complex issues into simpler subproblems and then systematically solving them. This approach enables the programmer to efficiently solve a problem by solving its smaller subproblems and combining their solutions. Doing so eliminates the need for recomputing the key multiple times, thus saving time and memory space. This makes it ideal for many real-world applications, such as solving complex optimization problems, parsing natural language texts, AI planning and scheduling tasks, etc. When the function is called with a particular problem instance, it first checks whether the solution for that instance is already in the memoization table. If it is, the function returns the precomputed solution. Otherwise, it recursively computes the answer for that instance while storing the result in the memoization table for future use (Tarek et al., 2020).

The top-down approach of dynamic programming involves the following general steps:

1. **Identify the Subproblems:** Break down the problem into smaller subproblems. Identify the recurring patterns and overlapping subproblems.
2. **Define the Memoization Table:** Create a table that stores the solutions to the subproblems. This table can be a 2D array or a hash table, depending on the problem.

3. **Define the Base Cases:** Define the base cases for the subproblems. The base cases are the simplest subproblems that can be solved directly without further recursion.

4. **Define the Recursive Function:** Define a recursive function that solves the subproblems using the memoization table. This function should check the memoization table first to see if the solution to the subproblem has already been computed. If it has not, then the function should solve the subproblem recursively.

5. **Populate the Memoization Table:** Call the recursive function with the initial parameters and populate the memoization table with the solutions to the subproblems.

6. **Return the Final Solution:** Once the memoization table has been populated, return the solution to the original problem, which will be stored in the memoization table at the appropriate position.

Overall, the top-down approach involves breaking down the problem into smaller subproblems, solving them recursively using memoization to avoid redundant computations, and returning the solution to the original problem based on the solutions to the subproblems.

The essential advantage of the top-down approach is that it allows us to avoid recomputing the same subproblems multiple times. By caching the intermediate results, the exponential time complexity of the algorithm can be managed to a polynomial level.

Bottom-Up Approach of Dynamic Programming

The bottom-up approach of dynamic programming is a technique used to solve optimization problems by breaking them down into smaller subproblems and solving them iteratively. In this approach, we start by solving the subproblems and then combine their solutions to find the solution to the original problem.

We typically use a table to store the solutions to the subproblems to implement the bottom-up approach. The table is usually filled systematically, starting from the smallest subproblems and gradually building up to the larger ones until we solve the original problem.

Here are the general steps involved in implementing the bottom-up approach of dynamic programming:

1. **Identify the Subproblems:** Break down the problem into smaller subproblems. Identify the recurring patterns and overlapping subproblems.

2. **Define the Memoization Table:** Create a table that stores the solutions to the subproblems. This table can be a 2D array or a hash table, depending on the problem.

3. **Define the Base Cases:** Define the base cases for the subproblems. The base cases are the simplest subproblems that can be solved directly without further recursion.

4. **Populate the Memoization Table:** Fill in the memoization table with the solutions to the subproblems in a bottom-up manner. Start with the base cases and work up to the final solution.

5. **Return the Final Solution:** Once the memoization table has been fully populated, return the solution to the original problem, which will be stored in the memoization table at the appropriate position.

Overall, the bottom-up approach involves breaking down the problem into smaller subproblems, solving them iteratively using memoization to avoid redundant computations, and returning the solution to the original problem based on the solutions to the subproblems. The bottom-up approach of dynamic programming is usually more efficient than the top-down approach because it avoids the overhead of recursion and memoization. However, it may require more memory to store the table of solutions.

Applications of Dynamic Programming

Dynamic programming is a powerful algorithmic technique that can be applied to various problems. Here are some examples of its applications (Bellman, 1957; Rosso & Venturino, 2023; Terek, 2020):

- **Optimization Problems:** Dynamic programming can solve optimization problems where the goal is to maximize or minimize some function. Examples include the knapsack, traveling salesman, and most extended common subsequence problems.

- **Path-Finding Problems:** Dynamic programming can be used to find the shortest or longest path in a graph or grid. Examples include Dijkstra's algorithm and the Floyd-Warshall algorithm.

- **Game Theory:** Dynamic programming can be used to analyze and solve games, such as the minimax algorithm for two-player games.

- **Machine Learning:** Dynamic programming is used in various machine learning techniques, such as reinforcement learning, where an agent learns to make decisions by maximizing a reward function.

- **Image Processing:** Dynamic programming can be used for image analysis and processing tasks such as object tracking, segmentation, and feature detection.
- **Natural Language Processing:** Dynamic programming can be used in natural language processing tasks such as speech recognition, machine translation, and text summarization.
- **Bioinformatics:** Dynamic programming is widely used for sequence alignment, gene prediction, and protein structure prediction.
- **Financial Modeling:** Dynamic programming can model financial decisions such as portfolio optimization, option pricing, and risk management.

Dynamic programming is a versatile and powerful tool for solving complex problems across many domains. Further, this chapter presents a detailed discussion of various computational problems solved using dynamic programming – Fibonacci Series, Towers of Hanoi Puzzle, Checkered Board Problem, and Dijkstra's Algorithm (Li et al., 2020; Senaras et al., 2020; Li et al., 2020).

FIBONACCI SERIES

The Fibonacci series is an essential mathematical concept in computer science. It can solve many problems, such as computing the nth Fibonacci number and more.

Dynamic programming can be understood with a simple example of the Fibonacci series. Let us consider generating the "nth" term of the Fibonacci series as a complex problem to be solved. The Nth term of the Fibonacci series is equal to the sum of $(N-1)^{th}$ Fibonacci term and $(N-2)^{th}$ Fibonacci term. The Fibonacci series problem and the inherent recurrence of the subproblems are shown in Figure 1. Observe the subproblems being repeated (similarly colored for visual reference). In the figure showcasing the first two levels of problem division into smaller tasks or subproblems, it can be observed that subproblem-2 is repeated, and subproblem-11 is repeated.

The Fibonacci series problem inherently comprehends two features – its subproblem's solutions depend on previously calculated solutions, and subproblems repeatedly occur over time. Let us understand with the help of an example. For example, the complex problem is $F(5)$, where F is the Fibonacci function (the task is to generate the 5th term of the Fibonacci series). The process of $F(5)$ is described as follows.

a. To calculate $F(5)$, we need to calculate $F(4)$ and $F(3)$ terms as $F(5)$ is expressed as the sum of $F(4)$ and $F(3)$. ($F(4)$ and $F(3)$ are subproblems)

Figure 1. Fibonacci series problem and the inherent recurrence of the subproblems

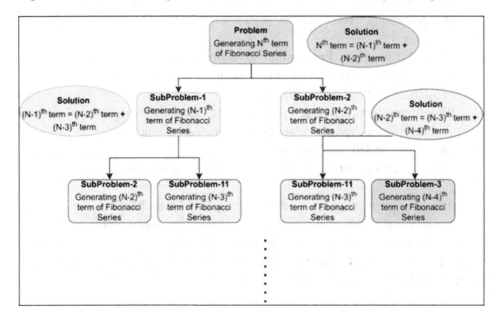

b. To calculate $F(4)$, we need to calculate $F(3)$ and $F(2)$ terms as $F(4)$ is expressed as the sum of $F(3)$ and $F(2)$. Here the subproblem $F(3)$ is repeated. ($F(3)$ and $F(2)$ are subproblems)

c. To calculate $F(3)$, we need to calculate $F(2)$ and $F(1)$ terms as $F(3)$ is expressed as the sum of $F(2)$ and $F(1)$. Here the subproblem $F(2)$ is repeated. ($F(2)$ and $F(1)$ are subproblems)

and so on.

This process of calculating the subproblems multiple times to obtain the optimal solution to obtain $F(5)$ is known as the overlapping of subproblems. Also, observe that solution of a Fibonacci series problem (or subproblem) depends on the resolution of its subproblems. Hence, the Fibonacci series problem inherently exhibits both the required features; therefore, dynamic programming is the best technique to solve the problem.

Generating Fibonacci Series Using Dynamic Programming With Python

One way to solve the problem of generating the first N Fibonacci terms is to use dynamic programming with a top-down approach. This approach utilizes memoization to store intermediate results and can significantly reduce the time complexity of a given problem. This section will explore using this approach to solve Fibonacci series-related problems. Dynamic programming for solving the Fibonacci series problem using a top-down approach works as follows - the concept is similar to the recursive technique. Still, the answers to any of the subproblems are preserved when the subproblems are encountered and solved for the first time. The held result will be used in the top-down approach whenever the subproblem is reencountered. As a result, each subproblem has to be solved precisely once. This provides savings in the computational time for solving the problem (Forootani et al., 2021; Xu & Wu, 2021; Xie et al., 2021).

The following is the Python code for generating the first *N* Fibonacci terms using dynamic programming (top-down approach). Sample input and output are also presented. We will start with a top-down approach to dynamic programming.

```python
# Initializing the first two terms of the Fibonacci Series
fib_list = [0, 1]
# Defining a function fibonac() to generate the Fibonacci
Series
def fibonac(n):
    # If the number 'n' is less than or equal to two, return
(n-1)th
    # Fibonacci term
    if n <= len(fib_list):
        return fib_list[n-1]
    # If the number 'n' is more significant than two, generate
the Fibonacci
    # Series
    else:
        # Computing the nth term in Fibonacci Series
        next = fibonac(n-1) + fibonac(n-2)
        # Storing the next term in the list
        fib_list.append(next)
        # Displaying the next term
        print((next), end = ' ')
        # Returning the Fibonacci term
        return next
# Prompting user to enter his choice for the number of
Fibonacci terms to # be generated
n = int (input ("How many Fibonacci terms are to be generated?
\
                (Enter any number > 2): "))
```

```
# Displaying the first two terms of the Fibonacci Series
print (0, 1, end = ' ')
# Calling function fibonac() to generate Fibonacci Series
fibonac(n)
```

Input: How many Fibonacci terms are to be generated? (Enter any number > 2): 5
Output: 0 1 1 2 3

In dynamic programming using the bottom-up approach, the subproblems are reordered for solving. Only two intermediate results are to be stored at a time, which will allow computing the solution to each subproblem only once. For instance, all that is required are the answers to $F(1)$ and $F(0)$ when trying to generate $F(2)$. Similarly, generating $F(2)$ and $F(3)$ requires that we have the answers to F(2) and F(1). As a result, the solution will consume less memory. The following is the Python code for generating the Fibonacci series using dynamic programming (bottom-up approach).

```
# Prompting user to enter his choice for the number of
Fibonacci
# terms to be generated
N = int (input ("How many Fibonacci terms will be generated?
                (Enter any number > 2): "))
# If the number 'N' is equal to zero or one, display the first
# ' N' Fibonacci terms and exit; If the number 'N' is greater
than # or equal to two, display the first 'N' Fibonacci terms
if N == 0:
    exit()
elif N == 1:
    print (0, end = ' ')
    exit()
elif N >= 2:
    print (0, 1, end = ' ')
# initializing the first two Fibonacci terms
A = 0
B = 1
# Generating the remaining Fibonacci terms
for i in range(3, N+1):
    # Calculate the next Fibonacci Term
    temp = A + B
    # Displaying Fibonacci term
    print (temp, end = ' ')
    # storing the most recent two Fibonacci terms
```

```
A = B
B = temp
```

Input: How many Fibonacci terms are to be generated? (Enter any number > 2): 8
Output: 0 1 1 2 3 5 8 13

For the top-down approach, each subproblem is solved only once. Since each subproblem takes a constant amount of time to solve, this gives an O(N) time complexity. However, since an array of size *N + 1* needs to be maintained to save all the intermediate results, the space complexity is *O(N)*. In the bottom-up approach, each subproblem is solved only once. So, the time complexity of the algorithm is O(N). However, only the most recent two Fibonacci terms are only to be maintained; the space complexity is a constant, which is O(1).

TOWERS OF HANOI PUZZLE

The Towers of Hanoi problem can be solved using dynamic programming using a memoization approach. The problem statement is as follows: given three towers and n disks (each of the disks of a different size), the objective is to move the entire stack of disks from one tower to another tower with the following restrictions:

- Only one disk can be moved at a time.
- Each move consists of taking the upper disk from one of the stacks and placing it on top of another.
- No disk may be placed on top of a smaller disk.

To solve this problem using dynamic programming, a function Hanoi(n, source, target, aux) that takes four arguments can be defined where:

- n: is the number of disks to move
- source: is the tower where the disks are initially located
- aux: is an auxiliary tower to help with the move
- target: is the tower where the disks should be moved to

The base case for this function is when n = 1. In this case, the top disk is moved from the source tower to the target tower. For n > 1, memoization can be used to avoid redundant computations. The result of each call to Hanoi (n, source, target, aux) shall be stored in a table, indexed by the values of n, source, target, aux. If a call to Hanoi (n, source, target, aux) already in the table is encountered, simply the stored result shall be returned. The recursive algorithm for Hanoi (n, source, target, aux) is as follows:

1. If n = 1, move the top disk from source to target.
2. Otherwise, recursively move n-1 disks from source to aux, using target as the auxiliary tower.
3. Move the largest disk from source to target.
4. Recursively move n-1 disks from aux to target, using the source as the auxiliary tower.

The Python code for the dynamic programming solution (top-down approach) to the Towers of Hanoi problem is as follows:

```
# define a memoization table to store the results of
subproblems
memo = {}
def Hanoi(n, source, target, aux):
    # Check if we have already computed the solution for this
    # subproblem
    if (n, source, target, aux) in memo:
        return memo[(n, source, target, aux)]
    # In the situation of the base case, the top disk has to be
moved
    # from the source tower to the target tower
    if n == 1:
        move(source, target)
        memo[(n, source, target, aux)] = 1
        return 1
    # In the situation of Recursive case, n-1 number of disks
have to
    # moved from the source tower to the auxiliary tower
    else:
        Hanoi(n-1, source, aux, target)
        move(source, target)
        Hanoi(n-1, aux, target, source)
        # Update the memoization table with the solution to
this
        # subproblem
        memo[(n, source, target, aux)] = memo.get((n-1, source,
aux,
```

```
            target), 0) + 1 + memo.get((n-1, aux, target,
source), 0)
        return memo[(n, source, target, aux)]
def move(source, target):
    print("Disk moved ", source, "->", target)
# example usage:
n = int(input("How many number of disks are to be moved?  "))
print("Total number of moves required:, "Hanoi(n, 'A', 'C',
'B'))
```

Input:
How many number of disks are to be moved? 3
Output:

Disk moved A -> C
Disk moved A -> B
Disk moved C -> B
Disk moved A -> C
Disk moved B -> A
Disk moved B -> C

Total Number of Moves Required: 7

This function takes four arguments: the number of disks to be moved (n), source tower (source), auxiliary tower (aux), and target tower (target). It also takes an optional memo dictionary, which stores the results of previous function calls. The function first checks whether the result of this particular call to Hanoi is already in the memo dictionary. If it is, it returns the stored result. Otherwise, it checks whether n is equal to 1. If it is, it simply moves the top disk from the source tower to the target tower and stores this move in the memo dictionary. If n is greater than 1, the function recursively calls itself to move n-1 disks from the source tower to the auxiliary tower, using the target tower as the auxiliary tower. It then stores the result of this recursive call in the memo dictionary. It then moves the largest disk from the source tower to the target tower and adds this move to the result list. Finally, it recursively calls itself to move n-1 disks from the auxiliary tower to the target tower, using the source tower as the auxiliary tower.

DIJKSTRA'S ALGORITHM

Dijkstra's algorithm is famous for finding the shortest path in a weighted graph with non-negative weights. Dynamic programming can be used to implement this algorithm efficiently, which involves breaking down a more significant problem into smaller subproblems and solving each subproblem only once. Dijkstra's algorithm is a popular approach for finding the shortest path from a source node to all other nodes in a weighted graph. The basic idea behind Dijkstra's algorithm is to start at the source node and repeatedly visit the unvisited neighbor with the smallest tentative distance until all nodes have been processed. It is commonly implemented using a priority queue to maintain the vertices that have not yet been processed.

A top-down approach to implementing Dijkstra's algorithm using dynamic programming involves the following steps:

1. Initialize the distance to the source node as 0 and the distance to all other nodes as infinity.
2. Create a priority queue (min heap) to maintain the set of unvisited nodes.
3. Insert the source node into the priority queue with a priority of 0.
4. While the priority queue is not empty, do the following:
   a. Extract the node with the smallest tentative distance from the priority queue.
   b. For each unvisited neighbor of the extracted node, do the following:
      i. Calculate the tentative distance to the neighbor by adding the weight of the edge between the two nodes to the distance of the extracted node.
      ii. If the tentative distance is smaller than the neighbor's current distance, update the neighbor's distance in the distance array and insert the neighbor into the priority queue with the new distance as its priority.
5. After all, nodes have been processed; the distance array will contain the shortest distance from the source node to all other nodes.

This top-down approach uses memoization to avoid redundant calculations. It is beneficial when the graph is large and sparse, allowing us to focus on the subproblems needed to find the shortest path. A Python code implementation top-down dynamic programming solution to find the shortest distance between a start node to all the other nodes in the weighted graph using Dijkstra's algorithm is as follows:

```
import heapq as hp
# Dijkstra() function returns a list of shortest distances from
```

```
the
# start node to all the other nodes in the graph
def dijkstra(graph, start):
    # Initialize distances to all nodes
    distances = {node: float('inf') for node in graph}
    distances[start] = 0
    # Create a heap to store nodes that need to be processed
    heap = [(0, start)]
    # Iterate until all nodes have been processed
    while heap:
        # Get the node with the smallest distance from the heap
        (curr_dist, curr_node) = hp.heappop(heap)
        # If the current distance is > than the previously
        # calculated distance, skip it
        if curr_dist > distances[curr_node]:
            continue
        # Update the distances of all the neighbors of current
node
        for neighbor, weight in graph[curr_node].items():
            distance = curr_dist + weight
            # Update the distance of current node if required
            if distance < distances[neighbor]:
                distances[neighbor] = distance
                # Add the neighbor to the heap to be processed
                hp.heappush(heap, (distance, neighbor))
    # Return the list of shortest distances
    return distances
# Sample graph
graph = {
    1: {2: 2, 3:4, 4:2},
    2: {3: 3, 4:1},
    3: {1: 4},
    4: {3:1}
}
# Sample function call to find shortest routes from node 1 to
all
# other nodes
d = dijkstra(graph, 1)
print(d)
```

Output:

{1: 0, 2: 2, 3: 3, 4: 2}

The graph parameter in the above code is assumed to be a list of adjacency lists, where graph[i] is a list of pairs {j: w} representing the edges going out from node i, where j is the index of the neighbor node and w is the weight of the edge. 'start' is the starting node for the algorithm. The algorithm uses a heap to store the graph nodes that need processing. The heap is maintained with the nodes with the smallest distance from the start node at the top. The algorithm iterates until all nodes have been processed, updating the distances to each neighbor of the current node if the new distance is shorter than the current distance (Gouse et al., 2019; Reshma et al., 2022).

CHECKERED BOARD PROBLEM

The Checkered Board Problem is a classic puzzle in mathematics. The problem can be stated as follows:

Given a checkered board of size n x n, where n is an even number, and two types of tiles - black and white, how many ways are there to fill the checkered board with these tiles such that no two adjacent tiles have the same color?

The Checkered board problem can be solved using the top-down dynamic programming approach. Let us define a function countWays(i, j, color) that calculates the number of ways to fill the checkered board of size "i x j" with the given color of the top-left cell. The color parameter can be either "B" or "W" for black or white.

The base cases of the function are as follows:

1. If the size of the board is 1 x 1, return 1.
2. If the board size is 1 x 2, return 2 if the top-left cell has the same color as the second cell; otherwise, return 1.
3. If the board size is 2 x 1, return 2 if the top-left cell has the same color as the second cell; otherwise, return 1.

For the recursive case, we need to consider two issues:

1. If the top-left cell has the same color as the second cell, we can only fill the rest of the board with alternating colors. So, we need to calculate the number of ways to fill the remaining board with the opposite color. This can be done

by calling the countWays(i-2, j, oppositeColor) function, where oppositeColor is the contrasting color of the top-left cell.

2. If the top-left cell has a different color than the second cell, we can either fill the second cell with the same color as the top-left cell or with the opposite color. So, we need to calculate the number of ways to fill the remaining board in both cases and add them up. This can be done by calling the countWays(i-2, j, sameColor) and countWays(i-2, j, oppositeColor) functions, where sameColor is the same color as the top-left cell and oppositeColor is the opposite color of the top-left cell.

Finally, we need to memoize the results of the function to avoid redundant computations. Here is the Python code for the solution:

```
memo = {}
def countWays(rows, cols, color):
    if (rows, cols, color) in memo:
        return memo[(rows, cols, color)]
    if rows == 1 and cols == 1:
        return 1
    elif rows == 1 and cols == 2:
        return 2 if color == "B" else 1
    elif rows == 2 and cols == 1:
        return 2 if color == "B" else 1
    sameColor = color
    oppositeColor = "B" if color == "W" else "W"
    if color == "B":
        oppositeColor = "W"
    else:
        oppositeColor = "B"
    if color == "B":
        if (rows-2, cols, oppositeColor) not in memo:
            memo[(rows-2, cols, oppositeColor)] = \
                        countWays(rows-2, cols, oppositeColor)
        return memo[(rows-2, cols, oppositeColor)]
    else:
        if (rows-2, cols, sameColor) not in memo:
            memo[(rows-2,cols,sameColor)]= \
                        countWays(rows-
2,cols,sameColor)
print(countWays(2,1,"B"))
```

Output:

2

Since they make it possible to solve challenging computational problems, algorithms are crucial to computer programming. Dynamic programming is an algorithmic technique that addresses optimization challenges with overlapping subproblems by dividing issues into smaller ones and memorizing the solutions. Mathematical optimization is a crucial element of dynamic programming that enables long-term problem solutions. The importance of dynamic programming, its versatility, and how it may be used to solve problems are all emphasized in this chapter. Additionally, the chapter covers top-down and bottom-up problem-solving strategies utilizing dynamic programming and offers Python code as a resource (Gouse et al., 2018; Samanta et al., 2021; Gouse et al., 2021).

CONCLUSION

Dynamic programming is an algorithmic approach that enables us to solve complex problems by breaking them into smaller sub-problems and solving each optimally. It can identify which parts of the problem can be reused from previous attempts at solving it, thus saving time and resources. In this perspective, this chapter presented a detailed discussion of dynamic programming - its importance, mathematical optimization, skill in solving various problems, key attributes, and the top-down and bottom-up approaches for problem-solving. A few of the famous computational problems are undertaken to solve them efficiently using dynamic programming, and the Python code is provided for reference. Dynamic programming is a powerful tool for tackling complex issues, particularly involving large amounts of data or multiple inputs. This method is often used in robotics and artificial intelligence to improve efficiency and accuracy. It also has applications in finance, economics, logistics, computer vision, and natural language processing.

REFERENCES

Bellman, R. E. (1957). *Dynamic programming, ser. Cambridge Studies in Speech Science and Communication*. Princeton University Press.

Bertsekas, D. (2022). *Abstract dynamic programming*. Athena Scientific.

Cooper, L., & Cooper, M. W. (2016). *Introduction to Dynamic Programming: International Series in Modern Applied Mathematics and Computer Science* (Vol. 1). Elsevier.

Forootani, A., Tipaldi, M., Ghaniee Zarch, M., Liuzza, D., & Glielmo, L. (2021). Modelling and solving resource allocation problems via a dynamic programming approach. *International Journal of Control*, *94*(6), 1544–1555. doi:10.1080/0020 7179.2019.1661521

Gouse, G. M., & Ahmed, A. N. (2019). Ensuring the public cloud security on scalability feature. *Journal of Advanced Research in Dynamical and Control Systems*, *11*(1), 132–137.

Gouse, M. (2018). *Optimized Secure Scan Flip Flop to Thwart Side Channel Attack in Crypto-Chip*. Academic Press.

Gouse, M. (2021). Deep Neural Network Concepts for Classification using Convolutional Neural Network: A Systematic Review and Evaluation. *Technium Romanian Journal of Applied Sciences and Technology.*, *3*(8), 58–70. doi:10.47577/ technium.v3i8.4554

Kennedy, J. O. (Ed.). (2012). *Dynamic programming: applications to agriculture and natural resources*. Springer Science & Business Media.

Kool, W., van Hoof, H., Gromicho, J., & Welling, M. (2022, June). Deep policy dynamic programming for vehicle routing problems. In *Integration of Constraint Programming, Artificial Intelligence, and Operations Research: 19th International Conference, CPAIOR 2022, Los Angeles, CA, USA, June 20-23, 2022, Proceedings* (pp. 190-213). Cham: Springer International Publishing. 10.1007/978-3-031-08011-1_14

Li, G., Rana, M. N., Sun, J., Song, Y., & Qu, J. (2020). Real-time image enhancement with efficient dynamic programming. *Multimedia Tools and Applications*, *79*(41-42), 30883–30903. doi:10.100711042-020-09586-y

Li, X., Ye, X., & Lu, L. (2020). Dynamic Programming Approaches for Solving Shortest Path Problem in Transportation: Comparison and Application. In *Green, Smart and Connected Transportation Systems: Proceedings of the 9th International Conference on Green Intelligent Transportation Systems and Safety* (pp. 141-160). Springer Singapore.

Liu, D., Xue, S., Zhao, B., Luo, B., & Wei, Q. (2020). Adaptive dynamic programming for control: A survey and recent advances. *IEEE Transactions on Systems, Man, and Cybernetics. Systems*, *51*(1), 142–160. doi:10.1109/TSMC.2020.3042876

Reshma, G., Al-Atroshi, C., Nassa, V. K., Geetha, B. T., Sunitha, G., Galety, M. G., & Neelakandan, S. (2022). Deep Learning-Based Skin Lesion Diagnosis Model Using Dermoscopic Images. *Intelligent Automation & Soft Computing, 31*(1).

Rosso, A., & Venturino, E. (2023). A Dynamic Programming Approach to Ecosystem Management. *Algorithms*, *16*(3), 139. doi:10.3390/a16030139

Samanta, D., Dutta, S., Gouse, M., & Pramanik, S. (2021). *A Novel Approach for Web Mining Taxonomy for High-Performance Computing*. doi:10.1007/978-981-16-4284-5_37

Şenaras, A. E., İnanç, Ş., Sezen, H. K., & Şenaras, O. M. (2021). Shortest Route Application via Dynamic Programming in the Transportation Networks. In *Handbook of Research on Decision Sciences and Applications in the Transportation Sector* (pp. 362–371). IGI Global. doi:10.4018/978-1-7998-8040-0.ch017

Tarek, A., Elsayed, H., Rashad, M., & Hassan, M. (2020, October). Dynamic programming applications: a suvrvey. In *2020 2nd Novel Intelligent and Leading Emerging Sciences Conference (NILES)* (pp. 380-385). IEEE. 10.1109/NILES50944.2020.9257968

Taylor, C. R. (2019). *Applications of dynamic programming to agricultural decision problems*. CRC Press. doi:10.1201/9780429040917

Xie, F., Li, H., & Xu, Z. (2021). An approximate dynamic programming approach to project scheduling with uncertain resource availabilities. *Applied Mathematical Modelling*, *97*, 226–243. doi:10.1016/j.apm.2021.03.048

Xu, J., & Wu, S. (2021, April). Analysis and Application of Dynamic Programming. *Journal of Physics: Conference Series*, *1865*(4), 042023. doi:10.1088/1742-6596/1865/4/042023

Chapter 6
Exploratory Data Analysis in Python

R. Sruthi
Coimbatore Institute of Technology, India

G. B. Anuvarshini
Coimbatore Institute of Technology, India

M. Sujithra
Coimbatore Institute of Technology, India

ABSTRACT

Data science is extremely important because of the immense value of data. Python provides extensive library support for data science and analytics, which has functions, tools, and methods to manage and analyze data. Python Libraries are used for exploratory data analysis. Libraries in Python such as Numpy, Pandas, Matplotlib, SciPy, etc. are used for the same. Data visualization's major objective is to make it simpler to spot patterns, trends, and outliers in big data sets. One of the processes in the data science process is data visualization, which asserts that after data has been gathered, processed, and modelled, it must be represented to draw conclusions. As a result, it is crucial to have systems in place for managing and regulating the quality of corporate data, metadata, and data sources. So, this chapter focuses on the libraries used in Python, their properties, functions, how few data structures are related to them, and a detailed explanation about their purpose serving as a better foundation for learning them.

DOI: 10.4018/978-1-6684-7100-5.ch006

INTRODUCTION

The vital process of performing primary analyses on data to explore new trends, patterns, identify outliers, hypotheses, and cross-check assumptions using summary of data's statistics and graphical representations is known as exploratory data analysis. Exploratory Data Analysis (EDA) is not a formal procedure with rigid guidelines. The approach to EDA emphasizes open-mindedness and the exploration of various notions in the early stages of analysis. Some concepts utilized may succeed while others may fail, highlighting the beauty of EDA as a means of exploring uncertainty. Despite the availability of predefined methods and techniques, exploratory data analysis remains a crucial component in any data analysis. As research progresses, certain fruitful areas will be discovered, documented, and shared with others.

PYTHON LIBRARIES TO PERFORM EDA

Numpy

NumPy is a powerful Python library for efficient array manipulation and numerical computing (Harris et al., 2022). Originally known as "Numeric," it evolved into NumPy with enhanced capabilities. Its optimized C programming and extensive functions make it the standard for array computation, supporting tasks like linear algebra and Fourier transformations. With a vibrant community and easy accessibility, NumPy is widely used in data analysis, machine learning, and more.

Pandas

Pandas is a Python library that efficiently manipulates diverse data, collaborating seamlessly with other data science libraries like NumPy, Matplotlib, SciPy, and scikit-learn. It plays a vital role in machine learning by accurately exploring, cleaning, transforming, and visualizing data. Jupyter notebook facilitates easy execution of Pandas programs, enabling data visualization and analysis. Pandas expand Python's data analysis capabilities with essential procedures: data loading, manipulation, preparation, modeling, and analysis (Ateeq & Afzal, 2023).

SciPy

SciPy is a powerful Python library that builds upon NumPy, providing multidimensional arrays for scientific and mathematical problem-solving (Khandare et al., 2023). It eliminates the need for separate NumPy imports and is widely used in Machine

Learning, particularly for image processing. With modules for optimization, linear algebra, parallel programming, and integration, SciPy is favored by data scientists, analysts, and engineers, enabling efficient numerical computations and faster data processing with enhanced expressiveness compared to other tools and libraries.

Matplotlib

Matplotlib is a popular library that simplifies complex tasks and offers advanced capabilities for statisticians and analysts (Lafuente et al., 2021). It is widely used to create charts, such as bar graphs, histograms, and scatter plots. Matplotlib is versatile and can be used by beginners, experts, and professionals in Python scripts, shells, and Jupyter Notebooks. It also enables the creation of 3D charts and facilitates animated and interactive visualizations in Machine Learning.

Sci-Kit

Scikit-learn is a widely used Python library for machine learning, offering mathematical and statistical algorithms and specialized toolkits like Scikit-image (Ahmed et al., 2022). It is essential for Python-based machine learning in the software industry, assisting with data preparation, analysis, model development, and post-model analysis. Scikit-learn represents data as tabular datasets, utilizing x and y variables for supervised learning and only x variables for unsupervised learning, where x variables are independent, and y variable is dependent, describing samples in qualitative or quantitative manners.

Seaborn

Statistical analysis involves understanding relationships and their dependencies on other variables in a dataset, aided by visualizations that enable the human eye to detect patterns. Seaborn, a Python library built on Matplotlib, provides an intuitive interface for creating aesthetically pleasing and informative statistical graphs, making it easier to observe and interpret correlations within the data (Bisong, 2019).

PYTHON FUNCTIONS FOR EDA

These functions run only if the panda's library is imported to the Python coding platform (Mukhiya & Ahmed, 2020).

To obtain the needed information from our data:

```
Data.info()
```

This Python code helps obtain the attributes of our dataset or data frame (if in CSV format), their total non-null elements, and their data types for each attribute, field, or column name. Also, this .info() function in Python helps identify the number of instances or rows present in our data for further analysis.

```
data.describe()
```

This function in Python describes the data, which returns the descriptive statistics values of our data frame such as count, minimum, and maximum values out of all the elements under each attribute, mean, standard deviation, 25 percentiles, 50 percentiles, and 75 percentiles.

Duplicate Values

```
data.duplicated().sum()
```

This function is crucial in exploratory data analysis, finding duplicate values. When the values are duplicated, those can negatively impact our predictions and analysis because these duplicated values occur due to human error or misinterpretation. It is good when all the values are unique in the data and there are null duplicate values. (However, sometimes, duplicate values might occur based on the attribute type and data). Hence, the .duplicated().sum() function returns the total number of duplicated values in our data.

Representing Unique Values in the Data

```
data ['attribute_name']. unique()
```

The unique function in Python returns all the unique values for the specified attribute of the data frame. This function not only returns the unique values but also specifies the datatype of those unique values.

Unique Counts Visualization

To visualize the unique value counts for each data field, initially import the seaborn library.

```
sns. countplot (data ['attribute_name']). unique()
```

The above function displays a simple normal graph plotted to visualize the unique value counts for each field or column.

Capturing Null Values

Enhancing the quality of our data is very necessary. To check for the null values present in any of the fields, the following function is used:

```
data. isnull (). sum()
```

This function returns the total number of null values under each attribute. If there are no null values, the function returns zero. That does not mean the attribute has one null value, but the attribute has no null values.

Null Values Replacement

Capturing the null values alone is not essential, but we must also take measures to replace them.

```
data.replace  (np. nan,' 0', inplace = True)
```

Here, nan refers to the null values. This function replaces each null value in the whole data with zero. There are many optimized methods for replacing null values, like using the mean or median of the entire column and replacing it with the null value.

Attribute Datatypes

```
data. Dtypes
```

Use the above function to specifically know the data's datatype for all the columns (attributes).

Data Filtration

```
data [ data ['attribute_name'] = = specify_value ]. head()
```

When the data is extensive, but the required data is on a small scale, data filtration is one of the best choices. This function returns the values belonging to the class of that particular attribute. So, the required data is filtered from the actual data.

Plotting

```
data [ ['attribute_name ] ]. type_of_plot()
```

This function displays the graph of the variables of the mentioned type.

Correlation

```
data. corr()
```

A table of the correlated values for each attribute is displayed in matrix format under the function mentioned earlier. Correlation is a statistical concept that estimates the degree to which two defined variables move concerning each other. The correlation matrix values will usually lie between -1 and +1, where -1 denotes a high negative correlation, and +1 denotes a high positive correlation. The methods mentioned earlier are the fundamental and most important methods and functions in exploratory data analysis.

UNIVARIATE GRAPHICAL METHOD

Bar charts are excellent for categorical data. Histogram is a bar graph where each of the bars reflects the number of cases for a specific range of values. They can therefore be used for categorical or continuous data. They aid in comprehending the outliers, spread, and center trend. Another way to examine univariate data is through box plots, which can be graphically represented by 5 number summary of the first quartile, median, third quartile, minimum and maximum. From quartile to quartile, a box is drawn, with whiskers extending to the minimum and maximum values. Therefore, they use reliable statistics like the median and interquartile range to provide information about the central tendency, spread, symmetry, and outliers.

UNIVARIATE NON-GRAPHICAL METHOD

Univariate EDA involves analyzing sample distributions to understand population characteristics, including outlier detection and examining categorical and quantitative data. Measures such as mean, median, mode, variance, standard deviation, and interquartile range are used to assess central tendency, spread, and asymmetry. Tabulating frequency helps analyze categorical variables, while summary statistics provide insights into numerical data's center, spread, and outliers.

MULTIVARIATE NON-GRAPHICAL METHOD

Multivariate non-graphical EDA techniques employ cross-tabulation or statistics to analyze relationships between variables. This includes comparing statistics across levels of categorical variables and computing covariances or correlations for numerical variables. Cross-tabulated reports help understand counts or percentages of two categorical variables. Correlation, ranging from -1 to +1, helps determine the strength and direction of association between two quantitative variables, aiding feature selection in machine learning (Chemmalar Selvi, & Lakshmi Priya, 2020).

MULTIVARIATE GRAPHICAL METHOD

Bar plots are commonly used to represent categorical multivariate values, with each group representing a level of one variable and each bar indicating levels of another variable. Conversely, scatterplots effectively visualize two quantitative multivariate variables, with points representing data samples and variables plotted on the x and y axes. Side-by-side box plots and bars help display relationships between quantitative and categorical variables, while scatter plots can accommodate multiple variables using different sizes and shapes.

DATA VISUALISATION IN EDA

Exploratory data analysis (EDA) is crucial in understanding and formulating questions for data science research (Shamim & Rihan, 2023). Visual methods, such as various types of graphs, are emphasized in EDA to evaluate and extract meaningful information from the data. Python libraries like matplotlib and Seaborn provide tools for data visualization, enabling us to comprehend and analyze the data through visual representations quickly.

Univariate Enumerative Plots

These lists of plots display every observation in the data and reveal how the observations are distributed across a particular data variable. Now let us examine various enumerative plots. Let us consider the "Iris dataset" for understanding the types. The dataset columns are sepal width, length, and petal width and length.

Univariate Scatter Plot

Univariate scatter plot helps plot various observations of the same variable in correspondence to the index number of that data. A univariate scatter diagram with the matplotlib's plt.scatter() method can also be plotted. To plot, the scatter() function needs two parameters. Therefore, plotting the "sepal.width" variable in this example contradicts matching the number of observations kept as the data frame's index (df.index). Then, using the seaborn library's sns.scatterplot() function, depict the same plot while considering its diversity. Let us consider that we are plotting the 'sepal length(cm)' variable:

Line-Plots (Using Markers)

The data is visualized in a line plot using line segments to connect the data points. It looks like a scatter plot, but the measurement points are joined by straight-line segments and are organized differently (usually by their x-axis value). The line plot is given in Figure 2.

By default, the matplotlib plt.plot() method uses a line plot to plot the data. Although matplotlib does not offer such an automated option, one can utilize pandas' groupby() function to plot such a graph. The line plot can also be seen using the sns.lineplot() function.

Strip-Plots

Both scatter and strip plots are comparable. Strip plots are frequently used with a few other plot types for more accurate analysis. These plots display the data points distribution of a specified variable. Use the function sns.striplot () to plot a strip plot. The strip plot is given in Figure 3.

Swarm-Plots

A way for visualizing univariate data to see the range of values in a continuous variable is the swarm plot, which resembles a strip plot. The sole difference

Figure 1. Scatter plot

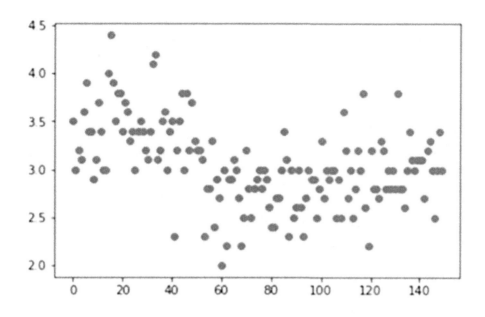

Figure 2. Line plot

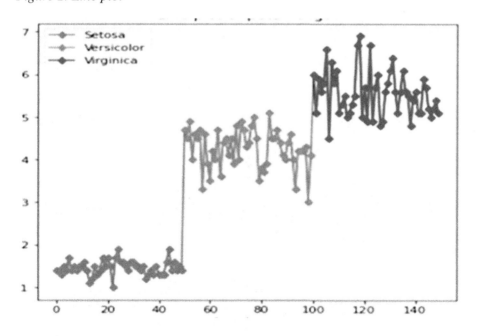

Figure 3. Strip plot

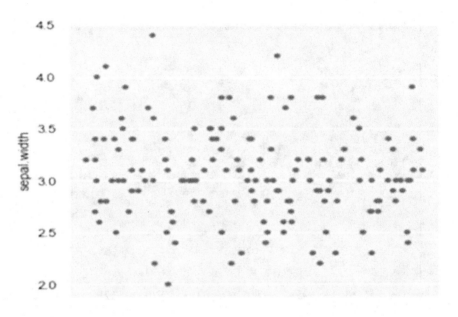

Figure 4. Swarm plot

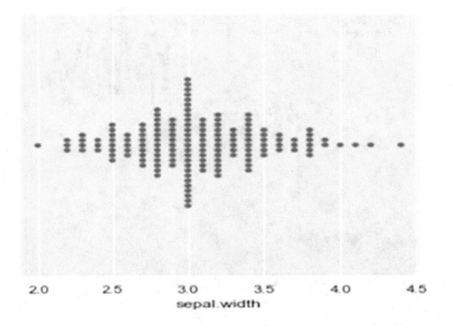

between the swarm-automatic plot and the strip plot, which produces a better visual representation of the data, is spreading the variable's data points to prevent overlap. Use the sns.swarmplot() function to plot a swarm-plot. An example of swam plot is presented in Figure 4.

Univariate Summary Plots

Compared with an enumerative plot, these plots give a more succinct representation of a variable's dispersion, position, diversity, and distribution. Though attaining every data value in a summary plot is impractical, it effectively portrays all data to draw more accurate inferences about the complete data set.

Histograms

Histograms resemble bar charts in appearance because they display counts or relative frequencies of values falling within specific class intervals or ranges. A histogram displays the shape and distribution of continuous sample data. It also aids in our comprehension of the data's skewness and kurtosis. In the matplotlib, plt.hist() function is used to plot a histogram. Figure 5 depicts the standard representation of the histogram.

Density Plots

The density plot mirrors a smooth histogram. The probability density function of the variable is typically displayed in density plots using the kernel density estimate. A continuous curve—the kernel—is created to estimate the density of the entire data set smoothly. Plotting the density plot for the 'petal.length' variable is given in Figure 6.

Rug Plots

Rug plots are a straightforward yet excellent legal technique to depict a distribution. Each data point has vertical lines in it. The height, in this case, is arbitrary. The density of the tick marks can be used to determine the distribution's density. The rug plot and histogram are directly related since a histogram makes bins with data range, and then a bar is drawn with a height equal to the ticks count in each bin. In the rug plot, each data point is represented by a single tick mark or line on a single axis. The rug plot's readability of the distribution reduces slightly compared to a marginal histogram. Figure 7 illustrates the representation of the Rug plot.

Figure 5. Histogram

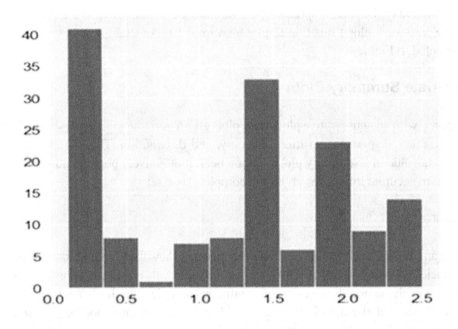

Figure 6. Density plot

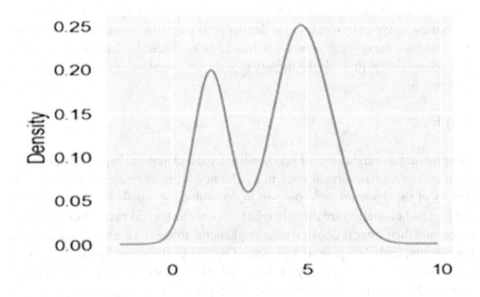

Figure 7. Rug plot

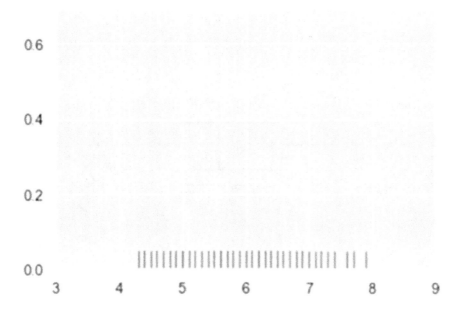

Box Plots

A box plot is a beneficial and standard method when depicting the data diversity by a 5-number description or summary (first quartile, second quartile (median), third quartile, maximum, and minimum). It greatly aids in identifying outliers and aids in comprehending these characteristics of the data distribution. Figure 8 illustrates the representation of the Box Plot.

Distplot

Earlier, the seaborn library's distplot() function was mentioned in the rug plot portion. The seaborn kdeplot() and rugplot() functions are combined with the matplotlib hist() function in this function. Figure 9 showcases the representation of the Dist Plot.

Violin Plots

With a rotating kernel density plot on either side, the box plot resembles the violin plot. In order to allow for comparison, it displays the diversity of data (quantitative) across several levels with a single (or more) categorical variable. The function plt. violinplot() is utilized, setting the Boolean parameter "show medians" to "True"

Figure 8. Box plot

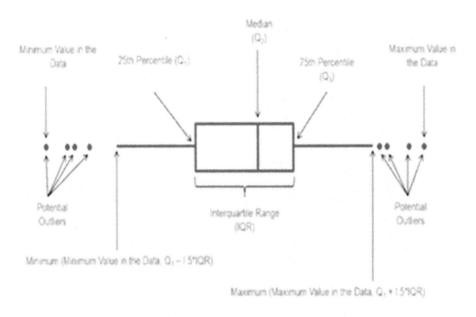

Figure 9. Dist plot

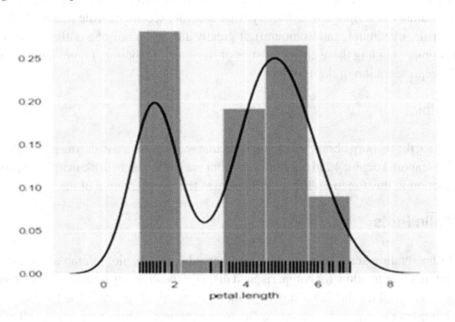

136

Figure 10. Violin plot

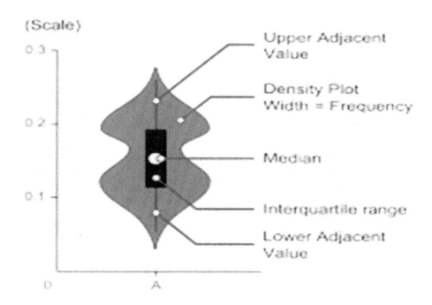

to mark the medians for each variable. The violin plot aids in comprehending the estimated density of the variable.

Bar Charts

A 2-D axis representation of univariate data is a Bar Plot. The category axis, which displays the category, is the first axis. The value axis, which displays the numerical value of the category as indicated by the length of the bar, is the second axis. A category variable is shown on the plot. Bar() produces a bar graph. A series holding the counts of the variable's unique values is returned by the function value counts(). The bar plot is a two-dimensional axis depiction of univariate data. The first axis is the category axis, which displays the category, and the second axis is the value axis, which displays the category's numerical value as represented by the length of the bar. A categorical variable is plotted using the plot.bar() function as a bar plot.

Pie Chart

The most popular method for representing the numerical percentages held by each category is a pie-plot or pie-chart. To simulate a pie-chart, use the plt.pie() function. Separate the parts equally in pie-chart because each category will be spread

Figure 11. Bar chart

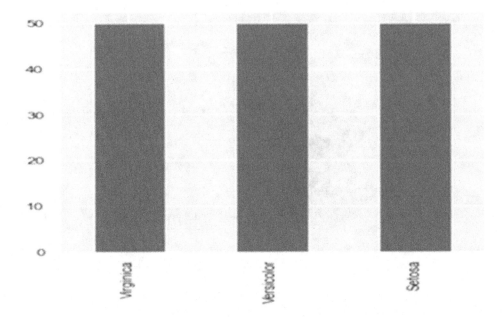

equally. Passing values in an array to the 'labels' option will then add the labels. The DataFrame.sample() function can be used to generate a random sample. The division of items that are to be returned in axis is indicated by frac argument of sample() function. The pie() function spins literally everything anti-clockwise at a specified angle using 'startangle' option. Additionally, startangle's default value is 0. One can use Python string formatting to display the percentage value using the 'autopct' argument. Figure 12 illustrates the representation of the Pie Chart.

BIVARIATE ANALYSIS

When it's necessary to investigate the link between two distinct variables, bivariate analysis is utilized (Dugard et al., 2022). In the end, this is what needed to accomplish in order to develop a strong model. Multivariate analysis is the process of combining more than two variables for analysis. For both Bivariate and Multivariate Analysis, will work on several charts. More variables are taken into account at once in multivariate analysis. Only two variables at a time are considered and concentrate on bivariate analysis. For visualization random datasets are considered.

Three categories of visual methods can be taken into account for bivariate analysis:

Figure 12. Pie chart

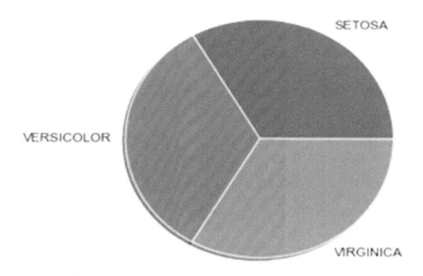

- Numerical and Numerical
- Numerical and Categorical
- Categorical and Categorical

NUMERICAL AND NUMERICAL

In this instance, two number variables are compared. The scatter plot, which shows the location where the two variables overlap, is the most typical graph used to show how they relate (Cooksey, 2020).

Scatter Plot

Using a scatter graph or plot to show the association between two numerical variables is easy. Let's use a scatter plot to visualise the relationship between the overall cost and the tip given. Figure 13 illustrates the representation of the scatter plot.

Figure 13. Scatter plot

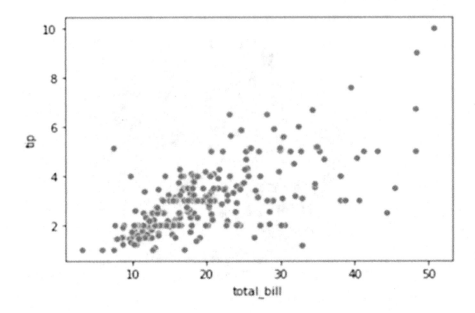

NUMERICAL AND CATEGORICAL

There are several plots that can be used for bivariate and multivariate analysis if one variable is numerical and the other is categorical (Kannan et al., 2019).

Bar Plot

By showing a numerical variable on the y-axis and a category variable on the x-axis, a bar plot is a simple graphic that may be used to investigate the relationship between two variables. Figure 14 illustrates the general representation of the Bar plot.

Boxplot

In the aforementioned Univariate analysis, boxplots is discussed in detail. For each variable, a separate boxplot can be created. A boxplot to investigate gender and age is given in Figure 15.

Figure 14. Bar plot

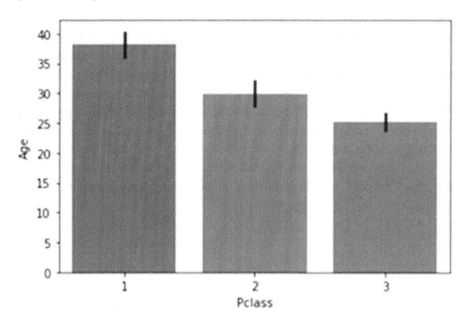

Figure 15. Box plot

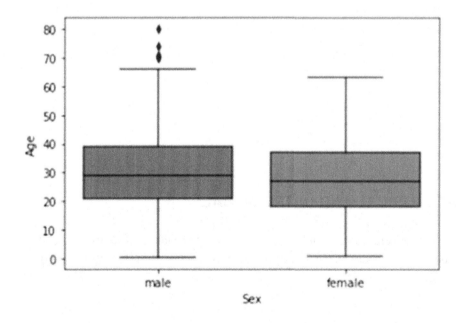

Distplot

By applying kernel density estimation, Distplot explains the PDF function (given in Figure 16). There is no hue option in Distplot, but can add one. Assume if want to determine whose survival probability is high compared to the age range of death ratio and want to see the chance of persons with an age range that of survival probability. The graph is clearly quite intriguing, as can see in Figure 16. The orange plot depicts the likelihood of survival, whereas the blue one displays the likelihood of dying. If observed, can see that children have a larger chance of surviving than dying, however it is the contrary for elderly individuals. This short analysis occasionally reveals important data insights and is helpful for crafting data narrative.

Figure 16. Dist plot

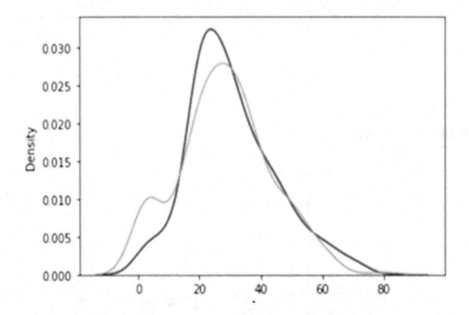

CATEGORICAL AND CATEGORICAL

There are several plots which can be used for bivariate and multivariate analysis if one variable is categorical and the other is categorical (Denis, 2020; Adams et al., 2021).

Heatmap

Heatmap is a visual depiction of only that, if you've ever used the crosstab function of pandas. It essentially displays how prevalent a particular category is in relation to another category in the dataset. To determine how many people survived and perished can use the heatmap. Figure 17 provides a visual depiction of the Heat map in a general form.

Figure 17. Heat map

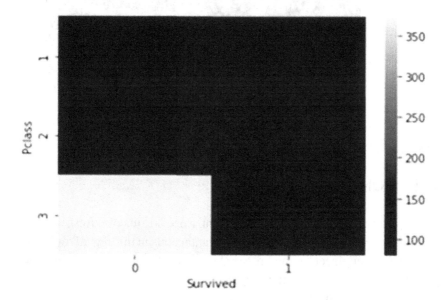

Cluster Map

To comprehend the link between two categorical variables, can also use a cluster map. In essence, a cluster map is a dendrogram that groups comparable behaviour categories together. Figure 18 visually represents a cluster map. If one is familiar with clustering methods, specifically DBSCAN, dendrograms are commonly used graphs in exploratory analysis.

Figure 18. Cluster map

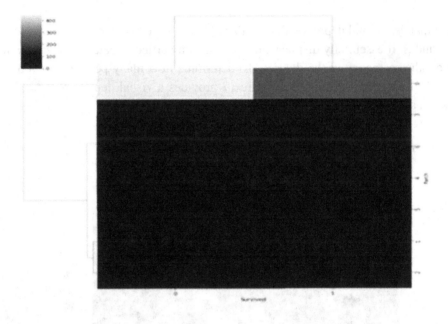

CONCLUSION

Exploratory data analysis is useful if a data scientist needs to uncover fresh information from a vast array of data sets. EDA can be advantageous in this regard for industries like data science, engineering, and research and development. As a result, current analytics are supported together with access to powerful computing today. For academics or data scientists, using EDA can be an exciting and interesting way to discover unanticipated value in a large number of complex data sets. From this chapter the various libraries used in EDA could be known and various visualization could also be learnt. The steps in EDA could also be known step by step.

REFERENCES

Adams, B., Baller, D., Jonas, B., Joseph, A. C., & Cummiskey, K. (2021). Computational skills for multivariable thinking in introductory statistics. *Journal of Statistics and Data Science Education, 29*(sup1), S123-S131.

Ahmed, T., Alam, M. A., Paul, R. R., Hasan, M. T., & Rab, R. (2022, February). Machine Learning and Deep Learning Techniques For Genre Classification of Bangla Music. In *2022 International Conference on Advancement in Electrical and Electronic Engineering (ICAEEE)* (pp. 1-6). IEEE. 10.1109/ICAEEE54957.2022.9836434

Ateeq, M., & Afzal, M. K. (2023). 10 Programming Languages, Tools, and Techniques. *Data-Driven Intelligence in Wireless Networks: Concepts, Solutions, and Applications*, 237.

Bisong, E. (2019). Matplotlib and seaborn. *Building Machine Learning and Deep Learning Models on Google Cloud Platform: A Comprehensive Guide for Beginners*, 151-165.

Chemmalar Selvi, G., & Lakshmi Priya, G. G. (2020). An Epidemic Analysis of COVID-19 using Exploratory Data Analysis Approach. *Predictive Analytics Using Statistics and Big Data: Concepts and Modeling*, 99.

Cooksey, R. W. (2020). Descriptive statistics for summarising data. *Illustrating statistical procedures: Finding meaning in quantitative data*, 61-139.

Denis, D. J. (2020). *Univariate, bivariate, and multivariate statistics using R: quantitative tools for data analysis and data science*. John Wiley & Sons. doi:10.1002/9781119549963

Dugard, P., Todman, J., & Staines, H. (2022). *Approaching multivariate analysis: A practical introduction*. Taylor & Francis. doi:10.4324/9781003343097

Harris, C. R., Millman, K. J., Van Der Walt, S. J., Gommers, R., Virtanen, P., Cournapeau, D., Wieser, E., Taylor, J., Berg, S., Smith, N. J., Kern, R., Picus, M., Hoyer, S., van Kerkwijk, M. H., Brett, M., Haldane, A., del Río, J. F., Wiebe, M., Peterson, P., ... Oliphant, T. E. (2020). Array programming with NumPy. *Nature*, *585*(7825), 357–362. doi:10.103841586-020-2649-2 PMID:32939066

Kannan, S., Dongare, P. A., Garg, R., & Harsoor, S. S. (2019). Describing and displaying numerical and categorical data. *Airway*, *2*(2), 64. doi:10.4103/ARWY. ARWY_24_19

Khandare, A., Agarwal, N., Bodhankar, A., Kulkarni, A., & Mane, I. (2023). Analysis of Python Libraries for Artificial Intelligence. In Intelligent Computing and Networking. *Proceedings of IC-ICN, 2022*, 157–177.

Lafuente, D., Cohen, B., Fiorini, G., García, A. A., Bringas, M., Morzan, E., & Onna, D. (2021). A Gentle introduction to machine learning for chemists: An undergraduate workshop using python notebooks for visualization, data processing, analysis, and modeling. *Journal of Chemical Education*, *98*(9), 2892–2898. doi:10.1021/acs.jchemed.1c00142

Mukhiya, S. K., & Ahmed, U. (2020). *Hands-On Exploratory Data Analysis with Python: Perform EDA techniques to understand, summarize, and investigate your data*. Packt Publishing Ltd.

Shamim, G., & Rihan, M. (2023). Exploratory Data Analytics and PCA-Based Dimensionality Reduction for Improvement in Smart Meter Data Clustering. *Journal of the Institution of Electronics and Telecommunication Engineers*, 1–10. doi:10.1080/03772063.2023.2218317

Chapter 7
Empowering Scientific Computing and Data Manipulation With Numerical Python (NumPy)

Tesfaye Fufa Gedefa

ⓘD https://orcid.org/0000-0001-5405-5320
Space Science and Geospatial Institute, Ethiopia

Galety Mohammed Gouse

ⓘD https://orcid.org/0000-0003-1666-2001
Samarkand International University of Technology, Uzbekistan

Garamu Tilahun Iticha
Debre Markos University, Ethiopia

ABSTRACT

NumPy is a Python library for performing numerical data structures and specialized computing. It improves the components of N-dimensional arrays and provides operations and tools to interface with these arrays. NumPy implements the N-dimensional array, or ndarray, and provides Python-specific scientific methods for performing realistic array and matrix operations. When compared to array programming in other languages, it will allow us to do a wide range of mathematical operations and data manipulations. NumPy can be used with other Python packages and programming languages such as C and C++. NumPy now supports object-oriented programming as well. For example, a class called ndarray may be an N-dimensional array with multiple ways of performing various data structure operations and characteristics.

DOI: 10.4018/978-1-6684-7100-5.ch007

INTRODUCTION

NumPy is an essential package for systematic computing in Python. The library gives an N-dimensional array question and different inferred objects (such as masked arrays and matrices) (NumPy Developers, 2008-2022). It is a mixture of sequences for fast procedures on arrays, with mathematical, logical, and shape manipulation; sorting; selecting; input/output; discrete Fourier transforms; introductory linear algebra; basic statistical techniques; arbitrary simulation; and more (Johansson, 2019). NumPy delivers the numerical backend for nearly every scientific or technical library for Python. It provides an N-dimensional array object, a robust data structure that has become Python's standard numerical data representation (Millman, 2011). It is, therefore, a vital part of the scientific Python ecosystem (Johansson, 2019). Its goal is to create the cornerstone of a suitable environment for scientific computing. As stated (Agathiya Raja, 2022), the Python library plays a significant role in different application areas for analyzing complex networks, data science, and big data; analyzing and visualizing the networks using Python offers good insights about the networks to end-users using the python library. To better understand the people surrounding NumPy, at the core of the NumPy package is the ndarray object (Alammar, 2022).

This encapsulates n-dimensional arrays of the same data types, with many operations performed in the accumulated code for performance. NumPy is an essential bundle for scientific computing in Python, and it provides an n-dimensional array object and numerous derived things (such as screened arrays and matrices). The ndarray object is at the heart of the NumPy bundle. However, NumPy arrays and standard Python sequences differ in several ways (Johansson, 2019; Albenis Pérez-Alarcón, 2021).

Python extends Python with robust mathematical operations that provide practical guarantees in calculations with arrays and matrices. NumPy stores a massive library of high-level mathematical functions that work on these arrays and matrices. NumPy aims to deliver an array object faster than traditional Python lists. As a result, Python is the fastest to read fewer bytes of memory or has contiguous memory. It assists with different operations like slicing, indexing, and broadcasting; matrix computational functions; and has the benefits of single instruction multiple data vector processes (SIMD). In addition, NumPy completely supports an object-oriented approach, and it is an N-dimensional array named ndarray, a class possessing various techniques and qualities. Functions mirror several methods in the outermost NumPy namespace. This lets the languages code in whatever makes the most sense.

Installing Numpy

This chapter strongly recommends using a technical Python source to install NumPy. In this chapter, looking for the complete commands to mount NumPy on the operating system, see Connecting NumPy and if there is already installed Python, easily connect NumPy with the following:

```
pip install NumPy, or > conda install NumPy
```

Importing Numpy

Importing Modules: To use the NumPy library in this chapter, import it into the program. The NumPy module is often imported using the alias np. NumPy should be imported as np.

```
import NumPy as np
```

After this, this chapter can access functions and classes in the NumPy module using the np namespace. It shortens the imported name to np for better readability (alias) of the code using NumPy. This is a widely adopted convention, so anyone working with code can easily understand it.

NUMPY DATATYPES

The most common way to manipulate values in NumPy is through ndarray objects (Johansson, 2019). Because ndarrays can hold any number of quantities, they can represent any data type, such as scalars, vectors, matrices, or tensors. They are similar to Python lists but can have multiple dimensions. The basic numeric information types saved by NumPy are listed in Figure 1. Non-numerical data sortings, such as text, objects, and custom compound sorts, are also accessible. Datasets for Basic Numeric Data that may be accessed using NumPy Scalar: A scalar is a single integer with zero dimension, and NumPy has one. As a result, instead of Python int, NumPy data types utilize collations such as uint8, int8, uint16, and int16. Strings, objects, and complicated data types the user creates are also supported.

Figure 1. Basic numerical data types NumPy
Source: NumPy Developers (2008-2022)

dtype	Variants	Description
int	int8, int16, int32, int64	Integers
uint	uint8, uint16, uint32, uint64	Unsigned (nonnegative) integers
bool	Bool	Boolean (True or False)
float	float16, float32, float64, float128	Floating-point numbers
complex	complex64, complex128, complex256	Complex-valued floating-point numbers

Scalar

Scalar and NumPy are terms for single numbers with a dimension of zero. As a result, this book chapter may pass the value to NumPy's array function to generate a NumPy array that holds a scalar instead of Python's int types, such as uint8, int8, uint16, and int16. It returns an empty parenthesis to indicate that it has no dimensions (Mulani, 2022)

Vectors

It is a one-dimensional list of numbers. To create a vector, pass a Python list to the array function (Mulani, 2022).

Matrices

In Numpy, matrices are represented as lists of lists or 2D vectors. Like vectors, this chapter generates matrices using NumPy's array function. However, one must provide a list where each A list denotes a row rather than merely passing through a single list. Consequently, to make a three-by-three matrix using digits 1 through 9 (McKinney, 2012).

Tensors

N-dimensional ndarrays are tensors. They can include additional dimensions similar to vectors (Alammar, 2022).

NUMPY ARRAYS

A data structure that effectively stores and accesses multidimensional arrays is the NumPy array. A pointer to memory is included in Numpy, along with metadata used to convert the data stored there—particularly information sorting, shaping, and steps. The data sort shows the kinds of parts stored in an array. The information sorting process depicts the personalities of components organized into an array. A data sort is included in an array, and the memory requirements for each cluster element are the same (Harris, 16 September 2020). In Python, NumPy arrays are the standard way to store numerical data and allow numerical operations to be done in a high-level language. As stated by (Oliphant, 2006), an array is a form of data that stores multiple values using just two identifiers.

An array is a collection of data pieces that can be accessed by their directories and are organized sequentially. Lists of numerical data, vectors, and matrices are stored in NumPy arrays. The NumPy library has numerous procedures (built-in functions) for creating, modifying, and modifying NumPy arrays. Even though the Python programming language has an array data structure, it is less flexible, practical, and powerful than the NumPy array. The NumPy Connect memory location: Each position is only assigned to one piece of data, and the memory space needs to be partitioned into precisely sized areas (Stefan van der Walt, 2021). Contiguous memory allocation is now available: To ensure that memory space can be used, split the data into pieces and put them in different places.

Figure 2 shows that the metadata areas are connected to the NumPy array data structure. Ordering an array using cuts is what b is about. These forms give back a summary of the initial data. c. arrange an array using masks, scalar aids, or other clusters in a way that duplicates the initial data. An array is ordered with different arrays in the bottom example, broadcasting the ordering disputes before the lookup of the original data. The bottom example discloses the indexing arguments before the lookup by indexing an array with several arrays. d. The use of vectorization allows operations to be applied to groups of elements. e. As two-dimensional arrays increase, so does broadcasting. f, acting in conjunction with one or more tomahawks while reducing operations. In this scenario, an array is added to a few tomahawks to produce a vector continuously or two tomahawks to produce a scalar. Using two consecutive axes to construct a scalar is explained in g, an illustration of NumPy code. An example, the NumPy code in g, demonstrates some of these ideas.

Figure 2. The NumPy array incorporates various fundamental features of the Array
Source: Harris (2020)

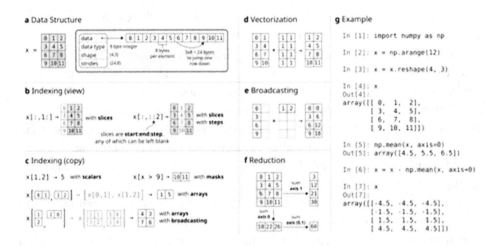

THE DIFFERENCE BETWEEN A NUMPY ARRAY AND A LIST

There are three benefits to using a Python NumPy array instead of a list. Less memory, faster, and more convenient. The Python NumPy array should be the first option because it uses less memory than a list. Then, it is relatively quick to implement and works well with NumPy simultaneously.

Figure 3. The difference between a NumPy array and a list
Source: Alammar (2022)

List:

Numpy:

In Figure 3, the list and Numpy array store data in memory. However, there is a significant difference. Performing these operations on a list can be tedious and time-consuming when searching, updating, and manipulating data from memory. On the other hand, using a NumPy array is advantageous as it allows for efficient data manipulation directly from memory due to its sequential data storage.

Difference between List and ArrayTable

- **Changeability:** An array can keep the features of several different data types, but it can only store the basics of one data type.
- **Data Types Storage:** The list can store various data, while the Array provides equivalent data values.
- **Importing Packages:** Bringing in parcels No container is necessary before utilizing a list because the Python programming language is an inbuilt data structure. The Array, however, is not a feature of the NumPy language. Therefore, we must ingest the "collection" component before creating and utilizing arrays.
- **Arithmetical Process:** The NumPy module allows an array assembly to save data values and modify them quickly, which makes using an array advantageous during mathematical operations in Python. On the other hand, the outcomes are not shown in the list. Due to this, math operations with the list are still possible but less practical than those with the collection.
- **Alter Competences:** The list, on the other hand, is an in-built data construction and hence can be resized and adjusted very rapidly and efficiently, whereas the Array consumes very little memory, changing the memory position.

ARRAY OPERATIONS

When an array is declared, we can access its elements or carry out particular operations. The last session taught us how to access items. The various functions that can be used with arrays are covered in this section.

Arithmetic Operations

Mathematical operations on NumPy arrays are quick and straightforward. An essential arithmetic operation, such as addition, subtraction, multiplication, division, etc., is performed on each pair of components when applied to two collections. For example, combine two arrays, the first element from the first Array will be added to the first element of the second Array, and so on. Consider the subsequent element-wise operations on two arrays:

Array Transpose

To reverse the tensor swap using the keyword argument, use transpose (an argsort (axes)). Transposing a one-dimensional array produces an unchanged copy of the original Array.

Array Sorting

This involves pushing components in logical order. Any sequence with an element-based order, such as numeric or alphabetical, ascending or descending, is considered well-ordered. For example, a function called sort () on the NumPy n-dimensional array element sorts an array.

Concatenating Arrays and Splitting

Every code that came before it only operated on individual arrays. On the other hand, it is also possible to join many arrays into a single array, and it is also possible to break a single array into several arrays. The concatenation process refers to joining two or more arrays together. When arrays are concatenated, sequences are added one after the other in sequential order.

Array Reshaping

Reshaping entails changing an array's shape. The number of necessary elements in each length determines the form of an array. By reshaping, we can change the size of the Array, the number of elements in each, or both.

As shown in Figure 4, reshaping the Array with the help of NumPy to change the dimension as we want using rows and columns by changing the size of the Array.

Slicing and Indexing

This approach makes it possible to choose any item in an array depending on its N-dimensional index, allowing for more flexibility in the selection process. Every integer array has a representation of the total number of indexes for its respective dimension. When the index is composed of the same number of integer arrays as the dimensions of the ndarray being targeted, completing the operation becomes quite simple. NumPy uses the Python language's sophisticated indexing (McKinney, 2012) capability. Python's indexing features were initially developed in response to the demands of users who worked with numbers. Slicing is removing a chosen

Figure 4. Data reshaping
Source: Java Tutorial Developers (2022)

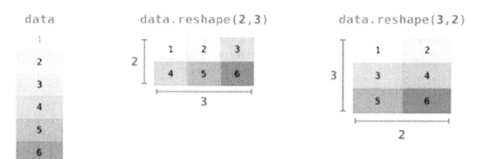

group of components from an array. This division process is comparable to the one used in the list. Think about the following:

Figure 5. Slicing a NumPy array
Source: Oliphant (2006)

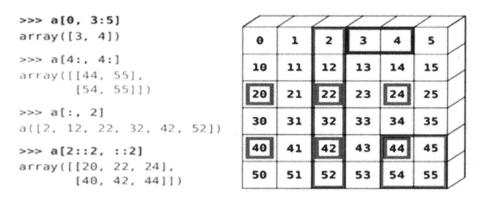

As described in Figure 5, the slicing of an array in NumPy is the way of removing a chosen group of components from a given an array.

Broadcasting

The ability of NumPy to handle arrays with varying dimensions appropriately while performing arithmetic operations is referred to as broadcasting. Arithmetic operations are often performed on items corresponding to one another when working with arrays. These procedures may be carried out without a hitch so long as the two

Figure 6. Numpy array broadcasting
Source: McKinney (2012)

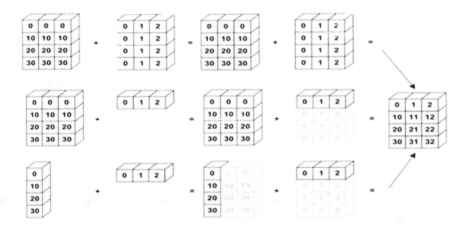

arrays being worked with have an identical structure. Vital processes on NumPy arrays are element-based. This works on arrays of the same degree. In any case, it is imaginable to perform actions on arrays of various sizes if NumPy can change them; this change is called broadcasting. Figure 6 gives an example of broadcasting.

In any case, it is also imaginable to perform actions on arrays of various sizes on the off chance that NumPy can change them/

SPECIAL FUNCTION OF NUMPY PYTHON

Numerous numerical capabilities in NumPy allow for a variety of numerical operations. Trigonometric aptitudes, arithmetic skills, and the capacity for working with complex numbers are all examples of numerical aptitudes (NumPy Developers, 2008-2022). Let us talk about the mathematical functions first, in any case.

Trigonometric Functions

Figure 7 shows that the trigonometric formulas for computing the sine, cosine, and tangents of various angles in radians are available in Numpy. The sin, cos, and tan functions return the trigonometric ratio for the supplied angles.

Figure 7. Trigonometric functions
Source: Mulani (2022)

```
import numpy as np
arr = np.array([0, 30, 60, 90, 120, 150, 180])
print("\nThe sin value of the angles",end = " ")
print(np.sin(arr * np.pi/180))
print("\nThe cosine value of the angles",end = " ")
print(np.cos(arr * np.pi/180))
print("\nThe tangent value of the angles",end = " ")
print(np.tan(arr * np.pi/180))
```

Rounding Functions

NumPy offers a variety of routines for truncating the value of a decimal number tuned to the accuracy of decimal digits. First, let us discuss the adjusting features—the numpy. The around () method works as intended. This task returns the corrected decimal value at the desired decimal location. Figure 8 contains the work's syntax.

Figure 8. Numpy rounding functions

SN	Parameter	Description
1	num	It is the input number.
2	decimals	It is the number of decimals which to which the number is to be rounded. The default value is 0. If this value is negative, then the decimal will be moved to the left.

Statistical Functions in NumPy

As shown in Figure 9, Numerous statistical functions offered by Numpy can be utilized to analyze statistical data. For instance, identifying the Array's most minor

Figure 9. Numpy statistical functions for maximum and minimum
Source: Millman (2011)

```
import numpy as np

a = np.array([[2,10,20],[80,43,31],[22,43,10]])

print("The original array:\n")
print(a)


print("\nThe minimum element among the array:",np.amin(a))
print("The maximum element among the array:",np.amax(a))

print("\nThe minimum element among the rows of array",np.amin(a,0))
print("The maximum element among the rows of array",np.amax(a,0))

print("\nThe minimum element among the columns of array",np.amin(a,1))
print("The maximum element among the columns of array",np.amax(a,1))
```

and extreme elements using NumPy.amin() and NumPy.amax() can find each array element's minimum and maximum values along the required axis.

NumPy Sorting and Searching

Numerous sorting and searching functions are available in Numpy. The sort () method is used to build several sorting algorithms, including quicksort, merge sort, and heapsort. The function call must specify the sorting algorithm utilized in the

Figure 10. NumPy sorting and search algorithms

SN	Algorithm	Worst case complexity
1	Quick Sort	O (n ^ 2)
2	Merge Sort	O (n * log(n))
3	Heap Sort	O (n * log(n))

sort operation. Let us talk about the sorting algorithm used by NumPy. Sort () is given in Figure 10.

Linear Algebra in NumPy

NumPy gives various capabilities to perform multiple algebraic calculations on the input data. Numpy linear algebra is shown in Figure 11.

Figure 11. NumPy linear algebra

SN	Function	Definition
1	dot()	It is used to calculate the dot product of two arrays.
2	vdot()	It is used to calculate the dot product of two vectors.
3	inner()	It is used to calculate the inner product of two arrays.
4	matmul()	It is used to calculate the matrix multiplication of two arrays.
5	det()	It is used to calculate the determinant of a matrix.
6	solve()	It is used to solve the linear matrix equation.
7	inv()	It is used to calculate the multiplicative inverse of the matrix.

Numpy Copies and Views

While executing the functions, some return a copy of the input array, while some return the view. When the contents are physically stored in another location, it is called Copy. If, on the other hand, a different view of the same memory content is provided, we call it a View (NumPy Developers, 2008-2022). A replica of the array object is not created by simply assigning values to its elements. Instead, it accesses it using the same id () used for the first Array. The id () method in Python is analogous to the pointer function in C in that it returns an object's universal identification. In addition, any changes that occur in one are immediately reflected in the other. For example, if one changes its form, this will cause the other to alter its shape as well.

CONCLUSION

Most of this chapter is devoted to examining the importance of NumPy and the applications that may use its various packages. When using Python for technical and scientific computing, grasping the NumPy package ecosystem is essential. How the packages are employed for computing is necessary to get the NumPy package ecosystem and how they are employed. This is because of the nature of the computing tasks that Python is used for. It was underlined that matrices, vectors, ndarray, tensors, reshaping array expressions, and arithmetic operators should all be employed to perform a realistic array analysis. This chapter briefly introduces the NumPy library, emphasizing its mathematical operations and benefits when dealing with data structures. NumPy is a library that is important for doing computations in Python, and it has the potential to serve as the basis for all other Python computational libraries. The Python Scientific Community first developed NumPy. The ndarray, which is NumPy's data structure for N-dimensional arrays, was the topic of our discussion at the outset of this subsection. Then, we looked at how the ndarray may be used to generate and manage arrays, count orders, solve issues with data structures, carry out mathematical calculations, design applications for data science, and clip off sections of arrays.

NumPy can be used with other Python packages and programming languages such as C and C++. In addition, NumPy now supports object-oriented programming as well. For example, a class called ndarray may be an N-dimensional array with multiple ways of performing various data structure operations and characteristics. In conclusion, NumPy gives users access to various functions that can execute basic mathematical operations. Users can design applications based on data structures, generate arrays with N dimensions with the aid of this package, and adjust the geometry of existing arrays. Users must consider every detail seriously to get any use out of computers.

REFERENCES

Agathiya Raja, G. K. (2022). *Introduction To Python for Social Network Analysis.* Wiley Online Library.

Alammar, J. (2022). *NumPy: the absolute basics for beginners.* Retrieved 10 25, 25, from http://jalammar.github.io/

Albenis Pérez-Alarcón, J. C.-A. (2021). *Alarconpy: a Python Package for Meteorologists.*

Harris, C. M. (2020). Array Programming with NumPy. *Nature*, 357–362.

Java Tutorial Developers. (2022). Retrieved from NumPy Tutorial: https://www.javatpoint.com/

Johansson, R. (2019). *1. Scientific Computing and Data Science Applications with Numpy, SciPy, and Matplotlib* (2nd ed.). Urayasu-shi.

McKinney, W. (2012). NumPy Basics: Arrays and Vectorized Computation. In *W. McKinney, Python for Data Analysis*. O'Reilly Media, Inc.

Millman, K. J., & Aivazis, M. (2011). Python for Scientists and Engineers. *Computing in Science & Engineering, 13*(2), 9–12. doi:10.1109/MCSE.2011.36

Mulani, S. (2022). *Python Advanced*. Retrieved from Vectors in Python: https://www.digitalocean.com/community/tutorials/vectors-in-python

NumPy Developers. (2008-2022). Retrieved from Numpy User Guide: https://numpy.org/doc/stable/user/whatisnumpy.html

Oliphant, T. E. (2006). *Guide to NumPy*. Academic Press.

Stefan van der Walt, S. C. (2021). The NumPy Array: A Structure for Efficient Numerical Computation. *IEEE, 13*(2), 22-30.

Chapter 8
Exploring Python's Powerful Data Collections

Mastan Vali Shaik
University of Technology and Applied Sciences, Ibri, Oman

Rajasrkaran Selvaraju
University of Technology and Applied Sciences, Ibri, Oman

ABSTRACT

One of the powerful data types for programmers that a Python supports is a list. A list is a mutable data structure that holds an ordered collection of items. Lists are useful to work with related data. A tuple is an immutable data type that stores values in a sequence. Slicing can be used to get a range of items. In Python, a set is variable that can store a variety of data, and different data types perform different operations. A set data type in Python is used to store multiple values in a single variable. In Python, dictionary is one of the built-in data types where elements are key: value pairs. In other programming languages, these are called associative memory or associative arrays. Dictionaries are faster in execution, provide easy lookups, and are implemented as hash tables. This chapter focuses on data collection in Python.

INTRODUCTION TO LIST

A list is a sequence of values and can be of any type. A list is a data structure that holds an ordered collection of items i.e., and you can store a sequence of items in a list. The values in the list are called elements or items. List values are accessed by using an index. The index value can be positive from 0 or negative from -1. Once you have created a list, you can add, remove or search for items in the list. Since

DOI: 10.4018/978-1-6684-7100-5.ch008

we can add and remove items, we say that a list is a mutable data type, i.e., this type can be altered (Learn to code for IoT with python essentials course, 2022). Figure 1 illustrates the list representation, while Table 1 provides information on accessing list values.

Example

```
List1 = [10, 20,15.7, 30, 40.2]
List2 = ['Chocolate', 'Juice', 'Burger', 'Pepsi']
List3 = []    #empty list
```

Accessing List Values

```
num = [ 2, 4, 1, 10, 5]
```

Figure 1. List representation

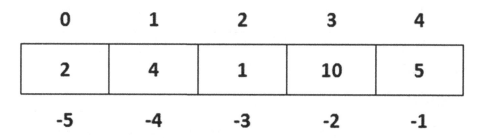

Index from front

0	1	2	3	4
2	4	1	10	5
-5	-4	-3	-2	-1

Index from rear

Slicing a List

The slicing operation takes a specific range of elements from the list (Moruzzi, 2020). Slice operation is performed on Lists with the use of a colon.

Table 1. Accessing list values

print(num[0]) → 2	print(num[-1]) → 5
print(num[2]) → 1	print(num[-3]) → 1
print(num[4]) → 5	print(num[-5]) → 2
print(num[5]) → IndexError	print(num[-6]) → IndexError

Syntax: list_name[index value]

Syntax

```
List_name[ start: end: step ]
```

Start is the starting index, End is the ending index (end value will be always the previous value of end) Step is the increment or decrement value for index. Table 2 outlines the slice operation.

Example

Consider the list with the name myList = ['a','b','c','d','e','f']

Table 2. Slice operation

List Slicing and Output	Description
myList[0: 3] = ['a', 'b', 'c']	Elements from index 0 to index 2
myList[3:] = ['d', 'e', 'f']	Elements from index 3 till the end
myList[: 4] = ['a', 'b', 'c', 'd']	starting index(0) to index 3
myList[1: 5: 2] = ['b', 'd']	Starting index 1, last index 4 and step by 2
myList[:] = ['a', 'b', 'c', 'd', 'e', 'f']	From first element to the last element
myList[:: 2] = ['a', 'c', 'e']	From start to last, step by 2
myList[:: -1] = ['f', 'e', 'd', 'c', 'b', 'a']	From the last element to the first one

Input to a List

Quite often, we need to give some input to a list. An input() can be used to read values to a List.

The following code inputs four values to a list and print.

Example

```
newlist=[]              #Empty list
for idx in range(4):
    val = int(input('Enter list value '))      #Take input
    newlist.append(val)                        #append value to
list
print(newlist)                                 #Print all list values
```

NESTED LIST

A List can have another list. The following code illustrates nested list and printing values.

Example

```
list_one = [10, 20, 12, [5, 9, 4], 17]
print(list_one)
print(list_one[3])
print(list_one[3][1])
```

Output

```
print(list_one) prints all values of a list
print(list_one[3])prints [5,9,4]
print(list_one[3][1]) prints 9
```

LIST METHODS

Table 3 provides the list methods in Python (Bisong, 2019).

Table 3. List methods

Method	Description	Example
append(val)	add one item at the end of the list	myList.append('M')
extend(seq)	add sequence of items at end	myList.extend('N','T')
insert(idx,val)	insert one item 'val' at index idx	myList.pop(3,'z')
remove(val)	remove first occurrence with value val	myList.remove('Z')
pop(idx)	remove & return item at index idx (default last)	Res = myList.pop(4)
sort()	sort and store in ascending order	myList.sort()
sort(reverse=True)	sort and store in descending	myList.sort(reverse=True)
len(list_name)	return items count	siz = len(myList)

Exercise

Consider the following list declaration and write Python statements.

```
mylist = [10, 2, 15, 17, 25, 8, 11]
```

Table 4 presents the exercise for Lists, including the associated questions.

Table 4. List exercise

Question	Answer
Print all values of list	
Print 2nd to 5th Value	
Find length of list	
Find maximum value	
Print 6th to 2nd value from reverse	
Print all values in reverse order	

LIST AND FUNCTIONS

We can have a user-defined function that takes the list as an argument and perform some operation. For example, the following code Initializes a list with some values. Write a user-defined function to find a number of positive numbers in that list (Kong et al., 2020).

Example

```
#List And User Defined Function
def mytest(mylist):
    pos=0
    n = len(mylist)
    for idx in range(n):
 if mylist[idx] > 0:
            pos = pos+1
    return pos
newList = [10, 2, -5, 17, -11, 8]
result = mytest(newList)
print(' Number of positive numbers in the list are ', result)
```

Practical Exercises

1. Read five values to the list and print the square root of each value.
2. Read seven integer values to the list and count number even numbers.
3. Read six integer values to the list and count the number of positive numbers.
4. Read seven integer values. Find average. Find and print the number of values below the average value.

INTRODUCTION TO TUPLE

A Tuple data structure is used when we have data that will not change over some time. A tuple is an ordered sequence of values separated by a comma. Tuples are helpful for group-related information such as student name, level, specialization, and grade. A tuple is heterogeneous Tuples are immutable. Once created can't be modified. Whereas a list is mutable. Since it is immutable, it faster execution. Tuple is represented in an optional parenthesis '(' and ')'. The three features of the tuple are immutable, indexed, and heterogeneous. Tuple can have duplicate values (Guttag, 2021; Johansson & John, 2019).

Creating and Printing a Tuple

Example

```
#working with tuples
student = ('76J1235',"Ahmed", 'Bachelor',3.2)
print("Student ID          : ", student[0])
print("Student name        : ", student[1])
print("Student level       : ", student[2])
print("Student grade score : ", student[3])
print("Length of tuple = ", len(student))
```

Output:
The above code prints the following output

```
Student ID          : 76J1235
Student name        : Ahmed
Student level       : Bachelor
Student grade score : 3.2
Length of tuple =  4
```

Figure 2. Tuple representation

Index	0	1	2	3

```
('76J1235',"Ahmed", 'Bachelor',3.2)
```

-4		-3		-2		-1	Index

In this example, *student* is the name of the tuple. The above example creates a tuple with four values. Tuple values are accessed using index *student[0]* refers to *'76J1235'* and *student[3]* refers to *3.2*. Positive index starts from 0, whereas negative indexing starts from -1, shown in Figure 2.

A *for* could be used to access tuple values as shown below.

Example

```
student = ('76J1235',"Ahmed", 'Bachelor',3.2)
for idx in student:
    print (idx)
```

TUPLE SLICING

Slicing operator:: is used to retrieve some elements of a tuple (Beri, 2019; Arulkumar, 2020).

```
Syntax:                    tuple_name(start: stop:  step)
```

Example:

```
student = ('76J1235',"Ahmed", 'Bachelor',3.2)
```

Table 5 provides examples of tuple slicing, including the input, output, and description for each example.

Table 5. Slicing a tuple

Slice	Output	Description
student[1]	Ahmed	Second value of the tuple
student[-1]	3.2	Using negative index. -1 represents last value of the tuple.
student[1::2]	('Ahmed', 3.2)	Starting from index 1 (Second value of the tuple), move until end of tuple with step 2.
student[::-1]	(3.2, 'Bachelor', 'Ahmed', '76J1235')	Tuples values in reverse order
student[0::3]	('76J1235', 3.2)	Starting from index 0 (Second value of the tuple), move until end of tuple with step 3.
student[-2::-2]	('Bachelor', '76J1235')	Starting index -2, step 2

TUPLE PACKING AND UNPACKING

Tuple packing refers to assigning multiple values to a tuple. Tuple unpacking refers to assigning a tuple to various variables (Unpingco, 2021).
Example:

```
        #Tuple packing
student = ('76J1235',"Ahmed", 'Bachelor',3.2)
#Tuple unpacking
(sid, name, level, grade) = student
```

```
print('student name  is: ', name)
print('student grade is: ', grade)
```

Tuple Examples

```
mark1 = (7,8,6,17,42)
print("maximum value in tuple is ", max(mark1))
print("Minimum value in tuple is ", min(mark1))
print("Length of tuple is ", len(mark1))
mark2 = sorted(mark1)
print("Before sorting: ",mark1, " After sorting:", mark2)
print(type(mark1), type(mark2))
name1 = ("Ahmed", "Rashid", "Omar")
name2 = ("ahmed", "rashid", "omar")
print("NAME1 = ", name1, " NAME2 = ", name2)
print(name1 == name2)
print(name1 < name2)
print(name1 > name2)
```

NESTED TUPLES

A tuple can be defined inside another tuple.

Example

```
emp = (('E101','Rashid', 3000), ('E105', 'Mohammed', 2900),
('E104','Omar',2810))
print("Emp ID \t Emp Name \t Emp Salary")
for k in range(len(emp)):
    print(emp[k][0],'\t', emp[k][1],'\t', emp[k][2])
```

The above course code generates the following output.

```
Emp ID Emp Name Emp Salary
E101 Rashid 3000
E105 Mohammed 2900
```

E104 Omar 2810

COUNT AND INDEX METHODS OF A TUPLE

count() returns the number of times a specified value is present. **index** () Searches the tuple for a specified value and returns the position of the value. index () generates ValueError if the value is absent in the tuple (Hill Christian, 2020).

Example

```
#initialize a tuple
tp = (2, 8, 5, 8, 7, 3, 6, 5, 1)
print("count(8) = ", tp.count(8))
print("count(3) = ", tp.count(3))
print("count(4) = ", tp.count(4))
print("index(7) = ", tp.index(7))
    #Value to search, starting index, End index
print("index(5) = ", tp.index(5,0,4))
```

The above code generates the following output:

```
count(8) =  2
count(3) =  1
count(4) =  0
index(7) =  4
index(5) =  2
```

INTRODUCTION TO SET

The word *set* is predominately used in set theory of mathematics (Haslwanter, Thomas, 2016). The implementation of *set theory* can efficiently carry through *set* data type in Python. A *set* is represented in curly braces{ }. Basically, *set* has the following properties:

1. A *set* is an unordered collection of data (The order of the set changes every time it is used)

2. *set* is an unindexed data type (Set items can appear in a different order every time you use them and cannot be referred to by index or key)
3. *set* doesn't have duplicate values (If items appear multiple times, only one will be recognized in the set)
4. *set* values are unchanged (we cannot change the items after the set has been created) *set* items are unchangeable, but you can remove and add new items.

INITIALIZING AND PRINTING A SET

Example

```
#initializing and printing a set
myset = {10, 8, 12, 7, 11}
myset2 = {'Oman', 'Iraq', 'USA', 'India'}
print(myset)
print(myset2)
```

The above code prints the following output

```
{7, 8, 10, 11, 12}
{'India', 'Iraq', 'USA', 'Oman'}
```

Example:

```
myset2 = {'Iraq', 'Oman', 'Iraq', 'USA', 'India', 'iraq',
'China'}
print(myset2)
```

The above code prints the following output:

```
{'iraq', 'USA', 'Iraq', 'China', 'Oman', 'India'}
```

The initialization statement *myset2* has multiple entries for 'Iraq'. The property of *set* is 'No duplicate values'. However, 'Iraq' and 'iraq' are different.

A *for* loop can also be used to print set values.

Table 6. SET methods

Method	Description	Example
add()	Add a value to the set.	myset2.add('Dubai')
discard()	Remove a value from given set	myset2.discard('iraq')
pop()	Removes an element from the set	myset2.pop()
clear()	Removes all elements from the set	myset2.clear()
remove()	Removes a specified element from the set	myset2.remove('USA')
update()	Update the set with another set, or any other iterable	myset2.update(myset3)

```
for inp in myset2:
        print (inp)
```

SET METHODS

Table 6 provides an overview of the set methods along with their descriptions and an illustrative example.

Example: Union, Intersection, Difference

Below is an example demonstrating the concepts of Union, Intersection, and Difference.

```
#set operations (union, intersection, difference)
itcourses = {'html','python','office','java','php'}
buscourses = {'office','tally','html'}
course1 = itcourses.union(buscourses)
course2 = itcourses.intersection(buscourses)
course3 = itcourses.difference(buscourses)
course4 = itcourses.symmetric_difference(buscourses)
print(course1)
print(course2)
print(course3)
print(course4)
print(itcourses.isdisjoint(buscourses))
print(itcourses.issubset(buscourses))
print(itcourses.issuperset(buscourses))
```

Table 7. SET methods

Method	Description	Example
union	Return a set. Combination (union) of two given sets	course1 = itcourses.union(buscourses)
intersection	Returns a set, that is the intersection of two or more sets	course2 = itcourses.intersection(buscourses)
difference	Returns a set. Contains difference between two sets	course3 = itcourses.difference(buscourses)
isdisjoint	Returns Boolean Value. Checks whether two sets have intersection or not.	itcourses.isdisjoint(buscourses)
issubset	Returns Boolean Value. Checks whether set-1 is subset of set-2	itcourses.issubset(buscourses)
issuperset	Returns Boolean Value. Checks whether set-1 is superset of set-2	itcourses.issuperset(buscourses)

The above code generates the following output:

```
{'office', 'php', 'java', 'python', 'html', 'tally'}
{'html', 'office'}
{'php', 'java', 'python'}
{'java', 'tally', 'php', 'python'}
False
False
False
```

Let's have a look on above methods. Table 7 presents a variety of set methods along with their descriptions and examples.

Example: Test and Analyze the Following Code

#Test the following code

```
st = {'Apple', 'Banana'}
while True:
    print(" 1. Add to set \n 2. Print Set \n 3. Delete from set
\n Other to Exit")
    ch = int(input(" Select one choice"))
    if ch==1:
        v = input('Enter fruit name to insert ')
```

```
        st.add(v)
    elif ch==2:
        print(' **** Fruit Set has ....')
        print(st)
    elif ch==3:
        a = input(' Enter fruit name to delete ')
        if a in st:
            st.discard(a)
            print(' **** delete success ')
        else:
            print(" *** No fruit available in set")
    else:
        print(' ****** Exit choice ')
        break
```

INTRODUCTION TO DICTIONARY

A dictionary is a collection which is ordered, changeable and does not allow duplicates. It is a Key: Value pair (Martelli et al., 2023) (Neelakandan, 2022). The following are some of the properties of a dictionary.

- Keys are immutable, case sensitive and unique.
- Dictionary values are accessed by using key.
- Dictionaries are used to store data values in key: value pairs.
- Dictionary items are ordered, changeable, and does not allow duplicates. Dictionary can be referred to by using the key name.
- Dictionary is created using { }

Example:

```
strength = {
    "java"  : 25,
    "python": 24,
    "sql"   : 19,
    "php"   : 13
}
```

Here, *strength* is the name of our dictionary with four *Key: Value* pairs. Now, it is very easy for us to access dictionary values. Even the value can be changed using *key*. A *key: value* can be deleted from the dictionary. A new *key: value* pair can be added dynamically.

CREATING A DICTIONARY

There are several methods to create a dictionary (McKinney Wes, 2022).

Example

```
#Empty dictionary
course = { }
#Empty dictionay using dict method
courseone = dict()
#dictionary with pre inserted values
coursetwo = {'math':30, 'physics': 24}
#dictionary with integer keys
mymark = {7: 'quiz', 10: 'test', 40: 'final'}
#dictionary using dict method
myaddress = dict({'street': 'alaqdar', 'city':'iraq'})
```

ACCESS DICTIONARY ITEMS

Using *print( )* to print dictionary values.

```
mycar={
    "brand":"Hyundai",
    "model":2022,
    "color":"red"
}
print("car details ", mycar)
print("car has ", len(mycar), " items")
print("data type is ", type(mycar))
```

mycar is the name of the dictionary with three *Key: Value* pairs. *print(mycar)* is used to print all dictionary values. l*en(mycar) is used to get length of dictionary.*
The above code generates the following output.

```
car details {'brand': 'Hyundai', 'model': 2022, 'color': 'red'}
car has 3 items
data type is <class 'dict'>
```

To get the value of a *mycar* key, we can use the following ways.

```
M = mycar['brand']
M = mycar.get('brand')
```

However, dictionary values can be changed as mycar['brand'] = 'Toyota'
A for loop is more effective to print keys and values.

Example

```
#Working with dictionary
mycar={
    "brand":"Hyundai",
    "model":2022,
    "color":"red"
}
print("---> Key names are ")
for k in mycar:
    print(k)
print("---> Values in dictionary are ")
for k in mycar:
    print(mycar[k])
```

The above code generates the following output. Off course, it prints all keys and values.

```
---> Key names are
brand
model
color
---> Values in dictionary are
```

```
Hyundai
2022
Red
```

Besides, the following methods are used to get keys and values of dictionary.

```
ky = mycar.keys()
val = mycar.values()
print("Dictionary keys are ", ky)
print("Dictionary values are ", val)
```

A simplest way to check whether the key is present in dictionary is:

```
if "model" in mycar:
    print("Model is one of the key in dictionary")
else:
    print("Model is not a key ")
```

ADDING AND REMOVING ITEMS

We can add a new item as dictionaryname[key] = value

```
mycar["price"]=2700
mycar["engine"]="1600CC"
```

There are several methods to remove:
Method-1:

```
        mycar.pop("price")
```

Method-2:

```
        mycar.popitem("price")
```

Method-3:

```
        del mycar["brand"]
```

Method-4: Deleted entire dictionary

```
del mycar
```

DICTIONARY METHODS

Table 8 showcases a range of dictionary methods along with accompanying descriptions and examples.

Table 8. Dictionary methods

Method	Example	Description
keys()	ky = mycar.keys()	Get all keys
values()	val = mycar.values()	Get all values associated with keys
len()	siz = len(mycar)	Return number of items in a dictionary
del()	del mycar	Delete entire dictionary
popitem()	mycar.popitem("price")	Remove most recently added item
pop()	mycar.pop("price")	Remove the specified item
clear()	mycar.clear()	Empty all values without deleting dictionary
copy()	Newcar = mycar.copy()	Return a copy of dictionary

CONCLUSION

A list is a flexible data type that can have heterogeneous items. List items are accessed through index number. This chapter emphasizes list operations. A list can be nested within another list. Tuples are used to group information such as employees, students, and books. Tuple slicing allows retrieval of some parts of required items. A tuple can be nested in another tuple. Tuple values are accessed by index. This chapter covers tuple initialization, accessing tuple values, functions, and the nesting of tuples. This chapter concisely explains set properties and practical methods in our daily programming life. Although the *set* has advantages, it has a few limitations too. For example, a *set* can't be embedded in another set. Also, a *set* can't have a list. A dictionary is a Key: Value pair that doesn't allow duplicate keys. There are several ways to access dictionary values. Dictionaries are sometimes called associative arrays. The dictionary provides faster execution than other data structures, such as lists.

REFERENCES

Arulkumar, N., Paulose, J., Galety, M. G., Manimaran, A., Saravanan, S., & Saleem, R. A. (2022). Exploring Social Networking Data Sets. *Social Network Analysis: Theory and Applications*, 205-228.

Beri, R. (2019). *Python Made Simple: Learn Python programming in easy steps with examples*. Bpb Publications.

Bisong, E. (2019). Python. *Building Machine Learning and Deep Learning Models on Google Cloud Platform: A Comprehensive Guide for Beginners*, 71-89.

Guttag, J. V. (2021). *Introduction to Computation and Programming Using Python: With Application to Computational Modeling and Understanding Data*. MIT Press.

Haslwanter, T. (2016). An Introduction to Statistics with Python. In *With Applications in the Life Sciences*. Springer International Publishing. doi:10.1007/978-3-319-28316-6

Hill, C. (2020). *Learning scientific programming with Python*. Cambridge University Press. doi:10.1017/9781108778039

Johansson, R., & John, S. (2019). *Numerical Python* (Vol. 1). Apress. doi:10.1007/978-1-4842-4246-9

Kong, Q., Siauw, T., & Bayen, A. (2020). *Python programming and numerical methods: A guide for engineers and scientists*. Academic Press.

Learn To Code For IoT With Python Essentials Course. (2022). Networking Academy. https://www.netacad.com/courses/programming/pcap-programming -essentials-python

Martelli, A., Ravenscroft, A. M., Holden, S., & McGuire, P. (2023). *Python in a Nutshell*. O'Reilly Media, Inc.

McKinney. (2022). *Python for Data Analysis*. O'Reilly Media, Inc.

Moruzzi, G. (2020). Python basics and the interactive mode. *Essential python for the physicist*, 1-39.

Neelakandan, S., Rene Beulah, J., Prathiba, L., Murthy, G. L. N., Fantin Irudaya Raj, E., & Arulkumar, N. (2022). Blockchain with deep learning-enabled secure healthcare data transmission and diagnostic model. *International Journal of Modeling, Simulation, and Scientific Computing*, *13*(04), 2241006. doi:10.1142/S1793962322410069

Unpingco, J. (2021). *Python Programming for Data Analysis*. Springer. doi:10.1007/978-3-030-68952-0

Chapter 9
Interactive Visualization With Plotly Express

Gurram Sunitha
School of Computing, Mohan Babu University, Tirupati, India

A. V. Sriharsha
iD https://orcid.org/0000-0003-4244-4243
Mohan Babu University, India

Olimjon Yalgashev
Samarkand International University of Technology, Uzbekistan

Islom Mamatov
iD https://orcid.org/0000-0002-7029-5890
Samarkand International University of Technology, Uzbekistan

ABSTRACT

Data visualisation is the process of visualizing data for the purpose of analyzing and correlating data to confirm complicated ideas and to spot visual patterns after an investigation. Data visualization allows data scientists to quickly identify visual patterns and trends that may not be immediately apparent from raw data. Visualization also enables us to build models that are easier for stakeholders to understand and apply. Data visualization is an essential tool for exploratory data analysis (EDA). Plotly Express is a terse, high-level Python visualization library. It is a wrapper module for Plotly library that provides simple interface for visualizing data in the form of various plots, maps, graph objects, layouts, traces, figures, etc. Plotly Express is a user-friendly, high-level interface to Plotly that generates easily styleable, interactive, beautiful, and informative figures visualizing various types of data. Plotly Express provides interactive visualizations.

DOI: 10.4018/978-1-6684-7100-5.ch009

IMPORTANCE OF DATA VISUALIZATION

Data visualization is converting data into visual representations, such as plots, graphs, charts, and maps, that may be used to explain the data and provide new perspectives. Data visualization is visualizing data to analyze and correlate data to confirm complicated ideas and spot visual patterns after an investigation. Data visualization plays a critical role in understanding and interpreting data. It can be used to uncover relationships in large, complex datasets and to make sense of the vast amounts of information available today. Data visualization allows data scientists to quickly identify visual patterns and trends that may not be immediately apparent from raw data. By presenting data visually, data scientists can promptly recognize outliers, patterns, and correlations that might otherwise be difficult to spot. Visualization also enables us to build more accessible models for stakeholders to understand and apply.

The main goal of data visualization is to make it easier for viewers to identify patterns, styles, and vendors in large datasets. By creating visual representations of data points such as charts, graphs, or maps, the most critical aspects of the data set can be highlighted while still conveying its complete story. This makes it easier for business analysts to interpret the underlying trends or correlations within the dataset, which ultimately helps them make better business decisions. Visual communication is a necessary talent for all managers in this era. Data visualization is an essential tool for Exploratory Data Analysis (EDA). It provides a way to gain insight into data by visually representing it and helps reveal patterns, correlations, outliers, and anomalies that may otherwise remain hidden. Data visualization allows business analysts to quickly observe trends in data, identify relationships between variables and understand the underlying structure of the data. This helps us form hypotheses about what might be causing specific patterns or behaviors in our data. Using data visualization techniques, we can more quickly and easily explore large data sets than possible by manually examining each observation. This makes it easier to discover meaningful insights from our data that can inform decisions and help guide further exploration.

PLOTLY EXPRESS FOR DATA VISUALIZATION

Plotly Express is a terse, high-level Python visualization library. It is a wrapper module for the Plotly library that provides a simple interface for visualizing data in various plots, maps, graph objects, layouts, traces, figures, etc. Plotly Express is a user-friendly, high-level interface to Plotly, which generates easily style able, interactive, beautiful, and informative figures visualizing various types of data.

Plotly Express provides interactive visualizations; for example, the Plotly figures are by default appended with hover text which the programmer can customize. An overview of Plotly Express can be referred to at (Plotly Express in Python, 2022). Table 1 illustrates the different types of plots supported by Plotly Express.

Table 1. Types of plots supported by Plotly Express

Plot Type	Various Types of Plots Supported by Plotly Express
Basic Plots	scatter, dot, line, area, bar, funnel, timeline
Part-of- Whole	pie, sunburst, treemap. icicle, funnel_area
1D Distributions	histogram, box, violin, strip, ecdf
2D Distributions	density_heatmap. density_contour
Matrix or Image Input	imshow
3-Dimensional	scatter_3d, line_3d
Multidimensional	scatter matrix, parallel_coordinates, parallel_categories
Tile Maps	scatter_mapbox, line_mapbox, choropleth_mapbox, density_mapbox
Outline Maps	scatter_geo, line geo, choropleth
Polar Charts	scatter_polar, line_polar, bar_polar
Ternary Charts	scatter_ternary, line_ternary

Plotly Express can create entire figures at once, thus reducing the burden on programmers in creating figures. All the figures created using Plotly Express are instances of plotly.graph_objects.Figure class. More than 30 functions are available in Plotly Express to develop various types of plots, maps, graph objects, layouts, traces, and figures. Throughout a data exploration session, it is simple to transition between multiple kinds of plots since the API for these functions was deliberately created to be as consistent and straightforward to understand as possible. Table 1 shows various types of plots that Plotly Express supports. The Plotly Express API for multiple plots, maps, graph objects, layouts, traces, and figures can be found at (Python API reference for Plotly Express, 2022). Plotly Express has various amicable features such as low code, user-friendly, simple API, automatic figure labeling, sensible & overridable default parameter settings, flexible input formats, automatic trace and layout configuration, uniform color handling, faceting, animations, etc.

INTERACTIVE VISUALIZATION WITH PLOTLY EXPRESS

This section presents a brief overview and sample Python code snippets for various types of plot visualizations – Scatter plot, Dot plot, Line plot, Area plot, Pie chart, Bar chart, Grouped bar chart, Stacked bar chart, Sunburst chart, Density heatmap.

Scatter Plot

The scatter plot is one of the types of relationship plot. A scatter plot primarily shows the relationship between two variables (bivariate data). A scatter plot can visually inspect the linear correlation between any two variables. Also, it allows us to visualize when one of the two variables is categorized. Clustered markers in a scatter plot, if any, enable the detection of data patterns. It is simple to determine whether there is a positive or negative or no correlation, strong or weak or no correlation, by simply looking at the visualization of the scatter plot. It frequently provides mathematicians with a solid beginning point for their research when they can quickly see how the two variables relate. The following Table 2 is the sample code snippet for visualizing the scatter plot for the considered data.

The Python libraries "plotly.express" and "pandas" have been imported (Lines 2 & 3). A dataset has been created of twenty individuals with their Gender ("Male", "Female"), Height (in centimeters), and Weight (in kilograms) (Line 5). A dataframe "health" has been created; it is initialized with the dataset "data", and the column names have been set for the dataframe (Line 7). "px.scatter()" function creates an entire figure with a scatter plot (Line 9).

The parameters for the "px.scatter()" function are set as follows

```
the dataset "health",
the x-axis variable (x="Height"),
the y-axis variable (y="Weight"),
the color of the marker (color = "Gender")
the symbol of the marker (symbol = "Gender")
the title of the scatter plot (title = "Scatter Plot - Height
vs Weight")
```

The marker color and the market shape are set differently based on Gender by setting the parameters as "color = "Gender" and symbol = "Gender". This trick allows to include of a third dimension, "Gender" into the scatter plot. The update_traces() function is used here to set marker size, marker border line width, and marker border line color (Line 11). The show() function will visualize the figure (Line 13). The Plotly Express API for the "scatter()" function can be referred to at (Plotly Express

Table 2. Scatter plot

```
1
2    # Importing the "pandas" and "plotly" libraries
3    import plotly.express as px
     import pandas as pd

4
5    # Creating a dataset of individuals "Gender", "Height" and "Weight".
     data = [["Male",180,84],["Female",150,60],["Female",154,55], ["Male",169,78],["Male",170,84],
     ["Female",157,56], ["Female",164,65],["Male",165,69], ["Male",172,73], ["Female",156,67],
     ["Female",184,55], ["Male",169,81], ["Male",178,90], ["Female",156,61], ["Female",168,55],
     ["Male",149,50], ["Male",181,80], ["Female",159,74], ["Female",169,85],["Male",151,48]]

     # Creating a dataframe with data and column names
6    health = pd.DataFrame(data, columns=["Gender", "Height", "Weight"])
7
     # Creating a scatter plot
8    fig = px.scatter(health, x="Height", y= "Weight", color = "Gender",
9    symbol = "Gender", title = "Scatter Plot - Height vs Weight")

     # Setting marker size, marker border width, and marker border-color
10   fig.update_traces(marker=dict(size=12,line=dict(width=2,
11   color= "DarkSlateGrey")))

     # Displaying the scatter plot
12   fig.show()
13
```

for scatter plot, 2022) (Plotly Express API for scatter plot, 2022). The Plotly Express API for the "update_traces()" function can be referred to at (Plotly Express API for Creating and Updating Figures, 2022). Figure 1 shows the scatter plot visualized using the above Python code snippet. Visual inspection shows that the attributes "Height" and "Weight" are positively correlated. Once the Plot is visualized, one can interact with the Plot by hovering the cursor over the Plot (Figure 2).

Dot Plot

The dot plot is one of the variations of the scatter plot. A scatter plot primarily shows the relationship between two numerical variables. In contrast, a dot plot's primary use is to observe and establish relationships between numeric and categorical variables. The linear correlation between a numeric variable and a categorical variable can be visually inspected using a scatter plot. The following is the sample code snippet for visualizing the dot plot for the considered data. The categorical variable "Gender" is considered on the x-axis of the Plot, and the numerical variable "Weight" is considered on the y-axis of the Plot. Figure 3 shows the dot plot visualized using the below Python code snippet. Table 3 shows the code for Dot Plot.

Figure 1. Data visualization using scatter plot

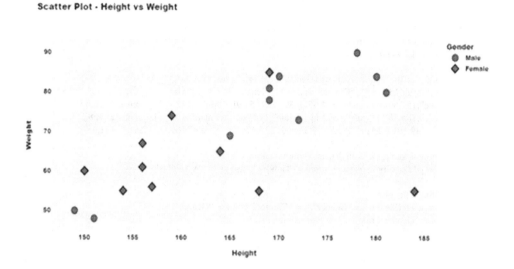

Line Plot

A line plot plots quantitative values of a subject/concept/entity/theme/class over a predetermined period (Dabbas, 2021). It is generally used to visually inspect the

Figure 2. Interaction with data visualized using scatter plot

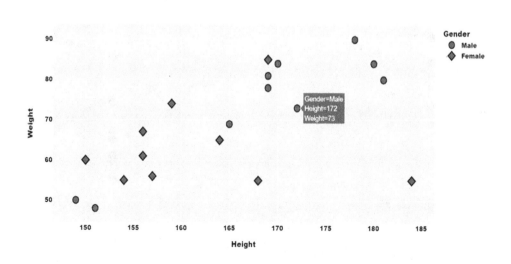

Table 3. Dot plot

1
2
3
 	
4
5
	# Importing the "pandas" and "plotly" libraries
	import plotly.express as px
	import pandas as pd
	
	# Creating a dataset of individuals "Gender", "Height" and "Weight".
	data = [["Male",180,84],["Female",150,60],["Female",154,55], ["Male",169,78], ["Male",170,84],
	["Female",157,56],["Female",164,65],["Male",165,69], ["Male",172,73], ["Female",156,67],
	["Female",184,55], ["Male",169,81], ["Male",178,90], ["Female",156,61], ["Female",168,55],
	["Male",149,50], ["Male",181,80], ["Female",159,74], ["Female",169,85],["Male",151,48]]

6
7
 	
8
9
	# Creating a dataframe with data and column names
	health = pd.DataFrame(data, columns=["Gender", "Height", "Weight"])
	
	# Creating a dot plot
	fig = px.scatter(health, x="Gender", y= "Weight", color = "Gender",
	symbol = "Gender", title = "Dot Plot - Gender vs Weight")

10 11	# Setting marker size, marker border width, and marker border-color fig.update_traces(marker=dict(size=12,line=dict(width=2, color= "DarkSlateGrey")))

12
13
	# Displaying the dot plot
	fig.show()

Figure 3. Data visualization using dot plot

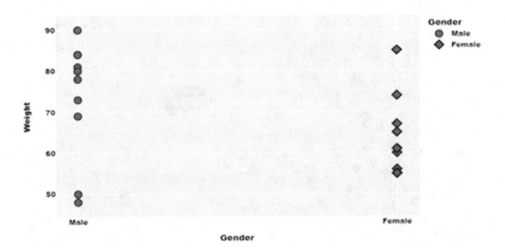

Table 4. Line plot

```
1    # Importing the "pandas" and "plotly" libraries
2    import plotly.express as px
3    import pandas as pd

4    # Creating a dataset of students "Test" and "Marks in Biology".
5    data = [["T1",48],["T2",51],["T3",56],["T4",64],["T5",59],["T6",69],
     ["T7",72],["T8",71], ["T9",73],["T10",79]]

6    # Creating a dataframe with data and column names
7    marks = pd.DataFrame(data, columns=["Test", "Marks"])

8    # Creating a line plot
9    fig = px.line(marks, x="Test", y="Marks",
     title = "Student 1 - Improvement in Biology")

10   # Displaying the line plot
11   fig.show()
```

trend of any subject/concept/entity/theme/class over some time. It is a plot between any two variables, and it shows the movement of change of one variable concerning the difference in the other variable. The following Table 4 is the sample code snippet for visualizing a line plot for the considered data.

A dataset has been created of "Student 1" who has attempted ten tests (T1 to T10) in a biology course (Line 5). A dataframe "marks" has been created; it is initialized with the dataset "data", and the column names have been set for the dataframe (Line 7). "px.line()" function creates an entire figure with line plot (Line 9).

The parameters for the "px.line()" function are set as follows –

```
the dataset "marks",
the x-axis variable (x= "Test"),
the y-axis variable (y= "Marks"),
the title of the line plot (title = "Student 1 - Improvement in
Biology")
```

The show() function will visualize the figure (Line 11). The Plotly Express API for the "line()" function can be referred to at (Plotly Express for line plot, 2022) (Plotly Express API for line plot, 2022). Figure 4 shows the line plot visualized using the above Python code snippet. By visual inspection, it can be observed that the student has clearly improved his knowledge, performed well, and shown considerable improvement in the biology course.

The line plot can include a third dimension by setting the "color" parameter. This parameter sets a different color for each line drawn on the line plot. The following

Figure 4. Data visualization using line plot

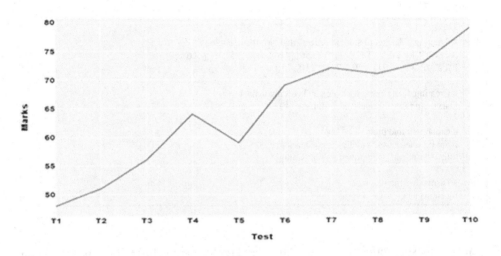

is the sample code snippet for visualizing a line plot with the third dimension for the considered data. The Table 5 code snippet draws multiple lines based on the "Subject". Figure 5 shows the line plot with the encoding column color visualized using the below Python code snippet.

Area Plot

Area plots are similar to line plots. First, the lines are drawn, and then the area between the lines and the axes is filled. Hence, these plots are called filled area plots. Generally, these plots are used to visualize multiple variables' data trends over time. The filled areas can be overlapped or stacked one over the other. These graphs are the standard approach to show stacked lines and often indicate accumulated totals over time. The following Table 6 is the sample code snippet for visualizing a filled area plot for the considered data.

A dataset has been created of "Student 1" who has attempted ten tests (T1 to T10) in biology and chemistry courses (Line 5). A dataframe "marks" has been created, it is initialized with the dataset "data", and the column names have been set for the dataframe (Line 7). "px.area()" function creates an entire figure with filled area plot (Line 9).

The parameters for the "px.area()" function are set as follows –

Table 5. Line plot with the encoding column color

```
1    # Importing the "pandas" and "plotly" libraries
2    import plotly.express as px
3    import pandas as pd

4    # Creating a dataset of students "Subject", "Test" and "Marks".
5    data= [["Biology","T1",48],["Biology","T2",51],["Biology","T3",56],
     ["Biology","T4",64], ["Biology","T5",59],["Biology","T6",69],
     ["Biology","T7",72], ["Biology","T8",71],["Biology","T9",73],
     ["Biology","T10",79],["Chemistry","T1",58],["Chemistry","T2",51],
     ["Chemistry","T3",56],["Chemistry","T4",62],["Chemistry","T5",64],
     ["Chemistry","T6",70],["Chemistry","T7",78],["Chemistry","T8",75],
     ["Chemistry","T9",79], ["Chemistry","T10",84]]

6    # Creating a dataframe with data and column names
7    marks = pd.DataFrame(data, columns=["Subject", "Test", "Marks"])

8    # Creating a line plot
9    fig = px.line(marks, x="Test", y="Marks", color = "Subject",
     title = "Student 1 - Improvement in Biology & Chemistry")

10   # Displaying the line plot
11   fig.show()
```

Figure 5. Data visualization using line plot with column encoding color

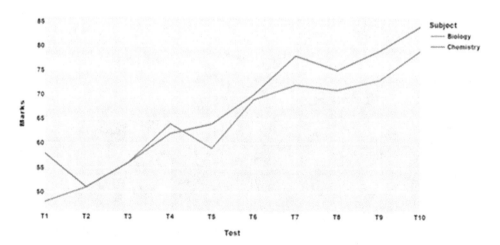

Table 6. Area plot

```
1    # Importing the "pandas" and "plotly" libraries
2    import plotly.express as px
3    import pandas as pd

4    #Creating a dataset of student's "Subject", "Test" and "Marks".
5    data= [["Biology","T1",48],["Biology","T2",51],
     ["Biology","T3",56],["Biology","T4",64],["Biology","T5",59],
     ["Biology","T6",69],["Biology","T7",72],["Biology","T8",71],
     ["Biology","T9",73],["Biology","T10",79],["Chemistry","T1",58],
     ["Chemistry","T2",51],["Chemistry","T3",56], ["Chemistry","T4",62],
     ["Chemistry","T5",64],["Chemistry","T6",70], ["Chemistry","T7",78],
     ["Chemistry","T8",75],["Chemistry","T9",79],["Chemistry","T10",84]]

6    # Creating a dataframe with data and column names
7    marks = pd.DataFrame(data, columns=["Subject","Test", "Marks"])

8    # Creating an area plot
9    fig = px.area(marks, x="Test", y="Marks", color = "Subject",
     title = "Student 1 - Improvement in Biology & Chemistry")

10   # Displaying the area plot
11   fig.show()
```

Figure 6. Data visualization using area plot

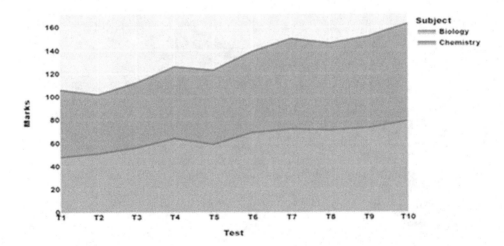

Table 7. Pie chart

```
1    # Importing the "pandas" and "plotly" libraries
2    import plotly.express as px
3    import pandas as pd

4    # Creating a dataset of population distribution in a country as per
     # gender (in millions).
5    data = [["Male",180], ["Female",150],["Others",25]]

6    # Creating a dataframe with data and column names
7    gender_distribution = pd.DataFrame(data,
     columns=["Gender", "Population"])

8    # Creating a pie chart
9    fig = px.pie(gender_distribution, values="Population", names="Gender",
     title = "Pie Chart - Gender Distribution")

10   # Displaying the pie chart
11   fig.show()
```

```
the dataset "marks",
the x-axis variable (x= "Test"),
the y-axis variable (y= "Marks"),
the color for the filling area (color = "Subject")
the title of the line plot (title = "Student 1 - Improvement in
Biology & Chemistry")
```

The Plotly Express API for the "area()" function can be referred to at (Plotly Express for filled area plot, 2022) (Plotly Express API for filled area plot, 2022). Figure 6 shows the filled area plot visualized using the above Python code snippet. By visual inspection, it can be observed that the student has clearly improved his knowledge, performed well, and has shown considerable improvement in both aggregated courses.

Pie Chart

A pie chart visualizes a part-in-the-whole relationship (Pattanaik, S. N., & Wiegand, R. P., 2021). If the data comprises categories where each contributes to a whole, then such partial contributions can be visualized using a pie chart. A pie chart is graphically visualized as a pie (circular-shaped) comprising slices, each representing a category in the data. In the pie chart, the size of a slice of a particular variety represents the proportional contribution of that category to the whole, i.e., each slice in the pie chart represents a proportion of data of each type. Using a pie chart, the

Figure 7. Data visualization using pie chart

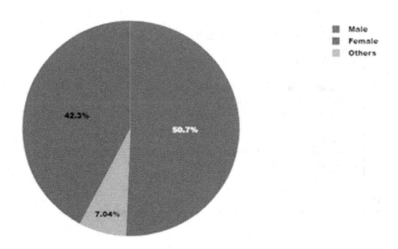

Pie Chart - Gender Distribution

importance/contribution of each category to the whole. The following Table 7 is the sample code snippet for visualizing a pie chart for the considered data.

A dataset has been created representing the population distribution in a country as per Gender (in millions) (Line 5). A dataframe "gender_distribution" has been completed; it is initialized with the dataset "data", and the column names have been set for the dataframe (Line 7). "px.pie()" function creates an entire figure with a pie chart (Line 9).

The parameters for the "px.pie()" function are set as follows –

```
the dataset "gender_distribution",
categories in the pie (the name for each slice in the pie)
(names="Gender"),
size of each slice in the pie (values="Population"),
the color for filling area (color = "Subject")
the title of the pie chart (title = "Pie Chart - Gender
Distribution")
```

The Plotly Express API for the "pie()" function can be referred to at (Plotly Express for pie chart, 2022) (Plotly Express API for pie chart, 2022). Figure 7 shows the pie chart visualized using the above Python code snippet. By visual inspection, it can be observed that the male population in the country contributes 50.7%, and the female population contributes 42.3%, which is less when compared to the male population.

Table 8. Bar chart

```
1    # Importing the "pandas" and "plotly" libraries
2    import plotly.express as px
3    import pandas as pd

4    # Creating a dataset of population distribution in the USA during 2019-
     # 2022 (in millions).
5    data = [["2019",328.24],["2020",331.5],["2021",331.89],
     ["2022",333.39]]

6    # Creating a dataframe with data and column names
7    population = pd.DataFrame(data, columns=["Year", "Population"])

8    # Creating the bar chart
9    fig = px.bar(population, x="Year", y="Population",
     title = "Bar Chart - Population")

10   # Setting the scale of the y-axis
11   fig.update_layout(yaxis_range=[325,335])

12   # Displaying the bar chart
13   fig.show()
```

Bar Chart

Bar charts can be used for displaying metrics of categories of data (Sievert, 2020). Bar charts can help compare multiple types of data or discrete data, provided there aren't too many categories to compare. The values are compared over time between the various groups using the bar chart. To track changes over time, bar graphs are utilized. For time series data, they are highly beneficial. The bars on the bar chart can be drawn horizontally or vertically. On the bar chart, each bar on the x-axis (or y-axis) represents a category. All the bars have uniform width (or height). The bar's height (or length) represents the category's value or metric on the y-axis (or x-axis). A bar chart is a statistical approach to defining the statistics of each type of data. Bar charts show the relationship between any two dimensions. On one axis, it represents the categories; on the other, it means the category's discrete values. The following is the sample code snippet for visualizing a bar chart for the considered data. There is one category in the data – "Year," and the statistical value for each class is the "Population." In the following code, the category "Year" is taken on the x-axis, and the y-axis represents the statistical data of each "Year." The height of the bar on the chart denotes the "Population" value for each "Year," while the width of the bar indicates the "Year" itself. Table 8 has the code for bar chart.

A dataset has been created representing the population distribution in a country per year (in millions) (Line 5). A dataframe "Population" has been completed; it

Figure 8. Data visualization using bar chart

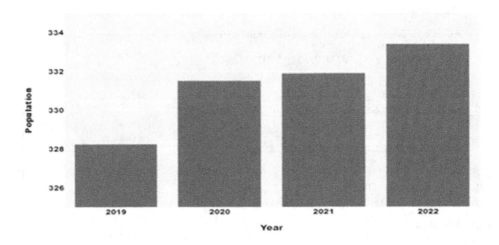

is initialized with the dataset "data", and the column names have been set for the dataframe (Line 7). "px.bar()" function creates an entire figure with bar chart (Line 9).

The parameters for the "px.bar()" function are set as follows –

```
the dataset "Population",
the x-axis variable representing the category (x = "Year"),
the y-axis variable representing the contribution of categories
to the whole (y = "Population"),
the title of the pie chart (title = "Bar Chart - Population")
```

The Plotly Express API for the "bar()" function can be referred to at (Plotly Express for bar chart, 2022) (Plotly Express API for bar chart, 2022). The update_layout() function is used to set the y-axis range. The y-axis scale ranges from a minimum value of 325 to a maximum of 335. Figure 8 shows the bar chart visualized using the above Python code snippet. By visual inspection, it can be how the population in a country has increased over the years 2019 to 2022.

Grouped Bar Chart

If the data contains two categories, a third dimension can be added to the bar chart, visualized as a grouped bar chart. The following is the sample code snippet for visualizing a bar chart for the considered data. There are two categories in the

Table 9. Grouped bar chart

1	# Importing the "pandas" and "plotly" libraries
2	import plotly.express as px
3	import pandas as pd
4	# Creating a population distribution dataset as per Gender in the USA during 2019-2022 (in millions.
5	data = [["2019","Male",161.66], ["2019","Female",166.58], ["2020","Male",164.21], ["2020","Female",167.29], ["2021","Male",164.38], ["2021","Female",167.51], ["2022","Male",165.13], ["2022","Female",168.26]]
6	# Creating a dataframe with data and column names
7	gender_distribution = pd.DataFrame(data, columns=["Year", "Gender", "Population"])
8	# Creating the grouped bar chart
9	fig = px.bar(gender_distribution, x="Year", y="Population", color="Gender", barmode='group', text_auto=True, title = "Grouped Bar Chart - Gender Distribution")
10	# Setting the scale of the y-axis
11	fig.update_layout(yaxis_range=[160,170])
12	# Displaying the grouped bar chart
13	fig.show()

data – "Year" and "Gender," and the statistical data is the "Population." In the following code, the category "Year" is taken on the x-axis, and the y-axis represents the statistical data of each "Year." The height of the bar on the chart denotes the "Population" value for each "Year," while the width of the bar indicates the "Year" itself. The other category, "Gender," is considered the third dimension where for each "Gender" subcategory, multiple bars will be visualized. They will be grouped for each "Year" on the x-axis, i.e., in the grouped bar chart, the bars representing the third dimension "Gender" are grouped for each x-axis value "Year". Table 9 has the code for Grouped Bar chart.

A dataset has been created representing the population distribution in a country per year (in millions) and Gender (Line 5). A dataframe "gender_distribution" has been completed; it is initialized with the dataset "data", and the column names have been set for the dataframe (Line 7). "px.bar()" function creates an entire figure with a bar chart (Line 9).

The parameters for the "px.bar()" function are set as follows –

```
the dataset "gender_distribution",
the x-axis variable representing the first category (x =
```

```
"Year"),
the y-axis variable representing the contribution of categories
to the whole (y = "Population"),
the second category is taken as a third dimension (color=
"Gender")
the mode of the bars of the third dimension (barmode = "group")
display of text on the bars ("text_auto=True")
the title of the pie chart (title = "Grouped Bar Chart -
Population")
```

Figure 9 shows the grouped bar chart visualized using the above Python code snippet. Observe that there are two bars visualized for each "Year" on the x-axis (one bar representing one subcategory ("Male", "Female") of the third dimension "Gender"). By visual inspection, it can be how various genders are contributing to the population in a country over the years 2019 to 2022.

Figure 9. Data visualization using grouped bar chart

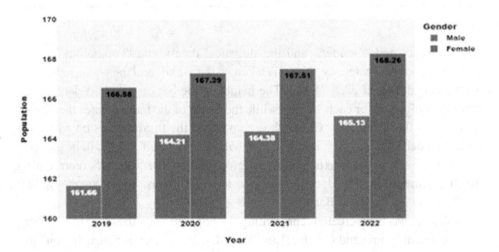

Stacked Bar Chart

With one aesthetic distinction, the stacked and grouped bar charts are comparable (Zhao, 2023). The bars representing the third dimension, "Gender," are stacked one

Table 10. Stacked bar chart

```
1    # Importing the "pandas" and "plotly" libraries
2    import plotly.express as px
3    import pandas as pd

4    # Creating a population distribution dataset per genders in USA # during 2019-2022 (in millions).
5    data = [["2019","Male",161.66], ["2019","Female",166.58],
     ["2020","Male",164.21], ["2020","Female",167.29],
     ["2021","Male",164.38], ["2021","Female",167.51],
     ["2022","Male",165.13], ["2022","Female",168.26] ]

6    # Creating a dataframe with data and column names
7    gender_distribution = pd.DataFrame(data,
     columns=["Year", "Gender", "Population"])

8    # Creating the stacked bar chart
9    fig = px.bar(gender_distribution, x="Year", y="Population",
     color="Gender", title = "Stacked Bar Chart - Gender Distribution",
     pattern_shape="Gender", pattern_shape_sequence=[".", "x"],
     text_auto=True)

10   # Displaying the stacked bar chart
11   fig.show()
```

over another rather than being grouped side-by-side. The following Table 10 has the sample code snippet for visualizing a bar chart for the considered data.

Observe that in the bar() function, the mode of the bars (barmode= "group") is not mentioned. If "barmode" is not mentioned, the bars representing the third dimension will be stacked rather than grouped. Also, different patterns and shapes can be used to fill the bars along with the color, if appropriate.

Two more parameters may be mentioned in the bar() function –

```
the filling patterns for the bars (pattern_shape = "Gender")
the filling shapes for the bars (pattern_shape_sequence = [".",
"x"])
```

Figure 10 shows the stacked bar chart visualized using the above Python code snippet. The third dimension, "Gender," is pictured as stacked bars. Only one bar represents each "Year" on the x-axis. Each subcategory ("Male", "Female") of the third dimension, "Gender" is visualized as part of the stacked bar.

Figure 10. Data visualization using stacked bar chart

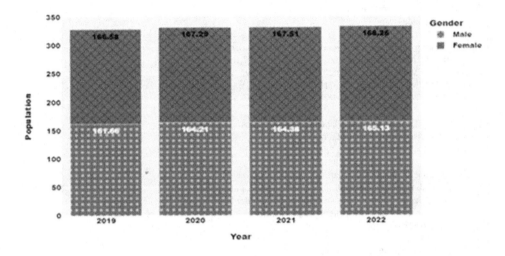

Sunburst Chart

The sunburst chart is a variation of the doughnut plot used to show a hierarchical structure (Rees & Laramee, 2019). Hierarchical data is best displayed with a sunburst chart. Without hierarchical information (only one level of categories), a sunburst chart resembles a doughnut. A sunburst plot shows discrete hierarchical data from the roots to the leaves. The root forms the core (innermost circle) of the Plot. Then,

Table 11. Sunburst chart

1	#Importing the "pandas" and "plotly" libraries
2	import plotly.express as px
3	import pandas as pd
4	# Creating a dataset of weekend planners.
5	data = dict(event=["Breakfast","Movie","Lunch","Shopping", "Drinks", "Concert","Gym","Brunch","Family Meet"], day=["Saturday","Saturday","Saturday", "Saturday","Saturday","Saturday","Sunday", "Sunday","Sunday"], hours=[1, 3, 2, 2, 1, 6, 2, 4, 4])
6	# Creating the sunburst plot
7	fig = px.sunburst(data, path = ["day", "event"],values="hours")
8	# Displaying the sunburst plot
9	fig.show()

Figure 11. Data visualization using sunburst chart

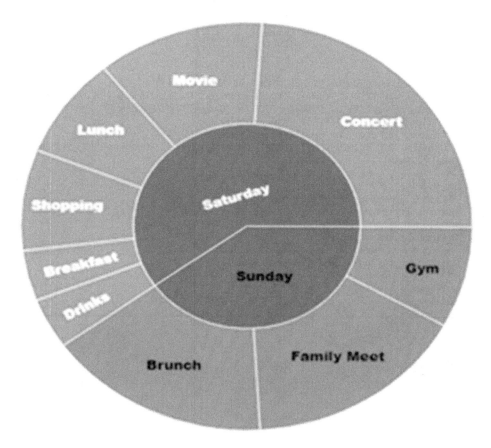

outer rings are added to the core as needed. One ring or circle represents each hierarchy level, with the innermost circle acting as the parent or root for all the data. Subsequent rings are divided into slices, and the size of each slice is proportional to the data value. Each ring demonstrates how the outer rings relate to the interior rings.

The following Table 11 has the sample code snippet for visualizing a sunburst chart for the considered data.

A dataset represents a two-level hierarchy of the weekend planner (Line 5). The attribute "day" is the sunburst plot's root (or core). The attribute "event" forms the outer ring (2nd level). The attribute "day" includes the data values that decide the size of each slice in the 2nd level ring. "px.sunburst()" function creates an entire figure with a bar chart (Line 7).

The parameters for the "px.sunburst ()" function are set as follows –

Table 12. Density heatmap

```
1    # Importing the "pandas" and "plotly" libraries
2    import plotly.express as px
3    import pandas as pd

4    # Creating a dataset of students "Subject", "Test" and "Marks".
5    data= [["Biology","T1",48],["Biology","T2",51],["Biology","T3",56], ["Biology","T4",64],["Biology"
     ,"T5",59],["Biology","T6",69], ["Biology","T7",72],["Biology","T8",71],["Biology","T9",73], ["Biolo
     gy","T10",79],["Chemistry","T1",58],["Chemistry","T2",51],
     ["Chemistry","T3",56],["Chemistry","T4",62],["Chemistry","T5",64],
     ["Chemistry","T6",70],["Chemistry","T7",78],["Chemistry","T8",75], ["Chemistry","T9",79],["Chem
     istry","T10",84]]

6    # Creating a dataframe with data and column names
7    marks = pd.DataFrame(data, columns=["Subject","Test", "Marks"])

8    # Creating an area plot
9    fig = px.density_heatmap(marks, x="Subject", y="Test", z = "Marks",
     title = "Student 1 - Improvement in Biology & Chemistry")

10   # Displaying the area plot
11   fig.show()
```

```
the dataset "data",
the path specifying the hierarchy of the hierarchical structure
(path = ["day", "event"]),
the data values (values = "hours"),
```

The Plotly Express API for "bar()" function can be referred to at (Plotly Express for sunburst chart, 2022) (Plotly Express API for sunburst chart, 2022). Figure 11 shows the sunburst chart visualized using the above Python code snippet.

Density Heatmap

In a heatmap, values for a primary variable plotted against two-axis variables are shown as a grid of colored squares (Berinato, 2019). The continuous color scale is used to represent the density of the primary variable, thus providing visual clues on the density or sparsity of the primary variable when compared against the two-axis variables. Darker colors on the color scale represent richer density levels, and sparse density levels are represented by lighter colors on the color scale. The following Table 12 has the sample code snippet for visualizing a density heatmap for the considered data.

Figure 12. Data visualization using density heatmap

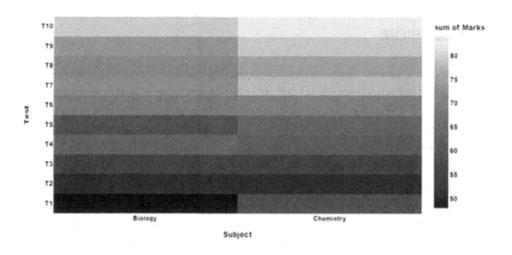

A dataset has been created of "Student 1" who has attempted ten tests (T1 to T10) in biology and chemistry courses (Line 5). A dataframe "marks" has been created, it is initialized with the dataset "data", and the column names have been set for the dataframe (Line 7). "px.density_heatmap()" function creates an entire figure with density heatmap (Line 9).

The parameters for the "px.density_heatmap()" function are set as follows –

```
the dataset "marks",
the x-axis variable (x= "Subject"),
the y-axis variable (y= "Test"),
the z-axis variable, which will be visualized as density
represented by variation of density on the color scale (z =
"Marks"),
the title of the density heatmap(title="Student 1 - Improvement
in Biology & Chemistry")
```

The Plotly Express API for "density_heatmap()" function can be referred to at (Plotly Express for density heatmap, 2022) (Plotly Express API for density heatmap, 2022). Figure 12 shows the density heatmap visualized using the above Python code snippet. By visual inspection, it can be observed that the student has clearly improved his knowledge, performed well, and has shown considerable improvement in both aggregated courses. Also, it can be observed that the student has performed well in the "Biology" approach than in "Chemistry" over tests.

CONCLUSION

Data visualization is visualizing data to analyze and correlate data to confirm complicated ideas and spot visual patterns after an investigation. By presenting data visually, data scientists can quickly recognize outliers, patterns, and correlations that might otherwise be difficult to spot. Visualization also enables us to build more accessible models for stakeholders to understand and apply. Data visualization is an essential tool for Exploratory Data Analysis (EDA).

Plotly Express is a terse, high-level Python visualization library. It is a wrapper module for the Plotly library that provides a simple interface for visualizing data in various plots, maps, graph objects, layouts, traces, figures, etc. Plotly Express is a user-friendly, high-level interface to Plotly, which generates easily designable, interactive, beautiful, and informative figures visualizing various types of data. Plotly Express provides interactive visualizations; for example, the Plotly figures are by default appended with hover text which the programmer can customize. More than 30 functions are available in Plotly Express to create various types of plots, maps, graph objects, layouts, traces, and figures. Throughout a data exploration session, it is simple to transition between multiple kinds of plots since the API for these functions was deliberately created to be as consistent and straightforward to understand as possible. Plotly Express has various amicable features such as low code, user-friendly, simple API, automatic figure labeling, sensible & overridable default parameter settings, flexible input formats, automatic trace and layout configuration, uniform color handling, faceting, animations, etc.

This chapter presents a brief overview of the importance of data visualization as part of Exploratory Data Analysis (EDA). Briefly, it explains the capabilities of the Plotly Express Python graphing library. Various types of plot visualizations such as Scatter plots, Dot plots, Line plots, Area plots, Pie charts, Bar charts, Grouped bar charts, Stacked bar charts, Sunburst charts, and Density heatmaps have been presented and discussed along with sample Python code snippets.

REFERENCES

Berinato, S. (2019). *Good charts workbook: Tips, tools, and exercises for making better data visualizations*. Harvard Business Press.

Dabbas, E. (2021). *Interactive Dashboards and Data Apps with Plotly and Dash: Harness the power of a fully fledged frontend web framework in Python–no JavaScript required.* Packt Publishing Ltd.

Pattanaik, S. N., & Wiegand, R. P. (2021). Data visualization. Handbook of Human Factors and Ergonomics, 893-946.

Plotly Express API for bar chart. (n.d.). Retrieved September 2022, from https://plotly.com/python-api-reference/generated/plotly.express.bar.html

Plotly Express for bar chart. (n.d.). Retrieved September 2022, from https://plotly.com/python/bar-charts/

Plotly Express API for Creating and Updating Figures. (n.d.). Retrieved September 2022, from https://plotly.com/python/creating-and-updating-figures/

Plotly Express API for density heatmap. (n.d.). Retrieved September 2022, from https://plotly.com/python-api-reference/generated/plotly.express.density_heatmap.html

Plotly Express API for filled area plot. (n.d.). Retrieved September 2022, from https://plotly.com/python-api-reference/generated/plotly.express.area.html

Plotly Express API for line plot. (n.d.). Retrieved September 2022, from https://plotly.com/python-api-reference/generated/plotly.express.line.html

Plotly Express API for pie chart. (n.d.). Retrieved September 2022, from https://plotly.com/python-api-reference/generated/plotly.express.pie.html

Plotly Express API for scatter plot. (n.d.). Retrieved September 2022, from https://plotly.com/python-api-reference/generated/plotly.express.scatter.html/

Plotly Express API for sunburst chart. (n.d.). Retrieved September 2022, from https://plotly.com/python-api-reference/generated/plotly.express.sunburst.html

Plotly Express in Python. (n.d.). Retrieved September 2022, from https://plotly.com/python/plotly-express/

Python API reference for Plotly Express. (n.d.). Retrieved September 2022, from https://plotly.com/python-api-reference/

Rees, D., & Laramee, R. S. (2019, February). A survey of information visualization books. *Computer Graphics Forum*, *38*(1), 610–646. doi:10.1111/cgf.13595

Sievert, C. (2020). *Interactive web-based data visualization with R, plotly, and shiny.* CRC Press. doi:10.1201/9780429447273

Zhao, P. (2023). Visualizing Data. In *Working with Data in Public Health: A Practical Pathway with R* (pp. 131–158). Springer. doi:10.1007/978-981-99-0135-7_8

Chapter 10

Enhancing Big Data Analytics and Recommendation Systems With Python:
Hierarchical Clustering and Filtering Using Slicing Technique

P. Thamilselvan
Bishop Heber College, India

ABSTRACT

The advancement of technology has led to an exponential increase in the volume, velocity, and variety of data generated, necessitating the development of effective methods for analyzing and extracting valuable insights from large datasets. This research focuses on enhancing big data analytics and recommendation systems using Python, specifically employing hierarchical clustering and a filtering approach with the slicing technique. This study proposes a novel approach to leverage Python's capabilities in processing and analyzing big data. Hierarchical clustering algorithms organize and structure data into hierarchical groups, enabling efficient exploration and extraction of relevant information. Additionally, a filtering mechanism is integrated with the slicing technique, allowing for identifying and extracting specific subsets of data based on predefined criteria. Experiments are conducted using real-world datasets in the context of recommendation systems to evaluate the approach's effectiveness.

DOI: 10.4018/978-1-6684-7100-5.ch010

INTRODUCTION

Big Data consists of vast data from diverse and independent sources, making traditional software difficult to manage (Beyer & Laney, 2012). Analyzing and extracting helpful information for future operations is a crucial challenge in Big Data applications. Recommendation Systems (RSs) are sophisticated instruments that aid consumers in making product or service selections. Recommendation systems confront two formidable challenges in applications containing enormous amounts of data. The first challenge is making decisions promptly. It is crucial that recommendation systems efficiently process and provide user-satisfying suggestions in light of the immense quantities of available data. The second challenge is generating optimal service recommendations from various alternatives. As the number of services and options increases, it becomes more challenging to identify the most relevant and customized offers for users. These obstacles must be surmounted for recommendation systems to provide timely and high-quality recommendations within the context of big data applications.

Clustering to integrate similar services has proven highly effective at reducing aggregate data size (Rajaraman & Ullman, 2012). Clustering and collaborative filtering are the two primary phases of this procedure (Zheng et al., 2013). Each subset corresponds to a discrete cluster consisting of services with similar characteristics. It is possible to considerably reduce computational time by limiting the number of services subject to the collaborative filtering phase to a subset within a particular cluster. Notably, this approach leverages the inherent relevance of ratings ascribed to similar services within a given cluster, significantly improving the accuracy of recommendations derived from user ratings (Bellogín et al., 2013).

CLUSTERING

Clustering has the potential to significantly reduce data volume by clustering together similar services (Rajaraman & Ullman, 2012). Clustering and collaborative filtration are the two fundamental phases of this procedure. Clustering is an essential preparatory step that facilitates the subdivision of enormous datasets into smaller, more manageable subsets (Zheng et al., 2013). Each cluster consists of services with comparable characteristics, enabling a more precise analysis. It is possible to significantly reduce computational time during the collaborative filtering phase by limiting the number of services within a cluster relative to the total benefits. Moreover, given the inherent relevance of ratings about services within a cluster as opposed to ratings about disparate services, the accuracy of recommendations based on user ratings can be substantially improved (Bellogín et al., 2013).

Clustering is a crucial element of data analysis and data mining applications (Zeng et al., 2010). Objects from the same category are more comparable than those from different types. A cluster is a collection of data objects distinguished by their unique attributes and inherent properties. Cluster analysis organizes data objects into meaningful groups by identifying similar features (Li et al., 2009).

Document clustering is advantageous because it eliminates the need for human intervention in the classification process (Havens et al., 2012). Instead, cluster membership is determined based on the distribution and composition of the data. A competent clustering method produces high-quality clusters characterized by high similarity within each cluster and low similarity between clusters. The effectiveness of a clustering result is exceptionally dependent on the similarity measure employed and its implementation (Liu et al., 2009). In addition, a clustering technique's efficacy is contingent on its ability to reveal underlying patterns, thereby illuminating the proximity of clusters through a distance function (Liu et al., 2009). When aggregating data using data mining techniques, adhering to a set of requirements is essential. Clustering-based strategies for collaborative filtering typically employ two distinct clustering algorithms.

RELATED WORK

Density-based clustering, a widely employed method for data partitioning based on density, involves separating high- and low-density points using a defined threshold (Ester et al., 1996). This technique serves as the foundation for density-based clustering algorithms. However, these algorithms lack inherent support for variable density, necessitating the development of alternative approaches to address this limitation.

An example of such an algorithm is OPTICS, proposed by Ankerst et al., which aims to overcome a significant constraint of DBSCAN by identifying meaningful clusters in datasets with varying densities. It achieves this by expanding the ordering of data points (Parimala et al., 2011). Another algorithm, VDBSCAN, was introduced by (Liu et al., 2011) to tackle the issue of variable density datasets within the DBSCAN framework. Before employing the conventional DBSCAN algorithm, VDBSCAN utilizes several techniques to determine the boundary parameter Eps based on a k-dist plot those accounts for varying densities. This enables the simultaneous discovery of clusters with diverse densities.

The VDBSCAN algorithm comprises five phases, including:

- Computation and storage of the k-dist for each data item, constructing k-dist plots
- Determination of the number of densities from the k-dist plot

- Automatic selection of Eps values for each density
- Scanning the dataset and clustering data points with different densities using the corresponding Eps values; and
- Visualization of the resulting valid clusters (Liu et al., 2007).

LDBSCAN, a density-based clustering algorithm based on local density, uses the Local Outlier Factor (LOF) to distinguish noise, setting it apart from other density-based clustering techniques (Duan et al., 2007). As proposed by Ram and Jalal, DVBSCAN introduces the density-variable DBSCAN algorithm (Ram et al., 2013) that can account for variations in local cluster density. AUTOEPSDBSCAN is an enhanced algorithm that chooses input boundaries autonomously, enabling the identification of clusters with variable densities, shapes, and sizes in large datasets comprising anomalies and noise. AUTOEPSDBSCAN outperforms the conventional DBSCAN algorithm by only requiring a single input boundary and producing superior results.

Borah and Bhattacharyya's DDSC algorithm is an effective method for detecting clusters with varying densities (Borah & Bhattacharyya, 2008). Even when discrete regions do not serve as apparent separators, DDSC attempts to identify cohesive groupings based on density by distributing local densities uniformly within a cluster and dividing local regions into separate clusters in the presence of significant density changes. VMDBSCAN, an extension of the DBSCAN algorithm, concentrates on detecting clusters with variable sizes, geometries, and local densities (Elbatta et al., 2011). This strategy entails identifying the "center" of each cluster generated by DBSCAN and then introducing "vibrations" to the cluster characteristics that impact these pivotal nodes most. VMDBSCAN facilitates the determination of the optimal number of clusters. These examples illustrate a variety of density-based clustering algorithms.

Despite the emergence of the big data paradigm (Ishwarappa, 2011), it has been discovered that the DBSCAN algorithm is inefficient when processing large data volumes on a single machine. Therefore, the most effective method for analyzing such massive datasets is to employ distributed computing technology (Akbar et al., 2015). Hadoop (Hadoop, 2009), an open-source platform, offers distributed storage and processing capabilities for administering vast amounts of data. It is founded on the MapReduce programming model (He et al., 2014), ideally suited for massive data processing. Mahran and Mahar (2008) developed the GriDBSCAN algorithm to resolve the deficiencies of DBSCAN. This algorithm builds multiple regular grids and assigns data points to similar grids, thereby producing partitions with distinct borders. Subsequently, DBSCAN is utilized to independently examine each section and its respective boundary points to merge. Nonetheless, regular grids in GriDBSCAN may divide datasets into high-density regions, producing many duplicate boundary points.

Given the obstacles mentioned earlier, He et al. (2014) proposed the MR-DBSCAN approach, which employs the Hadoop platform and MapReduce to facilitate distributed DBSCAN processing. Load balancing in large datasets is given special consideration to accelerate and efficiently scale skewed big data. The algorithm consists of three primary stages: data partitioning, local clustering, and global merging. In addition, Dai and Li developed the PRBP algorithm (Dai & Lin, 2012) to accomplish load balancing on individual nodes by choosing partition boundaries based on the distribution of data points. DBSCAN-MR, a MapReduce-based method, enables cloud-based parallel processing without requiring a global index. In addition, the inclusion of PRBP optimizes data partitioning. Bhardwaj and Das (Bhardwaj & Dash, 2015) developed a density-based approach for the DBSCAN-MR and VDMR-DBSCAN algorithms. Incorporating eps_diff into their merging strategy can prevent clusters of varying densities from sharing boundary points. Utilizing PRBP, the algorithm identifies clusters with varying densities within each partition, albeit at the expense of some inter-partition connectivity.

PROPOSED WORK

This research paper presents a HACE framework that proposes a data mining-based paradigm for managing Big Data. The framework encompasses multiple stages, including data acquisition from diverse sources, data extraction and analysis, modeling of user interests, and considerations for security and privacy. The advent of the data-driven model and the ongoing revolution in Big Data present unique challenges that can be effectively addressed. The capability to extract valuable insights from these vast datasets or data streams, referred to as Big Data mining, has emerged as a previously inconceivable prospect owing to the sheer volume, variability, and velocity of the data. The Big Data challenge represents an exciting opportunity to shape the future landscape. The term "Big Data" denotes datasets that exceed the capacity of our current systems and traditional data mining software tools in terms of size and complexity. This technology finds application in diverse domains, including credit card fraud detection and enterprise risk management, where large databases are utilized, owing to its significant performance enhancements over conventional data extraction and analysis techniques. The overall process of Big Data management is illustrated in Figure 1.

Figure 1. Process of bigdata

Data Preprocessing

It is impossible to exaggerate the significance of data preprocessing in preparing unstructured data for effective data mining analytics. Frequently, primary data are insufficient and formatted inconsistently, making subsequent analysis difficult. The quality of data formatting directly impacts the success of any data analytics endeavor. Data preprocessing entails essential operations like data purification and validation. Data validation aims to assess the accuracy and completeness of the data, thereby ensuring its reliability for further analysis. Data cleansing involves the elimination of errors and the administration of missing values through the use of manual intervention or automated software tools. Both database-driven and rule-based applications require data preprocessing to ensure data integrity and usability. Data preprocessing is essential in artificial intelligence for structuring large datasets in a manner that facilitates interpretation and processing by learning algorithms.

MULTI-DIMENSIONAL CONTENT DIFFICULTY RATING

Users may become frustrated and forsake their learning sessions if they find the content too difficult to comprehend. A dynamic strategy to regulate the difficulty of content based on the performance of each user across multiple dimensions is proposed as a solution to this problem. The first dimension focuses on classifying the difficulty of Big Data content by identifying repetitively complex or straightforward inquiries. The proficiency requirements for these queries are then adjusted for all users. The second dimension attempts to balance intended difficulty levels and learning progress by altering the content difficulty within each dataset based on the performance of individual users.

The development of distributed computing infrastructures has significantly accelerated the storage, processing, and distribution of enormous quantities of data. However, implementing reliable ranking mechanisms in search engine results and effectively supporting keyword-based queries present formidable challenges. Existing research primarily focuses on single-keyword questions and lacks appropriate ranking systems. We propose a flexible multi-keyword query method to circumvent this restriction. This algorithm considers keyword weights and user access history when compiling search results. The search results displayed on search engine results pages are generated by a multi-keyword search engine, a software application designed to retrieve data from immense data collections. These outcomes may contain web pages, images, and other relevant files.

Figure 2. Process of multi-dimensional content difficulty rating

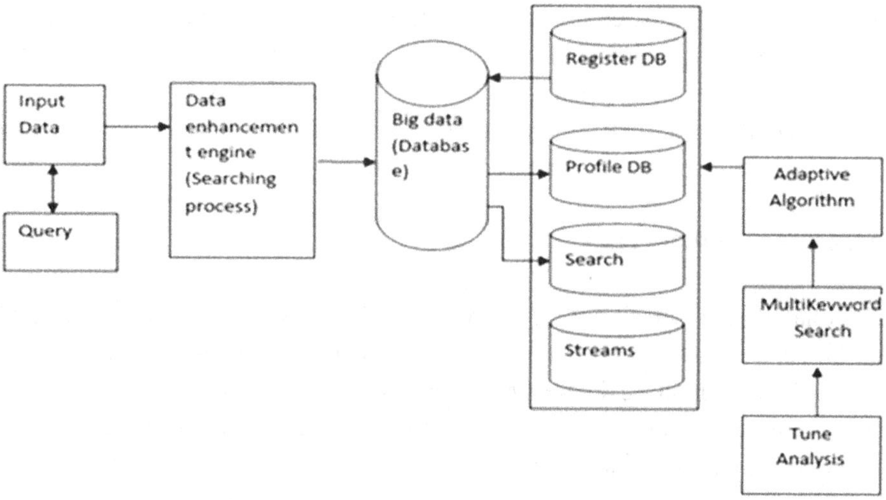

EXPERIMENTAL RESULT

The term "stem" in phonetics pertains to a constituent element of a word, and its meaning exhibits slight variations. In one usage, a stem is a structural foundation to which affixes can be attached. For instance, in the English word "fellowships," the stem "companion" provides the base form, to which the derivational suffix "-ship" is appended, resulting in the formation of the derived stem "friendship." Subsequently, the inflectional suffix "-s" is attached, forming the final stem "friendships." However, it is essential to note that the original root of the word (in this case, "companion") is not considered a stem in this particular interpretation.

Within this article, the term "stem" refers to the shared portion of a word in all its inflected forms. Hence, in this usage, all derivational affixes contribute to the stem.

For example, in the case of "friendships," the stem is "friendship," and the inflectional suffix "-s" is added. Cluster analysis, commonly called clustering, encompasses categorizing a collection of objects so that objects within the same group, known as clusters, exhibit more significant similarity to one another than to objects in other clusters. This analytical technique constitutes a fundamental aspect of exploratory data mining and serves as a standard procedure for statistical data analysis. Cluster analysis finds application in various domains, including machine learning, pattern recognition, image analysis, information retrieval, and bioinformatics.

Collaborative filtering (CF) is widely employed in multiple recommender systems. CF can be classified into two categories: extensive and restricted. Collaborative filtering generally involves extracting information or patterns through the interactions among various agents, perspectives, and data sources. Typically, the implementation of collaborative filtering entails the utilization of large-scale datasets. It has found applications in diverse domains such as sensing and monitoring data (e.g., mineral analysis, environmental sensing employing multiple sensors), financial data (e.g., financial institutions aggregating data from various financial sources), and e-commerce and web applications focused on user information.

Performance Analysis

The Collaborative Filtering (CF) method encompasses various strategies, such as item-based, user-based, and cluster-based approaches, which operate on the premise that individuals who have demonstrated agreement in the past are likely to continue exhibiting understanding. In item-based CF, the algorithm generates recommendations by identifying items similar to the user's previous choices. The CF methodology comprises two distinct stages: clustering and collaborative filtering.

Nevertheless, it is essential to note that the similarity calculation between each pair of users or services may prove to be computationally intensive, potentially surpassing the available processing capacity. Consequently, the timely relevance and feasibility of service recommendations based on similar users or services may be compromised. Furthermore, conventional CF algorithms often evaluate all services during the computation of service rating similarity, even though most of these services exhibit dissimilarities to the target service. Considering these different services in the rating calculation can impact the accuracy of the predicted ratings. For an overview of the performance analysis, please refer to Figure 3.

Clustering-based Collaborative Filtering (ClubCF) has been incorporated into the framework. Using the Markov chain model, it is feasible to distinguish between images based on unique keywords. The system retrieves and displays all associated images when a user searches for a specific keyword. The comparison between the current and proposed systems is illustrated in Figure 4.

Figure 3. Performance analysis diagram

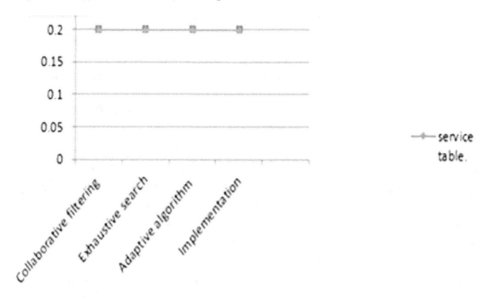

Figure 4. Existing vs. proposed system

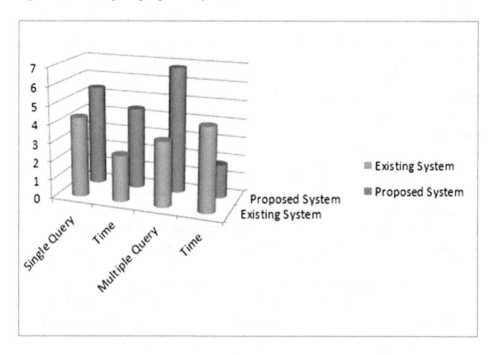

It is possible to decrease response time and expedite decision-making. Creating optimal recommendations from an extensive assortment of services can be challenging. A simple solution is to reduce the number of services requiring real-time processing. In addition, the accuracy of recommendations based on user ratings can be enhanced by giving similar services within a cluster a greater weight than other services.

Role of Python in Hierarchical Clustering and Filtering

Python is a flexible programming language that is frequently used for big data analytics and machine learning tasks, making it an ideal choice for hierarchical clustering and filtering algorithms (Perret et al., 2019). Python can be used to implement the hierarchical clustering algorithm in the research endeavor. Numerous Python libraries and frameworks, including scikit-learn and SciPy, provide efficient and versatile clustering analysis tools. These libraries provide ready-to-use hierarchical clustering functions and methods and can manage large-scale datasets, which are both necessary for big data analytics. Python can also be used to implement the research-described filtering strategies (de Aguiar Neto et al., 2020). It is possible to implement collaborative filtering algorithms using Python's libraries and frameworks, such as the clustering-based collaborative filtering technique mentioned. NumPy and other robust Python numerical computation utilities facilitate the efficient data manipulation and processing necessary for filtering operations (Subasi, 2020).

In addition, Python can be used to construct the segmentation method and CF algorithm. The array slicing capabilities of Python can be used to accomplish the goal of the slicing technique, which is to reduce computation time. In addition, Python's adaptability and extensive library ecosystem provide numerous implementation options for the CF algorithm, allowing the research to utilize Python's vast resources. Python is advantageous for implementing the hierarchical clustering and filtering methods described in the research paper. Its libraries, frameworks, and data processing capabilities make it ideal for big data analytics, enhancing search engine relevance, and enhancing user experience (Stančin & Jović, 2019).

The built-in data structures of Python, such as hierarchical clustering and filtering, play an important role in data analysis and processing, including big data analytics. These data structures facilitate the efficient storage, manipulation, and retrieval of data, thereby enhancing Python's ability to perform these tasks.

- **Lists:** Lists are one of Python's most versatile and pervasive data structures. They allow for the storage of heterogeneous data types and provide flexibility for dynamic resizing, appending, and indexing operations. In the context of hierarchical clustering and filtering, data elements, feature vectors, and cluster assignments can be retained and organized using lists.

Figure 5. Python's robust data structures

Lists	Arrays	Dictionaries	Sets	Trees and Graphs

- **Arrays:** Python arrays, in particular those provided by the NumPy library, offer efficient storage and operations for large homogenous numerical datasets. They enable vectorized operations, which facilitates the high-performance computations required to process vast quantities of data. In algorithms for hierarchical clustering and filtering, arrays are commonly used to store numerical data.
- **Dictionaries:** The key-value mapping provided by dictionaries enables efficient data access and retrieval based on unique keys. They facilitate the storage and retrieval of metadata or additional data associated with data points, clusters, or filtering criteria. Dictionaries can facilitate the organization and retrieval of pertinent data in hierarchical clustering and filtering processes.
- **Sets:** Sets are unordered collections of distinct elements that facilitate efficient membership testing and duplication elimination. They can be utilized for data preprocessing duties, such as eradicating redundant data points or filtering out irrelevant elements according to predetermined criteria. In hierarchical clustering and filtering algorithms for data cleansing and optimization, sets are advantageous.
- **Trees and Graphs:** Despite not being built-in, Python's libraries, such as networkx, provide efficient data structures for representing trees and graphs. Because they can represent hierarchical relationships between clusters or data elements, these data structures are advantageous for hierarchical clustering. Additionally, they can facilitate graph-based filtering techniques, such as collaborative filtering based on similarity graphs.

The leveraging python's robust data structures for efficient hierarchical clustering and filtering in big data analytics is given in Figure 5.

By leveraging these built-in and specialized data structures, Python enhances the efficiency and effectiveness of hierarchical clustering and filtering algorithms in big data analytics. The adaptability and capabilities of these data structures enable the efficient storage, retrieval, and manipulation of data, thereby facilitating the processing and analysis of enormous datasets.

CONCLUSION

This chapter focused on the application of hierarchical clustering and filtering techniques for slicing-based big data analytics. The study emphasized the importance of advanced techniques such as hierarchical clustering and collaborative filtering for analyzing vast amounts of data and augmenting search engine relevance and user experience. The research offers a data mining-based method for managing vast data sets. The framework incorporated data acquisition, extraction, analysis, user interest modelling, and security considerations. It was emphasized that hierarchical clustering and filtering algorithms can be implemented using Python's flexibility and vast library resources. The chapter emphasized the significance of data preprocessing in preparing unstructured data for data mining analytics. In addition, it introduced the concept of multivariate content difficulty rating to regulate content difficulty based on user performance across multiple dimensions.

Clustering and collaborative filtering were proposed as effective solutions to the problems encountered by recommendation systems when dealing with large amounts of data. It emphasized the benefits of clustering in terms of reducing data volume and increasing the accuracy of recommendations based on user ratings within clusters. In addition, the study evaluated the effectiveness of collaborative filtering methods and introduced the Cluster-based Collaborative Filtering (ClubCF) approach, which demonstrated substantial reductions in online processing computational time.

In addition, the conclusion identified two potential future research avenues. Inclusion of historical preferences derived from user-centric approaches in the absence of explicit ratings to generate recommendations. By emphasizing the significance of hierarchical clustering and filtering techniques, this article contributes to the field of big data analytics. It explores various aspects of data preprocessing, content difficulty classification, and collaborative filtering techniques. The findings and suggested future research directions offer valuable insights for enhancing recommendation systems and addressing the challenges posed by big data.

REFERENCES

Akbar, I., Hashem, T., Yaqoob, I., Anuar, N.B., Mokhtar, S., Gani, A., & Khan, S.A. (2015). The rise of "big data" on cloud computing: review and open research issues. *Inf Syst., 47*, 98–115.

Bellogín, A., Cantador, I., Díez, F., Castells, P., & Chavarriaga, E. (2013). An empirical comparison of social, collaborative filtering, and hybrid recommenders. *ACM Transactions on Intelligent Systems and Technology*, *4*(1), 1–37. doi:10.1145/2414425.2414439

Beyer & Laney. (2012). *The importance of "big data": A definition.* Gartner, Tech. Rep.

Bhardwaj, S., & Dash, S. K. (2015). VDMR-DBSCAN: varied density Mapreduce DBSCAN. *International conference on Big Data analytics.* 10.1007/978-3-319-27057-9_10

Borah, B., & Bhattacharyya, D. K. (2008). DDSC: A density differentiated spatial clustering technique. *Journal of Computers*, *3*(2), 72–79. doi:10.4304/jcp.3.2.72-79

Dai, B. R., & Lin, I.-C. (2012). Efficient Map/Reduce-based DBSCAN algorithm with optimized data partition. *Fifth International Conference on Cloud Computing.*

de Aguiar Neto, F. S., da Costa, A. F., Manzato, M. G., & Campello, R. J. (2020). Pre-processing approaches for collaborative filtering based on hierarchical clustering. *Information Sciences*, *534*, 172–191. doi:10.1016/j.ins.2020.05.021

Duan, L., Xu, L., Guo, F., Lee, J., & Yan, B. (2007). A local-density based spatial clustering algorithm with noise. *Information Systems*, *32*(7), 978–986. doi:10.1016/j.is.2006.10.006

Elbatta, M. T., Bolbol, R. M., & Ashur, W. M. (2011). *A vibration method for discovering density varied clusters.* Int Sch Res Not.

Ester, M., Kriegel, H. P., Sander, J., & Xu, X. (1996). A density-based algorithm for discovering clusters in large spatial databases with noise. In *2nd international conference on knowledge discovery and data mining.* Academic Press.

Gaonkar, M.N., & Sawant, K. (2013). AutoEpsDBSCAN: DBSCAN with Eps automatic for large dataset. *Int J Adv Comput Theory Eng.*, *2*(2), 2319–526.

Hadoop, W. T. (2009). *The definitive guide.* O'Reilly Media.

Havens, T. C., Bezdek, J. C., Leckie, C., Hall, L. O., & Palaniswami, M. (2012). Fuzzy c-Means Algorithms for Very Large Data. *IEEE Transactions on Fuzzy Systems*, *20*(6), 1130–1146. doi:10.1109/TFUZZ.2012.2201485

He, Y., Tan, H., Luo, W., Feng, S., & Fan, J. (2014). MR-DBSCAN: A scalable Map Reduce-based DBSCAN algorithm for heavily skewed data. *Frontiers of Computer Science*, *8*(1), 83–99. doi:10.100711704-013-3158-3

Ishwarappa, A. J., & Anuradha, J. (2011). A brief introduction on Big Data 5Vs characteristics and Hadoop technology. *Procedia Computer Science*, *48*, 319–324. doi:10.1016/j.procs.2015.04.188

Li, H. H., Du, X. Y., & Tian, X. (2009). A review-based reputation evaluation approach for Web services. *Journal of Computer Science and Technology*, *24*(5), 893–900. doi:10.100711390-009-9280-x

Liu, P., Zhou, D., & Wu, N. (2007, June). VDBSCAN: varied density based spatial clustering of applications with noise. In *2007 International conference on service systems and service management* (pp. 1-4). IEEE. 10.1109/ICSSSM.2007.4280175

Liu, X., Huang, G., & Mei, H. (2009). Discovering homogeneous web service community in the user-centric web environment. *IEEE Transactions on Services Computing*, *2*(2), 167–181. doi:10.1109/TSC.2009.11

Liu, Z., Li, P., & Zheng, Y. (2009). Clustering to find exemplar terms for keyphrase extraction. *Proc. 2009 Conf. on Empirical Methods in Natural Language Processing*, 257-266. 10.3115/1699510.1699544

Mahran, S., & Mahar, K. (2008). Using grid for accelerating density-based clustering. CIT 2008 IEEE international conference. doi:10.1109/CIT.2008.4594646

Parimala M, Lopez D, Senthilkumar N, (2011). A survey on density based clustring algorithms for mining large spatial databases. *Int J Adv Sci Technol.*, 31-59.

Perret, B., Chierchia, G., Cousty, J., Guimaraes, S. J. F., Kenmochi, Y., & Najman, L. (2019). Higra: Hierarchical graph analysis. *SoftwareX*, *10*, 100335. doi:10.1016/j. softx.2019.100335

Rajaraman, A., & Ullman, J. D. (2012). *Mining of massive datasets*. Cambridge University Press.

Ram, A., Jalal, S., & Kumar, M. (2013). A density based algorithm for discovering density varied clusters in large spatial databases. *IJCA*, *3*(6), 1–4.

Stančin, I., & Jović, A. (2019, May). An overview and comparison of free Python libraries for data mining and big data analysis. In *2019 42nd International convention on information and communication technology, electronics and microelectronics (MIPRO)* (pp. 977-982). IEEE. 10.23919/MIPRO.2019.8757088

Subasi, A. (2020). *Practical machine learning for data analysis using python.* Academic Press.

Wu, X., Zhu, X., & Wu, G. Q. (2014). Data mining with big data. *IEEE Transactions on Knowledge and Data Engineering, 26*(1), 97–107. doi:10.1109/TKDE.2013.109

Zeng, W., Shang, M. S., Zhang, Q. M., Lü, L., & Zhou, T. (2010). Can Dissimilar Users Contribute to Accuracy and Diversity of Personalized Recommendation. *International Journal of Modern Physics C, 21*(10), 1217–1227. doi:10.1142/S0129183110015786

Zheng, Z., Zhu, J., & Lyu, M. R. (2013). Service-generated Big Data and Big Data-as-a-Service: An Overview. *Proc. IEEE BigData*, 403-410. 10.1109/BigData. Congress.2013.60

Chapter 11

Optimizing Energy Consumption in Wireless Sensor Networks Using Python Libraries

Jency Jose
CHRIST University (Deemed), India

N. Arulkumar
CHRIST University (Deemed), India

ABSTRACT

Wireless sensor networks (WSNs) are widely utilized in various fields, including environmental monitoring, healthcare, and industrial automation. Optimizing energy consumption is one of the most challenging aspects of WSNs due to the limited capacity of the batteries that power the sensors. This chapter explores using Python libraries to optimize the energy consumption of WSNs. In WSNs, various nodes, including sensor, relay, and sink nodes, are introduced. How Python libraries such as NumPy, Pandas, Scikit-Learn, and Matplotlib can be used to optimize energy consumption is discussed. Techniques for optimizing energy consumption, such as data aggregation, duty cycling, and power management, are also presented. By employing these techniques and Python libraries, the energy consumption of WSNs can be drastically decreased, thereby extending battery life and boosting performance.

DOI: 10.4018/978-1-6684-7100-5.ch011

INTRODUCTION

Wireless Sensor Networks (WSNs) encounter several obstacles, such as data transmission and energy consumption restrictions, which immediately affect operational longevity (Abu-Baker et al., 2023). These obstacles can impede the extensive deployment and efficacy of WSNs in numerous application domains. Existing clustering techniques, such as LEACH, cannot resolve these obstacles effectively. To surmount these limitations and optimize energy consumption in WSNs, this Study introduces a novel Python library-based method. By strategically deploying sensor and relay nodes throughout the network, the proposed approach seeks to improve the energy efficiency of WSNs (Abdulzahra et al., 2023). The research uses relay sites to extend the data transmission range while reducing energy consumption. This method addresses the difficulties posed by limited transmission distance and the requirement for energy-efficient communication protocols in WSNs.

This Study demonstrates, through extensive testing and analysis, that the proposed technology reduces energy consumption without compromising the integrity of data transmission. The findings provide valuable insights into the optimization potential of Python libraries in wireless sensor networks. This research has enormous application-domain significance by contributing to developing energy-efficient wireless sensor networks. It enables the creation of more dependable and sustainable WSN solutions that can be deployed in various industries, such as environmental monitoring, smart cities, agriculture, healthcare, and industrial automation.

WIRELESS SENSOR NETWORKS

Wireless Sensor Networks (WSNs) are battery-operated data collection devices with sensors and communication capabilities. They are used extensively in environmental monitoring and industrial automation applications. Energy consumption is a crucial aspect of WSNs due to the deployment of numerous tiny sensors that rely on battery power for extended periods (Jondhale et al., 2022). It is crucial to effectively manage energy consumption in WSNs to maximize network lifetime and reduce maintenance costs.

Several protocols have been developed to address the challenges posed by energy consumption. These protocols aim to reduce network energy consumption and lifespan. Examples of notable protocols include Sensor Medium Access Control (SMAC), Energy-Efficient Medium Access Control (E-MAC), Threshold-sensitive Energy Efficient sensor Network protocol (TEEN), Berkeley Medium Access Control (B-MAC), and Traffic Adaptive Medium Access Control (T-MAC).

Using Python libraries to optimize the energy consumption of wireless sensor networks presents the following difficulties.

- Developing energy-saving techniques and algorithms that do not degrade network performance.
- Ensuring accurate and timely data acquisition by balancing the trade-off between transmission quality and energy consumption.
- Managing node sleep-wake cycles and duty cycling strategies for energy conservation and network upkeep.
- The optimizing data transmission paths by implementing efficient routing protocols for energy awareness.
- As the number of sensor nodes increases, the network must address scalability issues while maintaining energy efficiency.

By addressing these challenges and leveraging the capabilities of Python libraries, researchers can further refine the energy consumption of wireless sensor networks, leading to more sustainable and efficient deployments.

LITERATURE REVIEW

Specific constraints and needs determine the protocol choice for precision agriculture in wireless sensor networks—variables like transmission range, data rate, and deployment density significantly impact protocol selection. Several protocols have been proposed to optimize energy consumption in wireless sensor networks. SMAC (Sensor-MAC) is a protocol that uses a synchronized sleep schedule. By alternating between active and inactive states, SMAC reduces passive listening and overhearing, conserving energy (Chen et al., 2020).

E-MAC (Energy-efficient MAC) is another protocol that modifies node duty cycles in response to traffic demand (Soni & Selvaradjou, 2020). This adaptive approach helps conserve energy in wireless sensor networks. The TEEN (Threshold-sensitive Energy Efficient sensor Network) protocol is a threshold-based method created to minimize unnecessary data transfer and save energy. By establishing appropriate thresholds, TEEN decreases the energy consumption of wireless sensor networks.

B-MAC (Battery MAC) employs a randomized listening schedule and duty cycling to reduce idle listening and overhearing, thus conserving energy (Bria, 2019; Roopitha & Pai, 2020). The T-MAC (Traffic-aware MAC) protocol modifies the responsibility cycle of nodes based on their traffic volume in a dynamic fashion. This adaptive mechanism optimizes the energy consumption of sensor networks (Kim, 2019).

Several obstacles exist when refining energy consumption in wireless sensor networks utilizing Python libraries. Compatibility issues between the selected protocols and the employed Python libraries, efficient implementation of the protocols in Python, and the requirement for accurate energy modeling and measurement techniques within the Python environment may be among these obstacles. These obstacles must be overcome to optimize the energy consumption of wireless sensor networks with Python libraries.

Problem Identified From Literature Review

The existing energy-efficient routing protocols are not entirely effective based on parameters and factors for the dynamic environment in WSN. The efficiency of the current protocols can be enhanced in terms of being more adaptive and dynamic to sustain the node's lifetime, as they currently do not meet the energy efficiency standards for WSN in precision agriculture.

RESEARCH GAP IDENTIFIED

- Fixed cluster heads consume more energy to transmit data to the sink node.
- Sleep/wake cycles are not regulated in the current scenario for data transmission.
- We need a solution to adapt to the change in the field size because the additional sensors lead to multi-path routing.
- Existing protocols need improvement based on various unpredictable parameters and factors.
- Improper supplement of factors to the crops to be monitored to improve the quantity and quantity of the crop

Problem Statement

The existing energy-efficient routing protocols are not entirely effective based on parameters and factors for the dynamic environment in WSN. The efficiency of the current protocols can be enhanced in terms of being more adaptive and dynamic to sustain the node's lifetime, as they currently do not meet the energy efficiency standards for WSN in precision agriculture.

OBJECTIVES OF THE STUDY

Primary Objectives

- To design a framework that improves the energy efficiency of WSN, which reduces energy consumption and thus increases the lifetime of the network
- To compare the performance of the proposed model with the existing models

Secondary Objectives

- To implement the proposed model in the field of WSN for precision agriculture
- To perform experiments on a diverse set of large-scale scenarios

METHODOLOGY

To optimize the energy consumption of wireless sensor networks (WSNs), a thorough methodology was developed. Identifying the research voids in enhancing the energy efficacy of WSNs was the initial step. This analysis assisted in comprehending the extant obstacles and areas requiring additional research. Using this information as a foundation, the next phase centered on the development of a WSN specifically tailored for precision agriculture. This required the meticulous selection and deployment of sensors in strategic locations, taking into account crop types, terrain, and environmental conditions, among other factors.

After designing the WSN, the model was implemented and data collection began. Utilizing Python libraries streamlined the process and facilitated efficient data management. The collected data were then uploaded to a multi-tenant platform, enabling simple access and analysis by multiple parties. This platform not only enabled real-time monitoring, but also facilitated the energy efficiency comparison of various WSN protocols.

Extensive testing and experimentation were conducted to validate and enhance the model. The collected data was analyzed to assess the efficacy of various protocols and identify areas for enhancement. The data analysis tools provided by Python libraries enabled researchers to extract meaningful insights and draw accurate conclusions.

On the basis of the findings, an energy efficiency framework was proposed. This framework incorporated the knowledge acquired in the preceding stages and offered guidelines for optimizing energy consumption in WSNs. It included sensor placement, data transmission protocols, and power management strategies, among others. By implementing this framework, researchers and practitioners in the field of wireless sensor networks could increase the energy efficiency of their systems, thereby decreasing operational expenses and extending the network's lifecycle.

In conclusion, the above-described methodology addressed the optimization of energy consumption in wireless sensor networks. This study sought to contribute to the development of more sustainable and efficient WSN solutions by identifying research voids, designing a WSN for precision agriculture, comparing protocols, and proposing a framework for energy efficiency. Utilizing Python libraries throughout the process facilitated data manipulation, analysis, and model enhancement, demonstrating the strength of programming tools in advancing research in this field. The complete methodology is given below.

- Identify the research gaps in improving the energy efficiency of a WSN
- Designing a WSN for precision agriculture
- Implement the model and collect data into a multi-tenant platform
- Compare the energy efficiency of WSN protocols
- Validate and improve the model
- Propose the framework for energy efficiency

LIMITATIONS OF LEACH PROTOCOL

Its random cluster structure and cluster head rotation may help evenly distribute energy consumption among nodes. This is particularly crucial in farming environments where node failure due to weather, pests, or other factors is widespread. Due to the frequent transmission of control messages between nodes, the LEACH protocol incurs significant communication overhead, reducing network performance. The LEACH protocol uses a randomized technique to create clusters, which may result in some nodes being selected as cluster leaders more often than others, resulting in uneven energy usage and a shorter network lifetime (Daanoune et al., 2021). It is not scalable since the protocol requires centralized control and communication, which may result in a bottleneck as the number of nodes increases (Liang, 2019).

IMPORTANCE OF RELAY NODES

Relay nodes are essential in wireless sensor networks (WSN). Relay nodes are indispensable for extending the network's data transmission range and conserving energy (Su et al., 2019). By strategically positioning cluster heads and employing directional antennas, relay nodes in WSNs enable more reliable data transmission over greater distances with reduced energy consumption. The following are the importance of relay nodes in wireless sensor networks (WSNs):

- Network data transmission range depends on cluster head arrangement
- Data transmission range may be increased by carefully positioning cluster heads in areas with a high node density or a clear line of sight to the base station
- It can relay data between out-of-range nodes, extending the network's data transmission range and reducing energy consumption
- This strategy optimizes the energy consumption of WSNs while maintaining a reliable data transmission range
- Relay nodes can be used to extend the network's data transmission range and reduce energy consumption by employing directional antennas to increase the broadcast range

ENERGY CONSUMPTION OPTIMISATION IN WSN USING PYTHON

There are numerous ways to reduce the energy consumption of Wireless Sensor Networks (WSN). Increasing the LEACH protocol's data transmission range is one way to improve energy efficiency (Bharany et al., 2021). However, this increase in transmission capacity must be carefully weighed against energy consumption and network lifespan considerations. Adding more cluster leaders to the network is an additional strategy. Cluster heads capture and transmit data from member nodes to the base station. The network's transmission range can be increased by strategically placing cluster heads in areas with a high node density or a direct line of sight to the base station.

Additionally, directional antennas can be advantageous for extending broadcast range while simultaneously decreasing transmission power. In addition, relay nodes can facilitate data transmission between out-of-range nodes, thereby improving network efficiency. However, it is necessary to evaluate the benefits and drawbacks of each strategy in the context of the particular wireless sensor network application, considering the challenges associated with optimizing energy consumption (Thiagarajan, 2020).

Figure 1 presents a general sequence diagram illustrating the data transmission process in a WSN. The diagram encompasses the interactions among the Sensor Node, Base Station, and Relay Node, providing an overview of the data flow within the network.

Figure 1. Sequence diagram: WSN with sensor and relay nodes

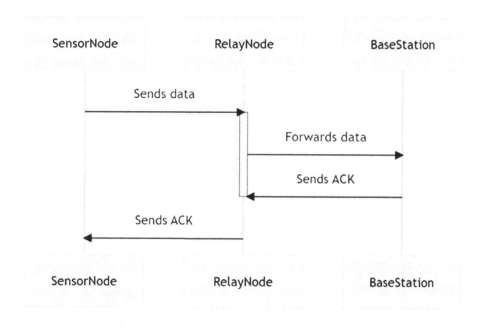

Steps to Implement Relay Nodes in WSN

The following steps are to implement relay nodes in WSN (Chauhan & Soni, 2021).

- Locate nodes out of range
- Place relay nodes strategically to efficiently transmit data between out-of-range nodes
- Identify the communication protocols to receive and transfer data
- Assess relay node performance
- Test and evaluate to optimize relay node locations to improve network performance

The flow diagram depicts the functioning of a wireless sensor network in Figure 2, including Sensor Nodes, Relay Nodes, and Base Stations.

- A SensorNode, represented by the color blue, initiates data transmission to a RelayNode and waits for an acknowledgment (ACK) in return.
- The RelayNode, depicted in red, receives the data from the SensorNode, forwards it to the base station, and waits for an acknowledgment (ACK) from

Figure 2. Proposed model with relay and sensor nodes

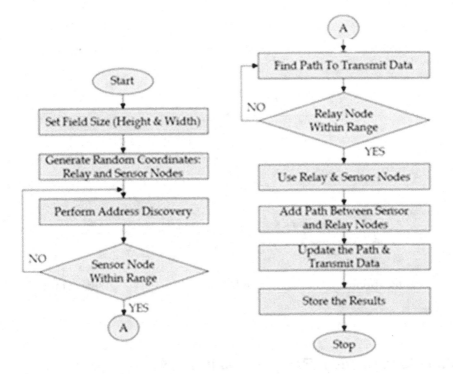

the base station. Subsequently, the RelayNode sends an ACK back to the SensorNode.

- The base station receives the data from the RelayNode and responds with an acknowledgment (ACK).

ADAPTIVE DUTY CYCLING WITH RELAY NODES

Duty cycling is a strategy for conserving energy that involves the intermittent deactivation of node radio transceivers (Khriji et al., 2022). However, data delays or loss may result if neighboring nodes are unavailable for relaying. To address this issue, strategically locating network relay nodes can assist in overcoming connectivity issues. These relay nodes function as intermediaries, transmitting data between out-of-range nodes. Using relay nodes increases network connectivity and decreases data loss caused by duty cycling (Sarwar et al., 2020).

When relay nodes are in use, adaptive duty cycling can be used to optimize energy consumption further. This technique allows nodes to dynamically adjust their duty

Figure 3. Implementation of the nodes and relay levels

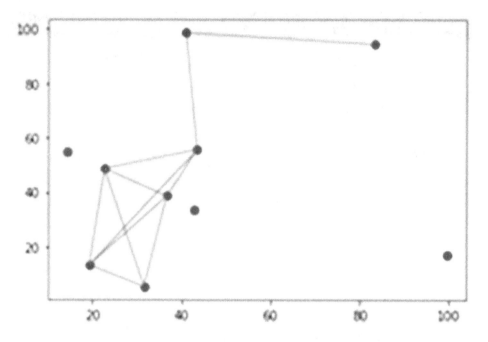

cycle based on the proximity of relay nodes. When a relay node is present, the duty cycle of a node can be decreased to conserve energy. If a relay node is unavailable, its duty cycle can be increased to maintain network connectivity. It is possible to balance network connectivity and energy conservation by integrating duty cycling and relay nodes. This strategy extends the network's lifetime and reduces the nodes' aggregate energy consumption (Abdalkafor & Aliesawi, 2022).

In Figure 3, sensor node and relay node coordinates are generated arbitrarily in a 2D plane representing an agricultural field. Also specified is the maximum transmission range for sensor and relay nodes. Based on their relative positions and transmission ranges, the code identifies all feasible data transmission lines between sensor nodes and relay nodes and between them. These data transmission paths are saved as tuples comprising the coordinates of the transmitting nodes. The code then depicts the nodes and data transmission lines using Matplotlib and displays the resulting graph. This code is intended to simulate a wireless sensor network employed in precision agriculture, in which relay nodes extend the transmission range of sensor nodes, enabling them to cover a more significant portion of the agricultural field.

Figure 4. Energy consumption using relay nodes

Figure 4 depicts the Energy Consumption of a Python system built with Relay Nodes. Figure 5 illustrates the system's Total Energy Consumption without Relay Nodes, also implemented using Python.

CONCLUSION

This research work describes a novel Python library-based method for maximizing energy efficiency in Wireless Sensor Networks (WSN). The proposed method strategically employs sensor and relay nodes to improve energy efficiency. The way overcomes the limitations of existing clustering techniques, such as LEACH, by extending the data transmission range and reducing relay sites' energy consumption. The research demonstrates through extensive testing and analysis that the proposed technology effectively reduces energy consumption while preserving the integrity of data transmission. The findings highlight the potential of Python libraries for optimizing WSNs and their implementations in numerous industries, including environmental monitoring, smart cities, agriculture, healthcare, and industrial

Figure 5. Total energy consumption without using relay nodes

automation. The Study emphasizes the importance of relay nodes in WSNs for extending the data transmission range and conserving energy. Also discussed is the significance of adaptive duty cycling in conjunction with relay nodes for optimizing energy consumption. This Study compares the energy consumption of WSNs with and without relay nodes and provides implementation guidelines for relay node integration into WSNs. Results indicate that integrating relay nodes into the network significantly reduces energy consumption, highlighting the energy-optimization benefits of relay node integration in WSNs. In the given scenario, the network's total energy consumption is 67.86 when relay nodes are not used, which is higher than the energy consumption with relay nodes. This indicates that incorporating relay nodes in the wireless sensor network (WSN) assists in optimizing energy consumption by the sensor nodes in the network.

REFERENCES

Abdalkafor, A. S., & Aliesawi, S. A. (2022, October). Data aggregation techniques in wireless sensors networks (WSNs): Taxonomy and an accurate literature survey. In AIP Conference Proceedings (Vol. 2400, No. 1, p. 020012). AIP Publishing LLC.

Abdulzahra, A. M. K., Al-Qurabat, A. K. M., & Abdulzahra, S. A. (2023). Optimizing energy consumption in WSN-based IoT using unequal clustering and sleep scheduling methods. *Internet of Things*, *22*, 100765. doi:10.1016/j.iot.2023.100765

Abu-Baker, A., Shakhatreh, H., Sawalmeh, A., & Alenezi, A. H. (2023). Efficient Data Collection in UAV-Assisted Cluster-Based Wireless Sensor Networks for 3D Environment: Optimization Study. *Journal of Sensors*, *2023*, 2023. doi:10.1155/2023/9513868

Bharany, S., Sharma, S., Badotra, S., Khalaf, O. I., Alotaibi, Y., Alghamdi, S., & Alassery, F. (2021). Energy-efficient clustering scheme for flying ad-hoc networks using an optimized LEACH protocol. *Energies*, *14*(19), 6016. doi:10.3390/en14196016

Bria, R., Wahab, A., & Alaydrus, M. (2019, October). Energy efficiency analysis of TEEN routing protocol with isolated nodes. In *2019 Fourth International Conference on Informatics and Computing (ICIC)* (pp. 1-5). IEEE. 10.1109/ICIC47613.2019.8985668

Chauhan, V., & Soni, S. (2021). Energy aware unequal clustering algorithm with multi-hop routing via low degree relay nodes for wireless sensor networks. *Journal of Ambient Intelligence and Humanized Computing*, *12*(2), 2469–2482. doi:10.100712652-020-02385-1

Chen, S., Zhang, L., Tang, Y., Shen, C., Kumar, R., Yu, K., Tariq, U., & Bashir, A. K. (2020). Indoor temperature monitoring using wireless sensor networks: A SMAC application in smart cities. *Sustainable Cities and Society*, *61*, 102333. doi:10.1016/j.scs.2020.102333

Daanoune, I., Abdennaceur, B., & Ballouk, A. (2021). A comprehensive survey on LEACH-based clustering routing protocols in Wireless Sensor Networks. *Ad Hoc Networks*, *114*, 102409. doi:10.1016/j.adhoc.2020.102409

Jondhale, S. R., Maheswar, R., Lloret, J., Jondhale, S. R., Maheswar, R., & Lloret, J. (2022). Fundamentals of wireless sensor networks. *Received Signal Strength Based Target Localization and Tracking Using Wireless Sensor Networks*, 1-19.

Khriji, S., Chéour, R., & Kanoun, O. (2022). Dynamic Voltage and Frequency Scaling and Duty-Cycling for Ultra Low-Power Wireless Sensor Nodes. *Electronics (Basel)*, *11*(24), 4071. doi:10.3390/electronics11244071

Kim, D. S., Tran-Dang, H., Kim, D. S., & Tran-Dang, H. (2019). Mac protocols for energy-efficient wireless sensor networks. *Industrial Sensors and Controls in Communication Networks: From Wired Technologies to Cloud Computing and the Internet of Things*, 141-159.

Liang, H., Yang, S., Li, L., & Gao, J. (2019). Research on routing optimization of WSNs based on improved LEACH protocol. *EURASIP Journal on Wireless Communications and Networking*, *2019*(1), 1–12. doi:10.118613638-019-1509-y

Roopitha, C. H., & Pai, V. (2020, January). Survey On Media Access Control Protocols In Wireless Sensor Network. In *2020 Fourth International Conference on Inventive Systems and Control (ICISC)* (pp. 163-168). IEEE. 10.1109/ICISC47916.2020.9171085

Sarwar, S., Sirhindi, R., Aslam, L., Mustafa, G., Yousaf, M. M., & Jaffry, S. W. U. Q. (2020). Reinforcement learning based adaptive duty cycling in LR-WPANs. *IEEE Access : Practical Innovations, Open Solutions*, *8*, 161157–161174. doi:10.1109/ACCESS.2020.3021016

Soni, G., & Selvaradjou, K. (2020). Performance evaluation of wireless sensor network MAC protocols with early sleep problem. *International Journal of Communication Networks and Distributed Systems*, *25*(2), 123–144. doi:10.1504/IJCNDS.2020.108875

Su, Y., Lu, X., Zhao, Y., Huang, L., & Du, X. (2019). Cooperative communications with relay selection based on deep reinforcement learning in wireless sensor networks. *IEEE Sensors Journal*, *19*(20), 9561–9569. doi:10.1109/JSEN.2019.2925719

Thiagarajan, R. (2020). Energy consumption and network connectivity based on Novel-LEACH-POS protocol networks. *Computer Communications*, *149*, 90–98. doi:10.1016/j.comcom.2019.10.006

Chapter 12

An Exploratory Study of Python's Role in the Advancement of Cryptocurrency and Blockchain Ecosystems

Agrata Gupta
CHRIST University (Deemed), India

N. Arulkumar
iD https://orcid.org/0000-0002-9728-477X
CHRIST University (Deemed), India

ABSTRACT

Blockchain is the foundation of cryptocurrency and enables decentralized transactions through its immutable ledger. The technology uses hashing to ensure secure transactions and is becoming increasingly popular due to its wide range of applications. Python is a performant, secure, scalable language well-suited for blockchain applications. It provides developers free tools for faster code writing and simplifies crypto analysis. Python allows developers to code blockchains quickly and efficiently as it is a completely scripted language that does not require compilation. Different models such as SVR, ARIMA, and LSTM can be used to predict cryptocurrency prices, and many Python packages are available for seamlessly pulling cryptocurrency data. Python can also create one's cryptocurrency version, as seen with Facebook's proposed cryptocurrency, Libra. Finally, a versatile and speedy language is needed for blockchain applications that enable chain addition without parallel processing, so Python is a suitable choice.

DOI: 10.4018/978-1-6684-7100-5.ch012

INTRODUCTION

In recent years, blockchain technology, the foundation of cryptocurrencies, has attracted a great deal of interest. It functions as an immutable distributed ledger that enables decentralized transactions. Transactions are distributed across an interconnected network of nodes and stored in segments. The owner's digital signature on the ledger provides security and prevents tampering. Consequently, cryptocurrency utilizes Blockchain technology, functioning as a decentralized and secure medium of exchange independent of centralized authorities like governments and institutions. Coin ownership records are stored in a database that employs cryptography to ensure transaction security, regulate coin production, and validate ownership transfers.

Current monetary systems are exposed to significant hazards and require sophisticated financial management. The fact that industries such as healthcare, supply chain, and the Internet of Things (IoT) use centralized processes makes decentralization essential. Numerous industries, such as agriculture, banking, healthcare administration, IoT, and governance, have the potential to be revolutionized by blockchain technology. It is the technology of the future, and nations including Japan, Germany, and France have already employed it in a variety of fields. The Indian state of Andhra Pradesh has already implemented blockchain technology in agribusiness. Despite Bitcoin's emergence in 2009, the financial applications of currencies and blockchain are still developing and will continue to do so.

Due to its high efficacy, robust security, and scalability, Python is the preferable programming language for Blockchain applications. It has a moderate learning curve, allowing programmers to acquire proficiency rapidly. Even inexperienced developers are able to contribute rapidly to blockchain projects. Python is a scripting language, unlike C++, which eliminates the need for compilation and increases developer productivity. Python also provides a large number of gratis programming utilities. Python makes it possible for developers to construct Blockchain applications with minimal code. In addition, Python facilitates the analysis, visualization, and forecasting of the prices and volatility of cryptocurrencies. Various models, including SVR, ARIMA, and LSTM, can be utilized to predict the price of cryptocurrencies.

However, the volatility and unpredictability of cryptocurrencies can make it difficult to make accurate predictions. Python packages such as Alpha Vantage, Pandas DataReader, YFinance, CrytpoCompare, IEX Cloud, and Twelve Data make it simple to retrieve cryptocurrency data. Additionally, Python enables us to construct our own cryptocurrency, as Facebook's recent introduction of Libra, which ignited global outrage, demonstrates. When developing a Blockchain application, it is crucial to enable anyone to contribute to the chain without requiring parallel transaction processing. For this reason, Python, a rapid and flexible programming language, is an excellent option. This article explores Python's key roles in Blockchain Technology and Cryptocurrency.

LITERATURE REVIEW

The blockchain technology was described in 1991 by the research scientist Stuart Haber and W. Scott Stornetta. They wanted to introduce a computationally practical solution for time-stamping digital documents so that they could not be backdated or tampered. In 1992, Merkle Trees were incorporated into the design, which made blockchain more efficient by allowing several documents to be collected into one block. In 2004, computer scientist and cryptographic activist Hal Finney introduced a system called Reusable Proof of Work (RPoW) as a prototype for digital cash. It was a significant early step in the history of cryptocurrencies. In 2008, Satoshi Nakamoto conceptualized the theory of distributed blockchains. The words block and chain were used separately in Satoshi Nakamoto's original paper but were eventually popularized as a single word, the Blockchain, by 2016.

In recent time, the file size of cryptocurrency blockchain containing records of all transactions that occurred on the network has grown from 20 GB to 100 GB (Larrier, 2021). On the other hand, the idea for cryptocurrency first began in the late 1980's, the idea was for a currency that could be sent untraceable and in a manner that did not require centralized entities (i.e., Banks). In 1995, American cryptographer David Chaum implemented an anonymous cryptographic electronic money called Digicash. Bit Gold, often called a direct precursor to Bitcoin, was designed in 1998 by Nick Szabo. It required a participant to dedicate computer power to solving cryptographic puzzles, and those who solved the puzzle received the reward (Aggarwal & Kumar, 2021). The focus on cryptocurrencies in the finance and banking sectors is gaining momentum.

The Bitcoin system only provides eventual consistency. For everyday life, the time to confirm a Bitcoin transaction is prohibitively slow (Decker, Seidel, & Wattenhofer, 2014). In this paper we propose a new system, built on the Bitcoin block chain, which enables strong consistency. Our system, Peer Census, acts as a certification authority, manages peer identities in a peer-to-peer network, and ultimately enhances Bitcoin and similar systems with strong consistency. Our extensive analysis shows that Peer Census is in a secure state with high probability. We also show how Discoin, a Bitcoin variant that decouples block creation and transaction confirmation, can be built on top of Peer Census, enabling real-time payments. Unlike Bitcoin, once transactions in Discoin are committed, they stay committed.

A purely peer-to-peer version of electronic cash would allow online payments to be sent directly from one party to another without going through a financial institution.

Digital signatures provide part of the solution, but the main benefits are lost if a trusted third party is still required to prevent double-spending. A solution is proposed to the double-spending problem using a peer-to-peer network. the objective of this research paper is to focuses on working framework of Block chain Technology and enlightens the security of Block chain technology through vulnerability (Nakamoto, 2008; Massias et al., 1999).

One of the first studies to attempt to predict cryptocurrency using non-linear neural networks—conducted by Maiti, Vyklyuk, and Vukovic and published in 2020—found that the non-linear models were preferable to linear models as the former's error was lower than the latter, giving more accurate predictions. This study also found that some elements of the cryptocurrency's historical data were not helpful in prediction, such as the volume (Maiti et al., 2020).

Another study released in 2022 to expand the prediction beyond merely yielding a direction; instead of reporting whether the price would go up or down, the model would report "the magnitude of the price change" (Critien et al., 2022). The study leveraged not only historical price data for Bitcoin, but also Twitter posts to glean public sentiment about the currency. An important distinction of this study is that it used a bidirectional LSTM, which is a model composed of two LSTMs: one for historical price data and one for Twitter posts. Its accuracy of 64.18% was achieved by using 450 days of historical data.

Furthermore, a 2022 study by Sarkodie, Ahmed, and Owusu used COVID-19 data, such as the number of cases and deaths, to determine whether cryptocurrencies such as Bitcoin would rise or fall in price. The study made use of the Romano–Wolf algorithm to test this correlation. In particular, it deemed Bitcoin to be very highly correlated with deaths due to COVID-19, correspondingly fluctuating 90.50% of the time. Lastly, a 2019 study by Azari utilized an autoregressive integrated moving average (ARIMA) approach to predict the price of Bitcoin. In this study, the model's effective-ness was evaluated by examining the mean-squared error; the findings reported a very low level of prediction error (Critien, et al., 2022).

Bitcoin was the first cryptocurrency introduced in the market by pseudonymous entity named Satoshi Nakamoto in 2009 but the real market for cryptocurrency started in 2013. Today there is more than 1650 different altcoins in the market. Bitcoin, the pioneer cryptocurrency, was conceived in 2008 by an individual or a group of researchers under the pseudonymous of Nakamoto (2008) and implemented in 2009 as an electronic payment system via a breakthrough application of blockchain technology.

THE FACTORS AND PARAMETERS

The study looks towards creating a comprehensive framework for predicting cryptocurrency prices using deep learning models. Several factors influence cryptocurrency prices. Market demand and supply dynamics play a crucial role, with increased demand driving prices up and oversupply causing them to decline. Investor sentiment and market psychology can significantly impact prices, with positive news and confidence-boosting prices, while negative developments and uncertainties can lead to declines. The regulatory environment, including government policies and regulations, can have a profound effect on cryptocurrency prices, as supportive regulations and institutional adoption tend to drive prices higher, while restrictive measures or bans can lead to price drops.

Technological advancements, upgrades, and innovations in blockchain technology or specific cryptocurrencies also influence prices, as improved features and utility attract more demand. Market liquidity, the ease of buying and selling cryptocurrencies, can affect prices, with higher liquidity generally leading to more stable prices. Moreover, market manipulation, integration and adoption into mainstream systems, macroeconomic factors, and global events all contribute to the complex dynamics that shape cryptocurrency prices. The parameters like MAE, RMSE, MSE, and MAPE are commonly used to evaluate the performance of predictive models; it's important to note that the choice of evaluation metrics may depend on the specific context and requirements of the cryptocurrency price prediction task or dataset. These metrics assess different aspects of prediction accuracy and can help identify the best-fit model.

PROBLEM STATEMENT

The accurate prediction of cryptocurrency prices and volatility poses a significant challenge in the market, with existing methods showing limited accuracy. To address this challenge, this research aims to develop a comprehensive framework using deep learning models to enhance the accuracy of cryptocurrency price and volatility prediction, evaluate volatility levels of different cryptocurrencies, and empower investors to make informed decisions in the dynamic and volatile cryptocurrency market.

OBJECTIVES OF THE STUDY

Primary Objective

- To develop an integrated framework of multiple deep learning models to accurately predict cryptocurrency prices, identify the most effective deep learning approach for enhanced accuracy, and forecast the volatility of various cryptocurrencies

Secondary Objectives

- To evaluate and compare the effectiveness of Deep Learning techniques in cryptocurrency price and volatility prediction against traditional statistical methods
- To develop a live dashboard that provides real-time tracking of daily cryptocurrency prices, incorporating the integrated framework of multiple Deep Learning models.

SCOPE OF THE STUDY

- The aim of this research is to develop a comprehensive framework that utilizes deep-learning models for predicting cryptocurrency prices and volatility more effectively.
- The study aims to provide investors with more accurate predictions, enabling them to make informed investment decisions and potentially increase their profits.
- Additionally, the research will focus on volatility prediction, aiding investors in making wise investment choices based on the expected fluctuations in cryptocurrency prices.

METHODOLOGY

The section that follows describes the research methodology used to achieve the primary and secondary goals of this study, which is to develop a comprehensive framework using deep learning models.

1. **Identify and Review:** Review the existing models and methods for predicting the price of the cryptocurrency.

2. **Data Collection:** Gather historical data on cryptocurrency prices, including the relevant features such as trading volume, market capitalization, and other market indicators. This data can be obtained from various sources like cryptocurrency exchanges, APIs, or online databases.

3. **Data Preprocessing:** Clean the collected data by removing any inconsistencies, missing values, or outliers. Perform necessary transformations, such as normalization or scaling, to ensure the data is in a suitable format for modeling.

4. **Feature Selection/Engineering:** Identify and select the most relevant features that can potentially influence cryptocurrency prices. Additionally, create new features or derive meaningful representations from the existing ones to improve the predictive power of the models. Consider factors like market sentiment, technical indicators, or macroeconomic data that might impact cryptocurrency prices.

5. **Split the Data:** Divide the dataset into training, validation, and testing sets. The training set will be used to train the prediction models, the validation set to tune model hyperparameters, and the testing set to evaluate the final model's performance.

6. **Model Selection:** Choose appropriate prediction models for cryptocurrency price forecasting. This can include traditional statistical models, machine learning algorithms (e.g., linear regression, random forests, support vector machines), or deep learning models (e.g., recurrent neural networks, long short-term memory networks, or transformer-based models).

7. **Model Training:** Train the selected models using the training dataset. Adjust the model parameters or hyperparameters through techniques like grid search, cross-validation, or Bayesian optimization to achieve optimal performance.

8. **Model Evaluation:** Evaluate the trained models using appropriate evaluation metrics such as MAE, RMSE, MSE, or MAPE. Compare the performance of different models to select the best-performing one.

9. **Model Validation:** Validate the selected model using the validation dataset. Assess its performance on unseen data to ensure its generalizability and robustness.

10. **Prediction and Analysis:** Apply the validated model to make predictions on new or future data. Monitor the predictions and analyze the results, comparing them with actual cryptocurrency prices to assess the accuracy and reliability of the model.

11. **Model Refinement:** Iterate and refine the model based on the feedback obtained from prediction analysis. Fine-tune the model parameters, update the feature selection/engineering process, or consider ensemble techniques to improve the prediction accuracy further.

TOOLS

Python Programming Language

Python is a widely used programming language in the field of data science and has become a popular tool for predicting cryptocurrency prices. Python offers several libraries, frameworks, and tools that facilitate data analysis, modelling, and visualization, making it suitable for developing cryptocurrency price prediction models. Python plays a crucial role in predicting cryptocurrency prices using deep learning methods. Here's how Python is involved: Here are some key Python tools commonly used in this context:

1. **Deep Learning Libraries:** Python offers popular deep learning libraries like TensorFlow, Keras, and PyTorch, which provide high-level APIs for building and training deep neural networks. These libraries enable the implementation of complex architectures such as recurrent neural networks (RNNs), long short-term memory networks (LSTMs), and convolutional neural networks (CNNs), which are commonly used in cryptocurrency price prediction.
2. **Data Pre-Processing:** Python, along with libraries like NumPy and Pandas, is used for data pre-processing tasks. This involves cleaning and transforming the cryptocurrency price data to prepare it for training deep learning models. Python's efficient data manipulation capabilities enable handling large datasets and performing necessary transformations, such as normalization or scaling.
3. **Feature Engineering:** Python allows for feature engineering tasks, where additional relevant features can be derived from the raw data. This may include technical indicators, sentiment analysis scores, or lagged values. Python libraries like Pandas make it easier to create new features or extract meaningful representations that enhance the predictive power of deep learning models.
4. **Model Development and Training:** Python's deep learning libraries provide a rich set of tools for building and training deep learning models. Developers can define the architecture of the model, configure its layers, and set hyperparameters. Python libraries facilitate the efficient training of models on large datasets using techniques such as mini-batch processing, regularization, and optimization algorithms.
5. **Hyperparameter Tuning:** Python libraries, like scikit-learn, provide tools for hyperparameter tuning, which involves searching for the optimal configuration of hyperparameters to improve model performance. Techniques like grid search or random search can be employed to find the best combination of hyperparameters for deep learning models.

6. **Model Evaluation and Validation:** Python enables the evaluation and validation of deep learning models. Various metrics, such as mean squared error (MSE), root mean squared error (RMSE), or mean absolute error (MAE), can be calculated to assess the model's performance. Python libraries for data visualization, such as Matplotlib and Seaborn, can be used to visualize model predictions and compare them with actual cryptocurrency prices.

7. **Deployment and Integration:** Python allows for easy deployment and integration of deep learning models into production systems or trading platforms. Python frameworks like Flask or Django can be used to develop web-based applications or APIs to serve the trained models. This enables real-time predictions and integration with other systems or trading algorithms.

Python's versatility, extensive deep learning libraries, and robust ecosystem make it a preferred choice for cryptocurrency price prediction using deep learning methods. It provides a flexible and efficient environment for model development, training, evaluation, and deployment, facilitating the entire prediction pipeline.

ANALYZING CRYPTO MARKET DATA WITH PYTHON

The code is separated into six portions: downloading the data and loading the necessary libraries, exploratory analysis, return series, Volatility, correlation, and moving average, respectively.

Figure 1 provides the Python code necessary for loading the required libraries.

Figure 1. Python code: Loading the necessary libraries

```
#Load the required libraries
import pandas as pd
import yfinance as yf
import seaborn as sns
import matplotlib.pyplot as plt
```

For instance, the desired Crypto data for Binance, Bitcoin, Ethereum, and XRP (Ripple) will be downloaded using their respective ticker symbols: BNB, BTC, ETH, and XRP (Shrivas, et al., 2022; Jamision et al., 2018).

Figure 2. Python code: List of crypto as ticker arguments

```
# list of crptocurrencies as ticker arguments
cryptocurrencies = ['BNB-USD','BTC-USD', 'ETH-USD', 'XRP-USD']
```

Figure 2, which presents Python code demonstrating how to convert ticker arguments to a list of crypto, providing readers with a practical and helpful example.

To observe the fluctuations in the cryptocurrency market during the Covid-19 pandemic, the analysis begins on January 1, 2020.

Figure 3 presents Python code that demonstrates how to load crypto data starting from the beginning of the Covid-19 pandemic.

Figure 3. Python code: Loading crypto data from the beginning of the COVID-19 pandemic

```
data = yf.download(cryptocurrencies, start='2020-01-01',
                end='2021-12-12')
data.head()

[**********************100%***********************]  4 of 4 completed
```

- After inspecting the data, it is determined that there are no missing values in the data frame. Consequently, the analysis can proceed, but it is necessary to understand the meaning of the features in the dataset first (Mohapatra et al., 2019).
- Through exploratory analysis, the time series plots reveal the fluctuation of stock prices over time. Due to the varying scales, direct comparison of the charts is not possible. Instead, the cumulative returns chart will be utilized, providing relative changes.

Figure 4, showcasing the graph with time-series plots, offering a visual representation of data trends and patterns.

Figure 4. Graph: Time-series plots

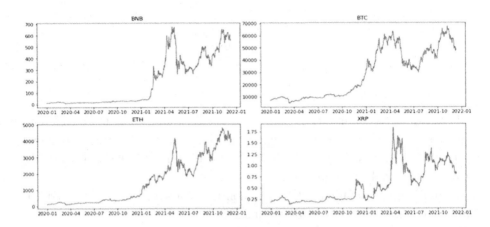

- The returns of an asset are more manageable compared to the price series, providing a comprehensive overview of the investment opportunity. Calculating the returns will be done using the pandas pct_change() function.

Figure 5. Python code: Relative price changes of the cryptocurrencies

```
# Returns i.e. percentage change in the adjusted close price and drop
the first row with NA's
returns = adj_close.pct_change().dropna(axis=0)
#view the first 5 rows of the data frame
returns.head()
```

Figure 5, which presents the Python code displaying the relative price changes of cryptocurrencies, offering a practical and insightful approach to understanding the dynamic nature of these digital assets. Figure 6, showcasing the Graph with Return Plot, enhances the chapter by providing visual representation and analysis of the data.

- XRP exhibits the highest volatility, with Binance being the next most volatile, while Bitcoin demonstrates the lowest volatility. A significant market crash can be observed across all cryptocurrencies around March 2020. Volatility, as measured by standard deviation, indicates the extent of price fluctuations in an asset (Molin & Jee, 2021). Figure 7, which presents the Python code for calculating the volatility and standard deviation of returns.

Figure 6. Graph: Return plot

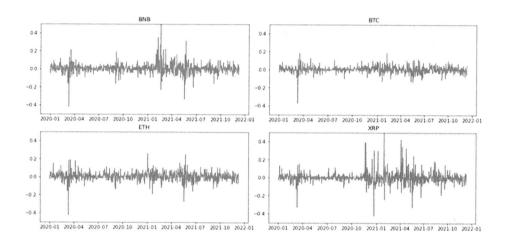

Figure 7. Python code: Volatility, standard deviation of the returns

```
#volatility, standard deviation of the returns
returns.std()

BNB-USD     0.065132
BTC-USD     0.040267
ETH-USD     0.053324
XRP-USD     0.071800
dtype: float64
```

- XRP (Ripple) exhibits the highest volatility among the four assets, whereas Bitcoin demonstrates the lowest volatility. Correlation will be computed based on return data to avoid biased results that can occur when using raw price data.
- Moving average (rolling average) is used to smooth out short-term fluctuations to identify long-term trends or cycles.

Figure 8, illustrating how to represent the correlation of cryptocurrencies, offering a practical and informative guide for analyzing and understanding the relationships between different digital currencies. The Python code for computing moving average is presented in Figure 9, providing a helpful resource for understanding and implementing this calculation.

Figure 8. Python code: Correlation of cryptocurrencies

```
#compute the correlations
returns.corr()
```

```
#plot the correlations
sns.heatmap(returns.corr(), annot=True, cmap='coolwarm')
plt.show()
```

Figure 9. Python code: Computing moving average

```
# compute a short-term 20-day moving average
MA20 = adj_close.rolling(20).mean()
# compute a long-term 50-day moving average
MA50 = adj_close.rolling(100).mean()
# compute a long-term 100-day moving average
MA100 = adj_close.rolling(100).mean()

# ploting the moving average
fig, axs = plt.subplots(2,2,figsize=(20,8),gridspec_kw ={'hspace':
0.2, 'wspace': 0.1})
axs[0,0].plot(adj_close['BNB-USD'], label= 'closing')
axs[0,0].plot(MA50['BNB-USD'], label= 'MA50')
axs[0,0].set_title('BNB')
axs[0,0].legend()
axs[0,1].plot(adj_close['BTC-USD'], label= 'closing')
axs[0,1].plot(MA50['BTC-USD'], label= 'MA50')
axs[0,1].set_title('BTC')
axs[0,1].legend()
axs[1,0].plot(adj_close['ETH-USD'], label= 'closing')
axs[1,0].plot(MA50['ETH-USD'], label= 'MA50')
axs[1,0].set_title('ETH')
axs[1,0].legend()
axs[1,1].plot(adj_close['XRP-USD'], label= 'closing')
axs[1,1].plot(MA50['XRP-USD'], label= 'MA50')
axs[1,1].set_title('XRP')
axs[1,1].legend()
plt.show()
```

- From the chart in Figure 10, it is evident that in mid-May 2021, the price falls below the 50-day MA, indicating a downward trend. Similarly, in mid-August, the price rises above the MA, signaling an upward trend.

Figure 10. Plotting moving average

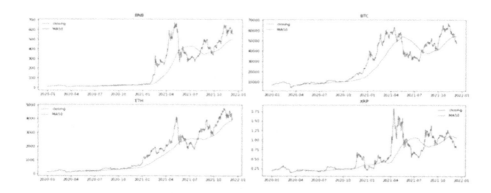

CREATING OUR OWN CRYPTOCURRENCY USING PYTHON

Governments, organizations, and individuals have been adopting blockchain technology to develop their own cryptocurrencies, aiming to stay relevant in the evolving landscape. An example that garnered significant attention worldwide was Facebook's introduction of its cryptocurrency, known as Libra (Opidi, 2019; Z, 2023; Yogeshwaran, 2019).

Figure 11 presents the fundamental design of the blockchain code in Python for creating the cryptocurrency (fccCoin), providing a clear and practical example for understanding the implementation of a blockchain.

CONCLUSION

This article demonstrates that Python is an excellent language for Blockchain projects. It offers a gentle learning curve, allowing developers to master it efficiently. With Python, developers can code a blockchain with minimal effort, and it simplifies cryptoanalysis. Utilizing Python packages like Alpha Vantage, Pandas DataReader, YFinance, CryptoCompare, IEX Cloud, Twelve Data, etc., facilitates seamless retrieval of cryptocurrency data. Python finds various applications in the cryptocurrency realm, including the ability to create custom crypto coins. Although an initially created coin may not meet the current market demands for stability, security, and user-friendliness, it can be enhanced by adding features for mining and financial transactions. In conclusion, Python is a versatile and efficient language.

Figure 11. Python code: To create crypto coin (fccCoin)

```python
class Block:

    def __init__():

    #first block class

        pass

    def calculate_hash():

    #calculates the cryptographic hash of every block


class BlockChain:

    def __init__(self):
       # constructor method
    pass

    def construct_genesis(self):
        # constructs the initial block
        pass

    def construct_block(self, proof_no, prev_hash):
        # constructs a new block and adds it to the chain
        pass

    @staticmethod
    def check_validity():
        # checks whether the blockchain is valid
        pass

    def new_data(self, sender, recipient, quantity):
        # adds a new transaction to the data of the transactions
        pass

    @staticmethod
    def construct_proof_of_work(prev_proof):
        # protects the blockchain from attack
        pass

    @property
    def last_block(self):
        # returns the last block in the chain
        return self.chain[-1]
```

REFERENCES

Aggarwal, S., & Kumar, N. (2021). History of blockchain-blockchain 1.0: Currency. *Advances in Computers*, *121*, 147–169.

Critien, J. V., Gatt, A., & Ellul, J. (2022). Bitcoin price change and trend prediction through twitter sentiment and data volume. *Financial Innovation*, *8*(1), 1–20.

Decker, C., Seidel, J., & Wattenhofer, R. (2016, January). Bitcoin meets strong consistency. In *Proceedings of the 17th International Conference on Distributed Computing and Networking* (pp. 1-10). Academic Press.

Jamison, M. A., & Tariq, P. (2018). Five things regulators should know about blockchain (and three myths to forget). *The Electricity Journal*, *31*(9), 20–23.

Larrier, J. H. (2021). A Brief History of Blockchain. *Transforming Scholarly Publishing With Blockchain Technologies and AI*, 85-100.

Maiti, M., Vyklyuk, Y., & Vuković, D. (2020). Cryptocurrencies chaotic co-movement forecasting with neural networks. *Internet Technology Letters*, *3*(3), e157.

Massias, H., Avila, X. S., & Quisquarter, J. J. (1999). Design of a secure timestamping service with minimal trust requirement. In *Symposium on Information theory in the Benelux* (pp. 79-86). Werkgemeenschap voor Informatie-en Communicatietheorie.

Mohapatra, S., Ahmed, N., & Alencar, P. (2019, December). KryptoOracle: A real-time cryptocurrency price prediction platform using twitter sentiments. *2019 IEEE international conference on big data*, 5544–5551.

Molin, S., & Jee, K. (2021). *Hands-On Data Analysis with Pandas: A Python data science handbook for data collection, wrangling, analysis, and visualization*. Packt Publishing Ltd.

Nakamoto, S. (2008). Bitcoin: A peer-to-peer electronic cash system. *Decentralized Business Review, 21260*.

Opidi, A. (2019, October 8). *How to Create Your Own Cryptocurrency Using Python*. freeCodeCamp.org. https://www.freecodecamp.org/news/create-cryptocurrency-using-python/

S, R. A. (2023, March 31). *What is Blockchain Technology? How Does Blockchain Work?* [Updated]. Simplilearn.com. https://www.simplilearn.com/tutorials/blockchain-tutorial/blockchain-technology

Shrivas, M. K., Hiran, K. K., Bhansali, A., & Doshi, R. (2022). *Advancements in Quantum Blockchain With Real-Time Applications*. IGI Global.

Yogeshwaran, S., Kaur, M. J., & Maheshwari, P. (2019, April). Project based learning: predicting bitcoin prices using deep learning. In *2019 IEEE Global Engineering Education Conference (EDUCON)* (pp. 1449-1454). IEEE.

Z. (2023, February 22). *Top 10 Useful Python Packages to Pull Cryptocurrency Data Seamlessly*. Analytics Insight. https://www.analyticsinsight.net/top-10-useful-python-packag es-to-pull-cryptocurrency-data-seamlessly/

Chapter 13
Exploring the Role of Python in Self-Supervised Contrastive Learning for Generating Medical Imaging Reports

Rahul Kumar
CHRIST University (Deemed), India

N. Arulkumar
CHRIST University (Deemed), India

ABSTRACT

This chapter investigates Python's involvement in self-supervised contrastive learning (SSCL) for medical imagery with report generation. The research highlights the relevance of SSCL as a method for creating medical imaging reports and the benefits of implementing it using Python. The literature review gives a complete overview of SSCL approaches in medical imaging and shows the advantages of SSCL implementation using Python libraries such as PyTorch, TensorFlow, and Keras. The study's methodology describes the research topics, survey design, methods of data gathering, and analytic procedures. The study named SSCL-GMIR findings indicate that several practitioners utilize SSCL in medical imaging using Python modules. This study highlights Python's significance in implementing SSCL for creating medical imaging report documents, offering researchers and practitioners a more efficient and effective method for producing accurate and informative reports and diagnoses.

DOI: 10.4018/978-1-6684-7100-5.ch013

INTRODUCTION

Self-Supervised Contrastive Learning for Medical Images with Report Generation heavily relies on implementing Python data structures and algorithms. Self-Supervised Contrastive Learning is a machine learning technique that constructs data representations by comparing various perspectives of the same data, which helps generate relevant reports or diagnoses in medical imaging. Python data structures such as dictionaries, lists, and arrays store and process the data. To extract valuable insights from these structures, it is necessary to use algorithms such as k-means clustering or PCA. Other techniques, such as gradient descent or backpropagation, may be used to train a neural network for representation learning (Li Zhiyuan et al., 2023; Mohan et al., 2023; Upadhye et al., 2023).

Once the data representations have been learned, they can generate reports or diagnoses. For instance, decision trees or random forests can categorize images and provide relevant reports. Python's implementation is highly advantageous for Self-Supervised Contrastive Learning for Medical Images with Report Generation. Python's data structures and algorithms facilitate efficient data manipulation, information extraction, model training, and evaluation, resulting in more accurate and informative reports and diagnoses (Mishra et al., 2023; Saravanan et al., 2023; Neelakandan et al., 2022).

LITERATURE REVIEW

Medical imaging is a potent, non-invasive diagnostic tool essential for diagnosing and treating various diseases because it permits the observation of the internal structures of human organs, tissues, and bones. SSCL, a methodology that trains visual representations via unsupervised Learning, has been a potential method for producing accurate medical reports and diagnoses. TensorFlow and Keras are some of the tools and frameworks the popular programming language Python provides for SSCL applications in medical imaging (Najma et al., 2023). Python's simplicity, readability, and scalability make it popular among medical imaging academics and industry professionals. Using Python for SSCL implementation in medical imaging presents unique problems, such as managing massive datasets and enhancing algorithm performance, but these obstacles may be solved with proper planning and design.

Chen et al. (2019) analyzed the challenges of finding enough labeled medical images to train deep-learning models and the need to include unlabeled data to improve model performance. The authors propose a context restoration-based self-supervised learning method to maximize medical image analysis using unlabeled images. The suggested context restoration strategy improved classification, localization, and segmentation performance. The proposed self-supervised learning strategy, which uses context restoration, may enhance machine learning models for medical imaging applications by acquiring semantic information.

In a unique self-supervised pre-training strategy for medical picture analysis, extra pixel-level information and scale information are directly included in high-level semantics (Zhou et al., 2023). PCRLv2 integrates multi-scale pixel restoration with siamese feature comparison in a feature pyramid for 3D medical imaging using a non-skip U-Net and sub-crop. The system outperforms self-supervised algorithms for segmenting brain tumors, identifying chest pathologies, detecting lung nodules, and segmenting abdominal organs, sometimes with little annotations.

CheSS, a publicly available chest X-ray pre-trained model, employs self-supervised contrastive Learning to learn various radiograph representations (Cho et al., 2023). Disease categorization, bone suppression, and nodule creation verify the model trained on 4.8 million CXR pictures. CheSS enhanced accuracy by 28.5% on the 6-class classification test dataset and 1.3% on the CheXpert dataset. The article concludes that CheSS may help researchers overcome data imbalance, inadequacy, and medical image-collecting inaccessibility.

Problem Identified From Literature Review

The review of relevant literature reveals a number of significant findings in the field of self-supervised contrastive learning for medical image texture generation. Despite the progress made, the following challenges and improvement opportunities have been identified:

- Traditional supervised methods rely heavily on manually annotated data, which can be time-consuming and costly to acquire. The difficulty lies in reducing this dependence and effectively utilising unlabelled data to enhance the learning process.
- Integration of diverse multi-organ datasets: In order to increase the efficacy of learned features, it is essential to integrate diverse multi-organ datasets with varying staining and resolution characteristics. The difficulty lies in developing methodologies that can handle the heterogeneity and complexity of such datasets.
- Clinical metadata, when incorporated into the self-supervised learning framework, can provide valuable contextual information and enhance the comprehension of medical images. However, additional research and the development of techniques to effectively utilise clinical metadata in the learning process are required.

- Self-supervised learning utilising contrastive learning and clustering methods has demonstrated superior performance in comparison to supervised learning, but there is room for improvement. Potentially enhancing the learning of visual features is the investigation of additional techniques or novel strategies beyond those currently employed.
- The effectiveness of attention mechanisms in medical image analysis, such as the detection of COVID-19, can be further optimised. Potentially increasing diagnostic precision and robustness is the investigation of alternative attention mechanisms or the refinement of the existing ones.
- Exploration of alternative ensemble strategies: The hybrid ensemble model proposed for detecting COVID-19 has shown promise. However, alternative ensemble strategies could be investigated to improve the overall performance of diagnostic models.
- While self-supervised learning has demonstrated promising results, it is necessary to investigate the potential advantages of using smaller sample sizes and fewer training steps. For practical implementation, it is essential to comprehend the trade-offs between computational requirements and output quality.
- Enhanced pre-training strategies for medical image classification Self-supervised learning has proven to be an effective pre-training strategy for medical image classification. In order to improve the accuracy of medical image classifiers, future research can concentrate on refining self-supervised learning techniques and exploring novel methods for constructing more informative positive pairs for self-supervised learning.
- The proposed self-supervised learning technique for abnormality detection in chest radiography has improved performance through model optimisation and training diversity. To improve its robustness and generalizability, the model must undergo additional optimisation and training on a more diverse set of images.

Reducing reliance on manually annotated data, handling diverse multi-organ datasets, incorporating clinical metadata, refining self-supervised learning techniques, optimising attention mechanisms, examining alternative ensemble strategies, analysing computational requirements, enhancing pre-training strategies for medical image classification, and enhancing model optimisation and training diversity are some of the identified problem areas. Addressing these obstacles will advance self-supervised contrastive learning with texture generation for medical images.

RESEARCH GAP

- If the number of instances is proportional to the intractable number of classes, labelling unlabelled images will become challenging.
- The existing research with K-Means clustering with contrastive learning has resulted in a only 3% improvement in accuracy, which falls short of a perfect 100% improvement.
- A novel approach is needed to enhance the effectiveness of contrastive learning with text, specifically for the purpose of detecting abnormalities.
- Despite the vast amount of research on contrastive learning for detecting abnormalities in text, there is a gap in the literature on incorporating the generation of texture to facilitate a seamless experience for end-users.

RESEARCH QUESTIONS

- What are the core techniques for increasing accuracy of medical image annotation
- How can medical texture generation be achieved using Self-Supervised learning or any other methods?
- What additional augmentation technique can be applied to generate multiple images from the same image?
- What is the importance of improving self-supervised contrastive learning in healthcare?

THE FACTORS AND PARAMETERS

The study looks towards annotation for medical images using self-supervised contrastive learning. It also aims to provide the texture generation of medical images. Data augmentation techniques including cropping, rotation, flipping, and color jittering are high factors. The parameters could be the softmax function with vector of numbers as input, the size of the contrastive loss batch, the learning rate, the quantity of training data, the size of the embedding space, and the regularization techniques like dropout, weight decay, or early stopping. The suggested self-supervised contrastive learning framework for medical image analysis and texture generation performs more effectively due to these characteristics and parameters, which are essential in predicting sections of the input data from other portions of the same input data.

PROBLEM STATEMENT

The lack of accurate and robust labelling for medical images has been a significant challenge in the field of medical image analysis. To address this challenge, this research aims to design a self-supervised method and model that improves the classification of unlabelled medical images. This research aims to implement texture description about disease and anomalies in medical images and to perform integration of self-supervised method with texture generation method. Overall, this research will contribute to the development of more accurate and reliable medical image analysis methods, which can help in the diagnosis and treatment of various medical conditions.

OBJECTIVES OF THE STUDY

Primary Objectives:

- To design a Self-Supervised method and model that improves the classification of unlabelled medical images
- To compare the performance of the proposed method and model with the existing models
- To provide accurate and robust labelling for medical images

Secondary Objectives:

- To implement the texture description of diseases and anomalies in medical images
- To perform integration of Self-Supervised method with texture generation method in API

SCOPE OF THE STUDY

- The study aims to develop a framework called the Advanced Contrastive Learning Approach with Text (ACLAT) for accurately labelling unlabelled images.
- The proposed framework intends to improve the accuracy of labelling and to enhance the performance of existing labelling methods and models.
- Upon implementation, the framework will generate a model capable of identifying anomalies and generating textures for end-users.

- This methodology can be applied to various domains, including the medical domain, to improve the accuracy of labelling and texture generation for unlabelled images.

METHODOLOGY

The section that follows describes the research methodology used to achieve the primary and secondary goals of this study, which is to develop a self-supervised contrastive learning framework for medical images with texture generation.

- Identify and review existing self-supervised methods and models for classification of unlabelled medical images.
- Designing a self-supervised method, ACLAT Framework, to enhance the accuracy and robustness of labelling with texture description.
- Implementation of the proposed framework within an API to generate the texture about diseases and abnormalities in images
- Compare the performance of the proposed ACLAT framework with existing models identified in the literature review.
- The proposed ACLAT framework is validated and assessed with a large dataset of unlabelled medical images to ensure accurate labelling.
- **Model Enhancement:** Based on the findings from the comparative analysis and validation, the ACLAT framework will undergo enhancements and optimizations to further improve its performance.

Application: The proposed methodology has the potential to enhance the accuracy of labeling and improve text generation for unlabeled images across different domains.

A STUDY ON EXITING VGG16 MODEL TO PREDICT LABELS

The code is separated into two portions. The first phase consists of downloading and preparing chest X-ray images for deep-learning models, while the second step employs the pre-trained VGG16 model to predict picture labels. The code searches the internet for photos, downloads them, adjusts their proportions, and eliminates broken images in the first stage. In the second stage, the pre-trained VGG16 model is loaded, pictures are processed for the model, predictions are generated, and probabilities are displayed next to labels (Sharma et al., 2023; Jaishankar et al., 2022; Kiran et al., 2021; Moussaid et al., 2023).

Downloading and Preprocessing

The following steps gather chest X-ray images and prepare them for use in deep-learning models. The code searches the internet for images, downloads them, modifies their dimensions, and removes broken images. The sample code for this task is given in Figure 1.

Steps

- *Use pip to install required packages for image processing.*
- *Import necessary packages.*
- *Define a function to search for images online and retrieve their URLs.*
- *Download the images using the retrieved URLs and save them in the directory.*
- *Resize the downloaded and save them in the same directory.*
- *Verify the downloaded images and delete any broken or corrupt images from the directory.*

VGG16 to Predict Labels

The provided code utilizes the pre-trained VGG16 model to predict labels for a collection of chest X-ray images. The sample code is given in Figure 2.

Steps

- *Load the pre-trained VGG16 model.*
- *Set the path to the directory containing the chest X-ray images.*
- *Get a list of all the image file names in the directory.*
- *Create an empty list to store the images.*
- *Loop over each image file in the directory and load the image.*
- *Preprocess the image by resizing it to 224x224 and converting it to an array.*
- *Append the image array to the list of images.*
- *Preprocess the images for the VGG16 model.*
- *Make predictions with the VGG16 model on the preprocessed images and decode the predictions.*
- *Print the predicted labels and their probabilities.*

Figure 1. Python code: Downloading and preprocessing the images

```
# Install Packages
pip install fastai

# Import Packages
from duckduckgo_search import ddg_images
from fastcore.all import *
from fastdownload import download_url
import fastai.vision.all as fv

# Define the Image Search Function
def search_images(term, max_images=10):
    """ This function will return us the URLs list"""

    print(f"Searching for {term}")
    return L(ddg_images(term, max_results=max_images)).itemgot('image')

# Download Images in Defined Folders
from time import sleep

searches = 'chest x-ray',
path = Path('ChestXRay')

for o in searches:
    dest = (path/o)
    dest.mkdir(exist_ok=True, parents=True)
    fv.download_images(dest, urls=search_images(f'{o} covid-chestxray-dataset'))
    sleep(10)
    fv.resize_images(path/o, max_size=400, dest=path/o)

# Handling Broken/Corrupt Images
failed = fv.verify_images(fv.get_image_files(path))
failed.map(Path.unlink)
len(failed)  #shows how many of them were corrupt
```

ROLE OF PYTHON TO PREDICT LABELS

Python is the programming language used to create the code. The code involves loading a pre-trained VGG16 model, preprocessing images, making predictions using the model, and printing the predicted labels and probabilities. Additionally, Python is used to install the necessary packages for image processing, import the required packages, define functions to search for and download images, process the downloaded images, and load the pre-trained model. These tasks are performed using Python (Alghamdi et al., 2023). The various role of Python in predicting labels is given in Figure 3.

Figure 2. Python code: VGG16 to predict labels

```python
# Import Necessary Python Packages
import os
import numpy as np
import tensorflow as tf
from tensorflow import keras
from tensorflow.keras.applications.vgg16 import VGG16
from tensorflow.keras.preprocessing import image
from tensorflow.keras.applications.vgg16 import preprocess_input

# Load the pre-trained VGG16 model
model = VGG16(weights='imagenet')

# Set the path to the directory containing the chest X-ray images
dir_path = "/content/ChestXRay/chest x-ray"

# Get a list of all the image file names in the directory
img_files = os.listdir(dir_path)

# Create an empty list to store the images
images = []

# Loop over each image file in the directory and load the image
for img_file in img_files:
    img_path = os.path.join(dir_path, img_file)
    img = image.load_img(img_path, target_size=(224, 224))
    img_array = image.img_to_array(img)
    images.append(img_array)

# Preprocess the images for the VGG16 model
images = np.array(images)
images = preprocess_input(images)

# Make predictions with the VGG16 model
preds = model.predict(images)

# Decode the predictions
decoded_preds = tf.keras.applications.vgg16.decode_predictions(preds, top=3)

# Print the predicted labels for each image
for i, img_file in enumerate(img_files):
    print("Image:", img_file)
    for j, label in enumerate(decoded_preds[i]):
        print("Prediction", j+1, ":", label[1], "- Probability:", label[2])
```

Figure 3. Python to predict labels

Image Processing: The chest X-ray pictures may be preprocessed using Python's many image processing packages, such as OpenCV, sci-kit-image, and Pillow. Image enhancement, noise reduction, and segmentation techniques may be used to segment the picture's areas of interest.

Deep Learning: Python is home to several deep learning frameworks, including TensorFlow, Keras, and PyTorch, which may be used to train a neural network model to recognize abnormalities in chest X-rays. This can include looking for pneumonia, pneumonia consolidation, or lung nodules.

Statistical Analysis: Python provides several libraries that may be used to analyze data statistically, such as NumPy, pandas, and SciPy. This may include examining the dataset's distribution of anomalies or comparing the effectiveness of various models.

Report Generation: To create PDF reports summarizing the results of the chest X-ray examination, Python offers several packages, including ReportLab and PyPDF2. The created reports may include images, graphs, and statistical summaries of the findings.

CONCLUSION

This chapter's conclusion emphasizes Python's significance in executing Self-Supervised Contrastive Learning for Medical Images with Report Generation. The research findings demonstrate that Python's data structures and algorithms allow fast data manipulation, information extraction, model training, and evaluation, resulting in more precise and comprehensive reports and diagnoses. The literature review highlights the benefits of utilizing Python frameworks like PyTorch, TensorFlow, and Keras for Self-Supervised Contrastive Learning and reinforces its applicability to medical imaging.

The potential impact of this study is immense, as medical imaging is a critical diagnostic tool that enables non-invasive examination of internal structures of human organs, tissues, and bones. Improving the accuracy of medical imaging reports and diagnoses can significantly impact patient care and treatment outcomes. Combining Python with Self-Supervised Contrastive Learning can enhance patient care by enabling medical professionals and researchers to generate more accurate and informative reports.

Future research could improve algorithm performance while overcoming challenges associated with managing large datasets and integrating self-supervised contrastive Learning with other machine learning techniques to enhance the accuracy and effectiveness of medical imaging reports and diagnoses. These findings suggest that Python and self-supervised contrastive learning have tremendous potential to improve patient care and treatment outcomes by developing more accurate and informative medical imaging reports and diagnoses. Continued research and improvements in this method could lead to significant advancements in medical care.

REFERENCES

Alghamdi, M. M. M., Dahab, M. Y. H., & Alazwary, N. H. A. (2023). Enhancing deep learning techniques for the diagnosis of the novel coronavirus (COVID-19) using X-ray images. *Cogent Engineering, 10*(1). doi:10.1080/23311916.2023.2181917

Chen, L., Bentley, P., Mori, K., Misawa, K., Fujiwara, M., & Rueckert, D. (2019). Self-supervised learning for medical image analysis using image context restoration. *Medical Image Analysis, 58,* 101539. doi:10.1016/j.media.2019.101539 PMID:31374449

Cho, K., Kim, K. D., Nam, Y., Jeong, J., Kim, J., Choi, C., Lee, S., Lee, J. S., Woo, S., Hong, G.-S., Seo, J. B., & Kim, N. (2023). CheSS: Chest X-Ray Pre-trained Model via Self-supervised Contrastive Learning. *Journal of Digital Imaging,* 1–9. doi:10.100710278-023-00782-4 PMID:36702988

Jaishankar, B., Vishwakarma, S., Mohan, P., Singh Pundir, A. K., Patel, I., & Arulkumar, N. (2022). Blockchain for Securing Healthcare Data Using Squirrel Search Optimization Algorithm. *Intelligent Automation & Soft Computing, 32*(3).

Kiran, S. V., Kaur, I., Thangaraj, K., Saveetha, V., Kingsy Grace, R., & Arulkumar, N. (2021). Machine Learning with Data Science-Enabled Lung Cancer Diagnosis and Classification Using Computed Tomography Images. *International Journal of Image and Graphics.*

Li, Z., Li, H., Ralescu, A. L., Dillman, J. R., Parikh, N. A., & He, L. (2023). *A Novel Collaborative Self-Supervised Learning Method for Radiomic Data.* arXiv preprint arXiv:2302.09807.

Mishra, A., & Soni, S. (2023, March). Summarization of Unstructured Medical Data for Accurate Medical Prognosis—A Learning Approach. In *Advances in Cognitive Science and Communications: Selected Articles from the 5th International Conference on Communications and Cyber-Physical Engineering (ICCCE 2022), Hyderabad, India* (pp. 825-838). Singapore: Springer Nature Singapore.

Mohan, P., Neelakandan, S., Mardani, A., Maurya, S., Arulkumar, N., & Thangaraj, K. (2023). Eagle Strategy Arithmetic Optimisation Algorithm with Optimal Deep Convolutional Forest Based FinTech Application for Hyper-automation. *Enterprise Information Systems*. doi:10.1080/17517575.2023.2188123

Moussaid, A., Zrira, N., Benmiloud, I., Farahat, Z., Karmoun, Y., Benzidia, Y., . . . Ngote, N. (2023, February). On the Implementation of a Post-Pandemic Deep Learning Algorithm Based on a Hybrid CT-Scan/X-ray Images Classification Applied to Pneumonia Categories. In Healthcare (Vol. 11, No. 5, p. 662). MDPI.

Najma, M., & Sekar, G. (2023, February). Novel CNN Approach (YOLO v5) to Detect Plant Diseases and Estimation of Nutritional Facts for Raw and Cooked Foods. In *Proceedings of Third International Conference on Sustainable Expert Systems: ICSES 2022* (pp. 305-329). Singapore: Springer Nature Singapore. 10.1007/978-981-19-7874-6_23

Neelakandan, S., Beulah, J. R., Prathiba, L., Murthy, G. L. N., Irudaya Raj, E. F., & Arulkumar, N. (2022). Blockchain with deep learning-enabled secure healthcare data transmission and diagnostic model. *International Journal of Modeling, Simulation, and Scientific Computing*, *13*(04), 2241006. doi:10.1142/S1793962322410069

Saravanan, S., Lavanya, M., Srinivas, C. M. V., Arunadevi, M., & Arulkumar, N. (n.d.). Secure IoT Protocol for Implementing Classified Electroencephalogram (EEG) Signals in the Field of Smart Healthcare. In Cyber Security Applications for Industry 4.0 (pp. 111-129). Chapman and Hall/CRC.

Sharma, S., & Guleria, K. (2023). A Deep Learning based model for the Detection of Pneumonia from Chest X-Ray Images using VGG-16 and Neural Networks. *Procedia Computer Science*, *218*, 357–366. doi:10.1016/j.procs.2023.01.018

Upadhye, S., Neelakandan, S., Thangaraj, K., Babu, D. V., Arulkumar, N., & Qureshi, K. (2023). Modeling of Real Time Traffic Flow Monitoring System Using Deep Learning and Unmanned Aerial Vehicles. *Journal of Mobile Multimedia*, 477-496.

Zhou, H. Y., Lu, C., Chen, C., Yang, S., & Yu, Y. (2023). A Unified Visual Information Preservation Framework for Self-supervised Pre-training in Medical Image Analysis. *IEEE Transactions on Pattern Analysis and Machine Intelligence*, 1–16. doi:10.1109/TPAMI.2023.3234002 PMID:37018263

Chapter 14
Python's Role in Predicting Type 2 Diabetes Using Insulin DNA Sequence

Aswathi Sasidharan
CHRIST University (Deemed), India

N. Arulkumar
ⓘ https://orcid.org/0000-0002-9728-477X
CHRIST University (Deemed), India

ABSTRACT

This chapter examines how Python can assist in predicting type 2 diabetes using insulin DNA sequences, given the substantial problem that biologists face in objectively evaluating diverse biological characteristics of DNA sequences. The chapter highlights Python's various libraries, such as NumPy, Pandas, and Scikit-learn, for data handling, analysis, and machine learning, as well as visualization tools, such as Matplotlib and Seaborn, to help researchers understand the relationship between different DNA sequences and type 2 diabetes. Additionally, Python's ease of integration with other bioinformatics tools, like BLAST, EMBOSS, and ClustalW, can help identify DNA markers that could aid in predicting type 2 diabetes. In addition, the initiative tries to identify unique gene variants of insulin protein that contribute to diabetes prognosis and investigates the risk factors connected with the discovered gene variants. In conclusion, Python's versatility and functionality make it a valuable tool for researchers studying insulin DNA sequences and type 2 diabetes prediction.

DOI: 10.4018/978-1-6684-7100-5.ch014

INTRODUCTION

Diabetes is a chronic disease that affects millions of people worldwide and is characterized by elevated blood sugar levels that can lead to various health complications. The two most common types of diabetes are type 1 and type 2 (Eizirik et al., 2020). Insulin-producing pancreatic cells are attacked and eliminated by the immune system in type 1 diabetes, an autoimmune condition. Type 2 diabetes, on the other hand, is marked by insulin resistance or inadequate insulin production to maintain normal blood sugar levels. The sequencing of DNA is a powerful tool that allows scientists to investigate the genetic basis of numerous diseases, such as diabetes. Researchers can identify genetic variants associated with an increased risk of developing type 2 diabetes by analyzing DNA sequences (Jurgens et al., 2020). The identification of these genetic markers could assist healthcare professionals in devising more individualized treatment plans for diabetic patients and in preventing the onset of diabetes in those at risk.

PREDICTING TYPE 2 DIABETES

Important for early intervention and disease prevention is the ability to predict type 2 diabetes. By identifying individuals at risk for developing type 2 diabetes, healthcare professionals can provide targeted interventions, such as lifestyle modifications or medication, to prevent or better manage the disease. Alterations in the insulin gene sequence can contribute to the development of type 2 diabetes, making the sequencing of insulin DNA a crucial component of predicting type 2 diabetes (Batista et al, 2020). Understanding the genetic basis of type 2 diabetes can lead to more effective interventions and therapies.

Predicting Type 2 Diabetes Using Insulin DNA Sequence

Multiple methods exist in which Python can contribute to research on predicting type 2 diabetes using insulin DNA sequences.

- **Data Administration and Analysis:** NumPy, Pandas, and Scikit-learn are Python libraries that can preprocess and analyze DNA sequence data. These libraries provide data manipulation, purification, analysis functions, and methods essential for predicting type 2 diabetes based on the insulin DNA sequence (Li et al., 2023).
- **Automatic Learning:** Python has become the most popular programming language for machine learning and artificial intelligence research due to

its simplicity and easy learning syntax. Using Python's machine learning libraries like Scikit-learn, TensorFlow, and Keras, it is possible to develop predictive models for identifying DNA markers that could be used to predict type 2 diabetes (Li et al., 2021).

- Visualization The powerful visualization libraries of Python, such as Matplotlib and Seaborn, can facilitate data visualization, such as DNA sequence data. With visualization, researchers can better comprehend and investigate the relationship between the numerous DNA sequences and type 2 diabetes.

- Integration with other tools Python is easily compatible with standard bioinformatics tools for DNA sequence analysis, such as BLAST, EMBOSS, and ClustalW. These tools can be used to compare the DNA sequence data for insulin with other DNA sequences in a database to identify similarities and differences that could aid in predicting type 2 diabetes (Rather et al., 2023).

Python provides data analysis, machine learning, visualization, and integration with other bioinformatics tools, thereby playing a crucial role in research on predicting type 2 diabetes based on the insulin DNA sequence.

THE MAIN OBJECTIVES OF THE RESEARCH

This chapter's primary objective is to study the existing machine-learning model that classifies the DNA sequence of the insulin gene to identify type 2 diabetes based on gene sequence transformation. This study will evaluate this machine-learning model's effectiveness compared to other extant models. In addition, the initiative endeavors to identify unique insulin gene variants that contribute to the prognosis of diabetes. In addition, the associated risk factors will be investigated. The study will highlight Python's role in facilitating this research and demonstrate its value as a tool for predicting type 2 diabetes based on the insulin DNA sequence.

Python is an integral component of each phase of this methodology.

- **Input:** Python can retrieve the DNA sequence for the insulin gene from Genebank using Biopython libraries.
- Python can handle one-hot encoding of DNA sequences, representing the DNA sequence as a binary code to make it compatible with machine learning algorithms.
- Python can divide data into train and test sets, a model training and evaluation requirement.

- **Model-Construction:** Using the training set, Python's machine learning libraries, such as Scikit-learn and Keras, can be used to construct the model (Liu, 2020).
- Python can be used to evaluate the model's performance in predicting type 2 diabetes and validate the model using metrics such as precision, recall, F1 score, and accuracy. Additionally, it can be used to visualize results with the Matplotlib and Seaborn libraries.
- The adaptability and functionality of Python make it an indispensable tool for each phase of this methodology.

THE ROLE OF PYTHON

Python is a popular programming language in various scientific fields, including genomics and bioinformatics. NumPy, Pandas, and Scikit-learn are just a few of Python's libraries for data manipulation, analysis, and machine learning. In addition, visualization tools such as Matplotlib and Seaborn can aid researchers in analyzing and comprehending the relationship between different DNA sequences and type 2 diabetes. The straightforward incorporation of Python with other bioinformatics tools, such as BLAST, EMBOSS, and ClustalW, enables the identification of DNA markers that may aid in predicting type 2 diabetes. Python's adaptability and functionality make it a valuable resource for scientists studying insulin DNA sequences and type 2 diabetes prediction.

Python Libraries for Data Handling, Analysis, and Machine Learning

Due to its extensive libraries that provide data manipulation, analysis, and visualization tools, Python is now the preferred language for data analysis and machine learning. This article concentrates on NumPy, Pandas, and Scikit-learn, the three most commonly used Python libraries for data manipulation, research, and machine learning. In the context of type 2 diabetes prediction based on the insulin DNA sequence, these Python libraries are indispensable for managing and manipulating DNA sequence data and constructing and evaluating predictive models. NumPy and Pandas are useful for preprocessing and analyzing DNA sequence data, whereas Scikit-learn helps build predictive models. Python and its libraries provide a robust and adaptable environment for analyzing and predicting complex biological data.

NumPy

NumPy (Numerical Python) is a Python library for scientific computing. It supports enormous multidimensional arrays and matrices and has a vast library of mathematical functions that operate on these arrays. Numerous other Python scientific libraries, including Pandas and Scikit-learn, significantly rely on NumPy. NumPy is a handy tool for manipulating and managing numerical data. Array-oriented programming simplifies the composition and execution of complex algorithms. NumPy also offers tools for linear algebra, Fourier transforms, and random number generation (Yalçın, 2021).

Pandas

Pandas is a Python data manipulation and analysis utility. It provides tools for reading and writing data in CSV, Excel, SQL databases, and JSON formats. Pandas is based on NumPy and offers the DataFrame object, a table-like data structure with rows and columns. Pandas provides tools for data purification, integration, filtering, and aggregation. Additionally, it offers robust data exploration and comprehension tools through its visualization capabilities. Pandas is particularly useful for working with time-series data because it allows for tools for resampling, time shifting, and window rotation (Betancourt, R. et al., 2019).

Scikit-Learn

Scikit-learn is a Python library for machine learning. It includes supervised and unsupervised learning techniques, data preprocessing, and model evaluation (Hao, J. et al., 2019). Scikit-learn is built upon NumPy and provides a standard API for working with different machine-learning algorithms. Scikit-learn includes classification, regression, clustering, dimensionality reduction, and model selection software. In addition, it provides tools for feature selection, extraction, model evaluation, and validation. Scikit-learn is especially useful for developing predictive models, as it allows for an extensive selection of machine learning algorithms and optimization tools.

VISUALIZATION TOOLS

Using Python's extensive library of visualization tools, DNA sequences associated with type 2 diabetes can be analyzed and comprehended. Matplotlib and Seaborn are well-known libraries that provide various visualization tools, including line charts, scatter plots, bar charts, and heatmaps. Using these tools, researchers can better understand the genetic factors contributing to type 2 diabetes and develop more effective treatments. As bioinformatics continues to develop, the significance of visualization tools for analyzing and understanding DNA sequences increases. Python offers vast libraries for data visualization, analysis, and interpretation. This article examines how two popular libraries, Matplotlib and Seaborn, can be utilized to comprehend the DNA sequences associated with type 2 diabetes.

Matplotlib

Matplotlib is a popular Python library for creating static, interactive, and animated plots. It provides, among other visualizations, line charts, scatter graphs, bar charts, and heatmaps (Klasen et al., 2023). Matplotlib can be used to visualize DNA sequences and identify patterns and anomalies. A scatter plot, for instance, can be used to depict the distribution of nucleotides in a DNA sequence. A line chart can be used to illustrate the evolution of the nucleotide sequence over time or to compare different DNA sequences. Heatmaps can depict associations between other nucleotides and their propensity to induce type 2 diabetes.

Seaborn

Seaborn is a Matplotlib-based Python library for data visualization that offers a high-level interface for creating informative and aesthetically appealing statistical visualizations (DSouza et al., 2020). Seaborn is notably useful for examining the relationships between variables and visualizing DNA sequence data. Seaborn can be utilized, for example, to visualize the distribution of different nucleotides in the DNA sequence and identify patterns indicative of type 2 diabetes. Seaborn can also generate heatmaps illustrating the associations between various nucleotides in the DNA sequence and the likelihood of developing type 2 diabetes.

ALGORITHMS IN PYTHON

This chapter examines five distinct machine learning approaches and how they could be used to predict type 2 diabetes using the insulin DNA sequence. In this context, the different algorithms are investigated convolutional neural networks, decision trees, random forests, logistic regression, and k-nearest neighbours. Decision tree classifiers can pinpoint the most important genetic factors associated with diabetes risk, unlike logistic regression, which may detect genetic markers and provide a prediction model for risk assessment. To improve predicted accuracy, the ensemble learning method known as random forest combines the predictions of several decision trees. Convolutional neural networks may extract pertinent traits from DNA sequence data to predict the likelihood of developing diabetes, unlike K-nearest neighbors, which may categorize people's DNA sequences into diabetic or non-diabetic groups based on similarity.

Logistic Regression

Logistic regression is a standard statistical technique for predicting results from a collection of independent variables or predictors. Logistic regression may be used to determine the relationship between the DNA sequence and a person's chance of acquiring diabetes when predicting type 2 diabetes using the insulin DNA sequence (Klarin et al., 2019). The existence or absence of type 2 diabetes would result from the dependent variable in this situation, while the insulin DNA sequence would be the predictor variable. To establish a prediction model for future occurrences, logistic regression may be performed to determine if specific DNA sequence changes or areas are linked to a greater risk of acquiring diabetes.

By looking at several measures like accuracy, precision, and recall, logistic regression may also be used to assess the model's efficacy. These criteria may be used to assess the model's propensity for prediction and clinical utility. Overall, by assisting in identifying pertinent genetic markers and developing a predictive model for risk assessment, logistic regression may significantly contribute to the prediction of type 2 diabetes by utilizing the insulin DNA sequence.

Decision Tree Classifier

Decision tree classifier, another well-liked machine learning method, uses the insulin DNA sequence as a predictor (Malik et al., 2022). A decision tree is a visual depiction of a collection of decision rules and their results. By using a variety of inputs, such as information on the insulin DNA sequence, the decision tree may be used to predict a person's chance of acquiring diabetes. The most significant traits or genetic variables linked to a higher risk of acquiring diabetes may be found using the decision tree classifier. It could be possible to comprehend the hereditary causes of diabetes by pointing forth potential points of intervention.

A prediction model that divides incoming instances into groups related to or unrelated to diabetes may be developed using the decision tree classifier. The right drugs may be given to patients with a high risk of acquiring diabetes by identifying them. Decision tree classifiers may also be used to calculate accuracy, precision, and recall metrics to assess the model's efficacy. These criteria may be used to assess the model's propensity for prediction and clinical utility. By selecting significant genetic markers, developing a predictive model, and assessing the model's performance, the decision tree classifier may significantly predict type 2 diabetes by utilizing insulin DNA sequence data.

Random Forest

Random forest is a machine-learning technique that may be used for classification and regression issues (Feng et al., 2021). It is a kind of ensemble learning approach that incorporates several decision trees to improve the model's predictive accuracy. The forecasts of all the individual decision trees, each trained using a random sample of the data and attributes, are combined to create the final forecast.

In the context of disease prediction using the Insulin DNA sequence, the Random forest may be utilized to find important DNA sequence characteristics linked to Type 2 Diabetes. The algorithm may be trained on a dataset including the DNA sequences of persons with and without Type 2 Diabetes and other relevant clinical data. A set of traits in the DNA sequence may point to the existence or absence of a particular mutation or variant. The Random Forest approach may then be used to identify the primary symptoms of the condition, and based on a patient's DNA sequence, it is possible to predict if they are likely to develop Type 2 Diabetes. This knowledge may be used to develop customized treatment plans for those more likely to get the ailment. Random forests are typically helpful in identifying relevant components in challenging datasets and may be used in various applications, including the analysis of genetic data and medical diagnostics.

K-Nearest Neighbours (K-NN)

Machine learning techniques like the K-NN algorithm are used for classification and regression analysis (Mezquita et al., 2021). It is often used for predictive modeling in many disciplines, including biology and genetics. The K-NN technique may be used to categorize an individual's DNA sequence as either belonging to a diabetic or non-diabetic group based on the similarity of their DNA sequence to other known DNA sequences in the context of predicting Type 2 Diabetes using insulin DNA sequence. The first step is to gather a large dataset of DNA sequences from people who are either diabetic or not to employ the k-NN technique for this. The next step would be to identify relevant qualities from these DNA sequences that may be used to predict the chance of acquiring diabetes.

The K-NN approach trains a model on the dataset after collecting features. The method locates a new DNA sequence's K-Nearest neighbors in the dataset and then utilizes the neighbors' class labels to predict the class label for the new sequence. When determining the value of k, the size of the dataset and the needed degree of precision are often considered. The K-NN algorithm may, in general, be a valuable tool for predicting the likelihood of developing Type 2 Diabetes based on knowledge of the insulin DNA sequence. However, it is essential to remember that the accuracy of the predictions will depend on the quality and volume of the dataset, the features used, and the value of k.

Convolutional Neural Networks (CNNs)

CNNs, a deep learning technique, are often employed in image recognition and classification applications (Alzubaidi et al., 2021). However, they may also be utilized in other domains, including bioinformatics, to predict outcomes based on DNA sequence data.

In order to predict Type 2 Diabetes using the insulin DNA sequence, CNNs may be utilized to extract relevant traits from DNA sequence data. Using a CNN, the system may automatically find connections and patterns in DNA sequence data that would not be apparent to the human eye. The DNA sequence data may be represented as a one-dimensional sequence of nucleotides (A, C, G, and T) as an input to the CNN. The CNN will next employ convolutional and pooling layers to extract features from the sequence data. Fully connected layers may further analyze these data to provide a forecast of the presence or absence of type 2 diabetes.

Overall, CNNs may help improve the accuracy of predictions generated using insulin DNA sequence data to predict Type 2 Diabetes by spotting important patterns and links in the data that may not be immediately obvious using traditional methodologies.

Long Short-Term Memory (LSTM)

Finding patterns and correlations in sequential data is a task that is especially well suited to recurrent neural networks (RNNs), specifically LSTM. LSTM algorithms may analyze the sequential data and provide predictions for Type 2 Diabetes based on insulin DNA sequence data analysis. When dealing with sequential data, such as DNA sequences, LSTMs can potentially develop long-term dependencies. DNA sequences may have significant patterns or links spread across the sequence at various locations. They are often relatively lengthy and complex. These tendencies may be recognized by LSTMs, which can then be utilized to make precise forecasts (Sansano et al., 2020).

The insulin DNA sequence may be seen as a time series using the information it contains, with each point in the sequence denoting a different time step. The patterns and connections it discovers in the sequential data may then be used to train the LSTM to predict whether or not a person has Type 2 Diabetes. The ability of an

LSTM technique to capture correlations and patterns over many time steps may be pretty helpful for investigating lengthy DNA sequences. Additionally, LSTMs can make predictions even in the presence of missing data, which often happens with data from DNA sequencing. Overall, by efficiently gathering patterns and correlations throughout the whole sequence of DNA data, the application of LSTM algorithms in predicting Type 2 Diabetes utilizing insulin DNA sequence data may assist in improving prediction accuracy.

BIOINFORMATICS TOOLS

Because of its flexibility and versatility, Python is the ideal programming language for integrating various bioinformatics tools to identify DNA markers associated with type 2 diabetes. This section will explain the three well-known bioinformatics software BLAST, EMBOSS, and ClustalW, and how they may be used with Python to find DNA markers (Lo, 2023).

BLAST

A bioinformatics method known as BLAST (Basic Local Alignment Search Technique) compares DNA sequences. The most comparable sequences are shown when a query sequence is compared to a database of known DNA sequences. Users may utilize BLAST capability inside Python by using one of the many Python libraries that includes a BLAST module, such as Biopython. It is feasible to compare and contrast the insulin DNA sequences of people with and without type 2 diabetes using BLAST, which one day might be used as DNA markers for the condition. Researchers may quickly analyze and compare enormous DNA sequence databases by combining Python with BLAST.

EMBOSS

A package of bioinformatics tools called EMBOSS is utilized for molecular biology tasks, including protein and sequence analysis. Among the more than 200 tools EMBOSS offers are sequence alignment, protein structure prediction, and sequence editing. Users may access EMBOSS capabilities from Python using the PyEMBOSS module for EMBOSS. In the context of predicting type 2 diabetes, EMBOSS may be used to evaluate insulin DNA sequences and identify any alterations or mutations that may potentially serve as DNA markers for the disease. By integrating Python with EMBOSS, researchers may speed up and increase the effectiveness of DNA sequence analysis.

ClustalW

ClustalW, a bioinformatics technique, may align multiple DNA or protein sequences. A multiple sequence alignment is produced by comparing sequences and identifying similarities and differences, which may be used to examine genetic linkages. The language supports the Biopython module of Python, which may be used to access ClustalW's functionality. ClustalW may be used to compare the insulin DNA sequences of people with and without type 2 diabetes to find similarities and differences that potentially act as DNA markers for the condition. Researchers can quickly compare and analyze enormous DNA sequence datasets using Python and ClustalW, making it simpler to find DNA markers for type 2 diabetes.

CONCLUSION

Python's ability to differentiate specific gene changes and risk variables makes it a helpful tool for forecasting diseases, notably type 2 diabetes. Through statistical analysis and machine learning algorithms, researchers may develop exact models for predicting the chance of developing diabetes and for producing customized medications. Python is the best programming language for integrating with several bioinformatics tools, such as BLAST, EMBOSS, and ClustalW, to swiftly analyze and compare huge DNA sequence datasets in search of DNA markers connected to type 2 diabetes. This insight may make the development of more potent treatments and drugs possible. To predict a patient's chance of getting type 2 diabetes, machine learning models created using Scikit-learn, TensorFlow, and Keras, three of the machine learning libraries available with Python, may be utilized. These models are based on the insulin DNA sequences. Additionally, by analyzing and displaying data using Python tools like Seaborn and Matplotlib, researchers may find patterns in patient data and improve the accuracy of the machine-learning model.

REFERENCES

Alzubaidi, L., Zhang, J., Humaidi, A. J., Al-Dujaili, A., Duan, Y., Al-Shamma, O., Santamaría, J., Fadhel, M. A., Al-Amidie, M., & Farhan, L. (2021). Review of deep learning: Concepts, CNN architectures, challenges, applications, future directions. *Journal of Big Data*, 8(1), 1–74. doi:10.118640537-021-00444-8 PMID:33816053

Batista, T. M., Jayavelu, A. K., Albrechtsen, N. J. W., Iovino, S., Lebastchi, J., Pan, H., ... Kahn, C. R. (2020). A cell-autonomous signature of dysregulated protein phosphorylation underlies muscle insulin resistance in type 2 diabetes. *Cell Metabolism*, *32*(5), 844–859. doi:10.1016/j.cmet.2020.08.007 PMID:32888406

Eizirik, D. L., Pasquali, L., & Cnop, M. (2020). Pancreatic β-cells in type 1 and type 2 diabetes mellitus: Different pathways to failure. *Nature Reviews. Endocrinology*, *16*(7), 349–362. doi:10.103841574-020-0355-7 PMID:32398822

Hao, J., & Ho, T. K. (2019). Machine learning made easy: A review of scikit-learn package in python programming language. *Journal of Educational and Behavioral Statistics*, *44*(3), 348–361. doi:10.3102/1076998619832248

Jurgens, S. J., Choi, S. H., Morrill, V. N., Chaffin, M., Pirruccello, J. P., Halford, J. L., Weng, L.-C., Nauffal, V., Roselli, C., Hall, A. W., Oetjens, M. T., Lagerman, B., vanMaanen, D. P., Abecasis, G., Bai, X., Balasubramanian, S., Baras, A., Beechert, C., Boutkov, B., ... Ellinor, P. T. (2022). Analysis of rare genetic variation underlying cardiometabolic diseases and traits among 200,000 individuals in the UK Biobank. *Nature Genetics*, *54*(3), 240–250. doi:10.103841588-021-01011-w PMID:35177841

Klarin, D., Lynch, J., Aragam, K., Chaffin, M., Assimes, T. L., Huang, J., Lee, K. M., Shao, Q., Huffman, J. E., Natarajan, P., Arya, S., Small, A., Sun, Y. V., Vujkovic, M., Freiberg, M. S., Wang, L., Chen, J., Saleheen, D., Lee, J. S., ... Damrauer, S. M. (2019). Genome-wide association study of peripheral artery disease in the Million Veteran Program. *Nature Medicine*, *25*(8), 1274–1279. doi:10.103841591-019-0492-5 PMID:31285632

Klasen, V., Bogucka, E. P., Meng, L., & Krisp, J. M. (2023). How we see time–the evolution and current state of visualizations of temporal data. *International Journal of Cartography*, 1-18. 10.1080/23729333.2022.2156316

Li, J., Chen, Q., Hu, X., Yuan, P., Cui, L., Tu, L., Cui, J., Huang, J., Jiang, T., Ma, X., Yao, X., Zhou, C., Lu, H., & Xu, J. (2021). Establishment of noninvasive diabetes risk prediction model based on tongue features and machine learning techniques. *International Journal of Medical Informatics*, *149*, 104429. doi:10.1016/j.ijmedinf.2021.104429 PMID:33647600

Li, X., Zhang, Y., Leung, J., Sun, C., & Zhao, J. (2023). EDAssistant: Supporting Exploratory Data Analysis in Computational Notebooks with In Situ Code Search and Recommendation. *ACM Transactions on Interactive Intelligent Systems*, *13*(1), 1–27. doi:10.1145/3545995

Liu, Y. H. (2020). *Python Machine Learning By Example: Build intelligent systems using Python, TensorFlow 2, PyTorch, and scikit-learn*. Packt Publishing Ltd.

Lo, Y. T. (2023). Bioinformatics for DNA Sequencing Data Analysis. In Authentication of Chinese Medicinal Materials by DNA Technology: Techniques and Applications (pp. 89-125). Academic Press.

Malik, M., Kaushik, A., & Khatana, R. (2022). Classification-Based Prediction Techniques Using ML: A Perspective for Health Care. In *Data Science for Effective Healthcare Systems* (pp. 43-56). Chapman and Hall/CRC.

Mezquita, Y., Alonso, R. S., Casado-Vara, R., Prieto, J., & Corchado, J. M. (2021). A review of k-nn algorithm based on classical and quantum machine learning. In *Distributed Computing and Artificial Intelligence, Special Sessions, 17th International Conference* (pp. 189-198). Springer International Publishing. 10.1007/978-3-030-53829-3_20

Rather, M. A., Agarwal, D., Bhat, T. A., Khan, I. A., Zafar, I., Kumar, S., Amin, A., Sundaray, J. K., & Qadri, T. (2023). Bioinformatics approaches and big data analytics opportunities in improving fisheries and aquaculture. *International Journal of Biological Macromolecules, 233*, 123549. doi:10.1016/j.ijbiomac.2023.123549 PMID:36740117

Sansano, E., Montoliu, R., & Belmonte Fernandez, O. (2020). A study of deep neural networks for human activity recognition. *Computational Intelligence, 36*(3), 1113–1139. doi:10.1111/coin.12318

Yalçın, O. G. (2021). Complementary Libraries to TensorFlow 2.x. *Applied Neural Networks with TensorFlow 2: API Oriented Deep Learning with Python*, 81-94.

Compilation of References

Abdalkafor, A. S., & Aliesawi, S. A. (2022, October). Data aggregation techniques in wireless sensors networks (WSNs): Taxonomy and an accurate literature survey. In AIP Conference Proceedings (Vol. 2400, No. 1, p. 020012). AIP Publishing LLC.

Abdulzahra, A. M. K., Al-Qurabat, A. K. M., & Abdulzahra, S. A. (2023). Optimizing energy consumption in WSN-based IoT using unequal clustering and sleep scheduling methods. *Internet of Things*, *22*, 100765. doi:10.1016/j.iot.2023.100765

Abu-Baker, A., Shakhatreh, H., Sawalmeh, A., & Alenezi, A. H. (2023). Efficient Data Collection in UAV-Assisted Cluster-Based Wireless Sensor Networks for 3D Environment: Optimization Study. *Journal of Sensors*, *2023*, 2023. doi:10.1155/2023/9513868

Adams, B., Baller, D., Jonas, B., Joseph, A. C., & Cummiskey, K. (2021). Computational skills for multivariable thinking in introductory statistics. *Journal of Statistics and Data Science Education, 29*(sup1), S123-S131.

Agathiya Raja, G. K. (2022). *Introduction To Python for Social Network Analysis*. Wiley Online Library.

Aggarwal, S., & Kumar, N. (2021). History of blockchain-blockchain 1.0: Currency. *Advances in Computers*, *121*, 147–169.

Ahmed, T., Alam, M. A., Paul, R. R., Hasan, M. T., & Rab, R. (2022, February). Machine Learning and Deep Learning Techniques For Genre Classification of Bangla Music. In *2022 International Conference on Advancement in Electrical and Electronic Engineering (ICAEEE)* (pp. 1-6). IEEE. 10.1109/ICAEEE54957.2022.9836434

Akbar, I., Hashem, T., Yaqoob, I., Anuar, N.B., Mokhtar, S., Gani, A., & Khan, S.A. (2015). The rise of "big data" on cloud computing: review and open research issues. *Inf Syst.*, *47*, 98–115.

Alammar, J. (2022). *NumPy: the absolute basics for beginners*. Retrieved 10 25, 25, from http://jalammar.github.io/

Albenis Pérez-Alarcón, J. C.-A. (2021). *Alarconpy: a Python Package for Meteorologists*.

Alcoz, A. G., Dietmüller, A., & Vanbever, L. (2020, February). SP-PIFO: Approximating Push-In First-Out Behaviors using Strict-Priority Queues. In NSDI (pp. 59-76). Academic Press.

Alghamdi, M. M. M., Dahab, M. Y. H., & Alazwary, N. H. A. (2023). Enhancing deep learning techniques for the diagnosis of the novel coronavirus (COVID-19) using X-ray images. *Cogent Engineering*, *10*(1). doi:10.1080/23311916.2023.2181917

Almadhoun, E., & Parham-Mocello, J. (2023). Students' difficulties with inserting and deleting nodes in a singly linked list in the C programming language. *Journal of Computer Languages*, *74*, 101184. doi:10.1016/j.cola.2022.101184

Alzubaidi, L., Zhang, J., Humaidi, A. J., Al-Dujaili, A., Duan, Y., Al-Shamma, O., Santamaría, J., Fadhel, M. A., Al-Amidie, M., & Farhan, L. (2021). Review of deep learning: Concepts, CNN architectures, challenges, applications, future directions. *Journal of Big Data*, *8*(1), 1–74. doi:10.118640537-021-00444-8 PMID:33816053

Arslan, B. (2022). *Search and Sort Algorithms for Big Data Structures*. Academic Press.

Arulkumar, N., Paulose, J., Galety, M. G., Manimaran, A., Saravanan, S., & Saleem, R. A. (2022). Exploring Social Networking Data Sets. *Social Network Analysis: Theory and Applications*, 205-228.

Ateeq, M., & Afzal, M. K. (2023). 10 Programming Languages, Tools, and Techniques. *Data-Driven Intelligence in Wireless Networks: Concepts, Solutions, and Applications*, 237.

Baka, B. (2017). *Python Data Structures and Algorithms*. Packt Publishing Ltd.

Bandopadhyay, S., & Shang, H. (2022). SADHANA: A Doubly Linked List-based Multidimensional Adaptive Mesh Refinement Framework for Solving Hyperbolic Conservation Laws with Application to Astrophysical Hydrodynamics and Magnetohydrodynamics. *The Astrophysical Journal. Supplement Series*, *263*(2), 32. doi:10.3847/1538-4365/ac9279

Batista, T. M., Jayavelu, A. K., Albrechtsen, N. J. W., Iovino, S., Lebastchi, J., Pan, H., ... Kahn, C. R. (2020). A cell-autonomous signature of dysregulated protein phosphorylation underlies muscle insulin resistance in type 2 diabetes. *Cell Metabolism*, *32*(5), 844–859. doi:10.1016/j.cmet.2020.08.007 PMID:32888406

Bellogín, A., Cantador, I., Díez, F., Castells, P., & Chavarriaga, E. (2013). An empirical comparison of social, collaborative filtering, and hybrid recommenders. *ACM Transactions on Intelligent Systems and Technology*, *4*(1), 1–37. doi:10.1145/2414425.2414439

Beri, R. (2019). *Python Made Simple: Learn Python programming in easy steps with examples*. Bpb Publications.

Besta, M., Peter, E., Gerstenberger, R., Fischer, M., Podstawski, M., Barthels, C., . . . Hoefler, T. (2019). *Demystifying graph databases: Analysis and taxonomy of data organization, system designs, and graph queries*. arXiv preprint arXiv:1910.09017.

Beyer & Laney. (2012). *The importance of "big data": A definition*. Gartner, Tech. Rep.

Bharany, S., Sharma, S., Badotra, S., Khalaf, O. I., Alotaibi, Y., Alghamdi, S., & Alassery, F. (2021). Energy-efficient clustering scheme for flying ad-hoc networks using an optimized LEACH protocol. *Energies*, *14*(19), 6016. doi:10.3390/en14196016

Bhardwaj, S., & Dash, S. K. (2015). VDMR-DBSCAN: varied density Mapreduce DBSCAN. *International conference on Big Data analytics*. 10.1007/978-3-319-27057-9_10

Bisong, E. (2019). Matplotlib and seaborn. *Building Machine Learning and Deep Learning Models on Google Cloud Platform: A Comprehensive Guide for Beginners*, 151-165.

Bisong, E. (2019). Python. *Building Machine Learning and Deep Learning Models on Google Cloud Platform: A Comprehensive Guide for Beginners*, 71-89.

Boockmann, J. H., & Lüttgen, G. (2020, May). Learning Data Structure Shapes from Memory Graphs. LPAR.

Borah, B., & Bhattacharyya, D. K. (2008). DDSC: A density differentiated spatial clustering technique. *Journal of Computers*, *3*(2), 72–79. doi:10.4304/jcp.3.2.72-79

Bria, R., Wahab, A., & Alaydrus, M. (2019, October). Energy efficiency analysis of TEEN routing protocol with isolated nodes. In *2019 Fourth International Conference on Informatics and Computing (ICIC)* (pp. 1-5). IEEE. 10.1109/ICIC47613.2019.8985668

Buckley, I. A., & Buckley, W. S. (2017). Teaching software testing using data structures. *International Journal of Advanced Computer Science and Applications*, *8*(4).

Carullo, G. (2020). Data Structures. *Implementing Effective Code Reviews: How to Build and Maintain Clean Code*, 27-42.

Chauhan, V., & Soni, S. (2021). Energy aware unequal clustering algorithm with multi-hop routing via low degree relay nodes for wireless sensor networks. *Journal of Ambient Intelligence and Humanized Computing*, *12*(2), 2469–2482. doi:10.100712652-020-02385-1

Chemmalar Selvi, G., & Lakshmi Priya, G. G. (2020). An Epidemic Analysis of COVID-19 using Exploratory Data Analysis Approach. *Predictive Analytics Using Statistics and Big Data: Concepts and Modeling*, 99.

Chen, L., Bentley, P., Mori, K., Misawa, K., Fujiwara, M., & Rueckert, D. (2019). Self-supervised learning for medical image analysis using image context restoration. *Medical Image Analysis*, *58*, 101539. doi:10.1016/j.media.2019.101539 PMID:31374449

Chen, S., Zhang, L., Tang, Y., Shen, C., Kumar, R., Yu, K., Tariq, U., & Bashir, A. K. (2020). Indoor temperature monitoring using wireless sensor networks: A SMAC application in smart cities. *Sustainable Cities and Society*, *61*, 102333. doi:10.1016/j.scs.2020.102333

Chen, Z., Wang, Y., Zhao, B., Cheng, J., Zhao, X., & Duan, Z. (2020). Knowledge graph completion: A review. *IEEE Access : Practical Innovations, Open Solutions*, *8*, 192435–192456. doi:10.1109/ACCESS.2020.3030076

Cho, K., Kim, K. D., Nam, Y., Jeong, J., Kim, J., Choi, C., Lee, S., Lee, J. S., Woo, S., Hong, G.-S., Seo, J. B., & Kim, N. (2023). CheSS: Chest X-Ray Pre-trained Model via Self-supervised Contrastive Learning. *Journal of Digital Imaging*, 1–9. doi:10.100710278-023-00782-4 PMID:36702988

Cooksey, R. W. (2020). Descriptive statistics for summarising data. *Illustrating statistical procedures: Finding meaning in quantitative data*, 61-139.

Critien, J. V., Gatt, A., & Ellul, J. (2022). Bitcoin price change and trend prediction through twitter sentiment and data volume. *Financial Innovation*, *8*(1), 1–20.

Daanoune, I., Abdennaceur, B., & Ballouk, A. (2021). A comprehensive survey on LEACH-based clustering routing protocols in Wireless Sensor Networks. *Ad Hoc Networks*, *114*, 102409. doi:10.1016/j.adhoc.2020.102409

Dai, B. R., & Lin, I.-C. (2012). Efficient Map/Reduce-based DBSCAN algorithm with optimized data partition. *Fifth International Conference on Cloud Computing*.

de Aguiar Neto, F. S., da Costa, A. F., Manzato, M. G., & Campello, R. J. (2020). Pre-processing approaches for collaborative filtering based on hierarchical clustering. *Information Sciences*, *534*, 172–191. doi:10.1016/j.ins.2020.05.021

Decker, C., Seidel, J., & Wattenhofer, R. (2016, January). Bitcoin meets strong consistency. In *Proceedings of the 17th International Conference on Distributed Computing and Networking* (pp. 1-10). Academic Press.

Denis, D. J. (2020). *Univariate, bivariate, and multivariate statistics using R: quantitative tools for data analysis and data science*. John Wiley & Sons. doi:10.1002/9781119549963

Domkin, V. (2021). Linked Lists. *Programming Algorithms in Lisp: Writing Efficient Programs with Examples in ANSI Common Lisp*, 75-99.

Duan, L., Xu, L., Guo, F., Lee, J., & Yan, B. (2007). A local-density based spatial clustering algorithm with noise. *Information Systems*, *32*(7), 978–986. doi:10.1016/j.is.2006.10.006

Dubois, P. F., Hinsen, K., & Hugunin, J. (1996). Numerical Python. *Computers in Physics*, *10*(3), 262–267. doi:10.1063/1.4822400

Dugard, P., Todman, J., & Staines, H. (2022). *Approaching multivariate analysis: A practical introduction*. Taylor & Francis. doi:10.4324/9781003343097

Dutta, S., Chowdhury, A., Debnath, I., Sarkar, R., Dey, H., & Dutta, A. (2020). The role of data structures in different fields of computer-science: A review. *Journal of Mathematical Sciences & Computational Mathematics*, *1*(3), 363–373. doi:10.15864/jmscm.1310

Eizirik, D. L., Pasquali, L., & Cnop, M. (2020). Pancreatic β-cells in type 1 and type 2 diabetes mellitus: Different pathways to failure. *Nature Reviews. Endocrinology*, *16*(7), 349–362. doi:10.103841574-020-0355-7 PMID:32398822

Elbatta, M. T., Bolbol, R. M., & Ashur, W. M. (2011). *A vibration method for discovering density varied clusters.* Int Sch Res Not.

Erciyes, K. (2021). *A Short Review of Python. In Algebraic Graph Algorithms.* Springer. doi:10.1007/978-3-030-87886-3

Ester, M., Kriegel, H. P., Sander, J., & Xu, X. (1996). A density-based algorithm for discovering clusters in large spatial databases with noise. In *2nd international conference on knowledge discovery and data mining.* Academic Press.

Gaonkar, M.N., & Sawant, K. (2013). AutoEpsDBSCAN: DBSCAN with Eps automatic for large dataset. *Int J Adv Comput Theory Eng., 2*(2), 2319–526.

Gibbons, P. B., & Matias, Y. (1999, January). Synopsis Data Structures for Massive Data Sets. In SODA (Vol. 10, pp. 909-910). doi:10.1090/dimacs/050/02

Goodrich, M. T., Tamassia, R., & Goldwasser, M. H. (2013). *Data structures and algorithms in Python.* John Wiley & Sons Ltd.

Guttag, J. V. (2021). *Introduction to Computation and Programming Using Python: With Application to Computational Modeling and Understanding Data.* MIT Press.

Guzdial, M., & Ericson, B. (2012, February). Listening to linked lists: Using multimedia to learn data structures. In *Proceedings of the 43rd ACM technical symposium on Computer Science Education* (pp. 663-663). 10.1145/2157136.2157358

Hadoop, W. T. (2009). *The definitive guide.* O'Reilly Media.

Hao, J., & Ho, T. K. (2019). Machine learning made easy: A review of scikit-learn package in python programming language. *Journal of Educational and Behavioral Statistics, 44*(3), 348–361. doi:10.3102/1076998619832248

Harris, C. M. (2020). Array Programming with NumPy. *Nature,* 357–362.

Harris, C. R., Millman, K. J., Van Der Walt, S. J., Gommers, R., Virtanen, P., Cournapeau, D., Wieser, E., Taylor, J., Berg, S., Smith, N. J., Kern, R., Picus, M., Hoyer, S., van Kerkwijk, M. H., Brett, M., Haldane, A., del Río, J. F., Wiebe, M., Peterson, P., ... Oliphant, T. E. (2020). Array programming with NumPy. *Nature, 585*(7825), 357–362. doi:10.103841586-020-2649-2 PMID:32939066

Haslwanter, T. (2016). An Introduction to Statistics with Python. In *With Applications in the Life Sciences.* Springer International Publishing. doi:10.1007/978-3-319-28316-6

Havens, T. C., Bezdek, J. C., Leckie, C., Hall, L. O., & Palaniswami, M. (2012). Fuzzy c-Means Algorithms for Very Large Data. *IEEE Transactions on Fuzzy Systems, 20*(6), 1130–1146. doi:10.1109/TFUZZ.2012.2201485

Hetland, M. L. (2017). *Beginning Python: From novice to professional.* Apress. doi:10.1007/978-1-4842-0028-5

He, Y., Tan, H., Luo, W., Feng, S., & Fan, J. (2014). MR-DBSCAN: A scalable Map Reduce-based DBSCAN algorithm for heavily skewed data. *Frontiers of Computer Science, 8*(1), 83–99. doi:10.100711704-013-3158-3

Hill, C. (2020). *Learning scientific programming with Python.* Cambridge University Press. doi:10.1017/9781108778039

Hunt, J. (2019). ADTs, Queues and Stacks. In *A Beginners Guide to Python 3 Programming* (pp. 407–414). Springer. doi:10.1007/978-3-030-25943-3_34

Inayat, Z., Sajjad, R., Anam, M., Younas, A., & Hussain, M. (2021, November). Analysis of Comparison-Based Sorting Algorithms. In *2021 International Conference on Innovative Computing (ICIC)* (pp. 1-8). IEEE.

Ishwarappa, A. J., & Anuradha, J. (2011). A brief introduction on Big Data 5Vs characteristics and Hadoop technology. *Procedia Computer Science, 48*, 319–324. doi:10.1016/j.procs.2015.04.188

Jaishankar, B., Vishwakarma, S., Mohan, P., Singh Pundir, A. K., Patel, I., & Arulkumar, N. (2022). Blockchain for Securing Healthcare Data Using Squirrel Search Optimization Algorithm. *Intelligent Automation & Soft Computing, 32*(3).

Jamison, M. A., & Tariq, P. (2018). Five things regulators should know about blockchain (and three myths to forget). *The Electricity Journal, 31*(9), 20–23.

Java Tutorial Developers. (2022). Retrieved from NumPy Tutorial: https://www.javatpoint.com/

Johansson, R. (2019). *1. Scientific Computing and Data Science Applications with Numpy, SciPy, and Matplotlib* (2nd ed.). Urayasu-shi.

Johansson, R., & John, S. (2019). *Numerical Python* (Vol. 1). Apress. doi:10.1007/978-1-4842-4246-9

Jondhale, S. R., Maheswar, R., Lloret, J., Jondhale, S. R., Maheswar, R., & Lloret, J. (2022). Fundamentals of wireless sensor networks. *Received Signal Strength Based Target Localization and Tracking Using Wireless Sensor Networks*, 1-19.

Jurgens, S. J., Choi, S. H., Morrill, V. N., Chaffin, M., Pirruccello, J. P., Halford, J. L., Weng, L.-C., Nauffal, V., Roselli, C., Hall, A. W., Oetjens, M. T., Lagerman, B., vanMaanen, D. P., Abecasis, G., Bai, X., Balasubramanian, S., Baras, A., Beechert, C., Boutkov, B., ... Ellinor, P. T. (2022). Analysis of rare genetic variation underlying cardiometabolic diseases and traits among 200,000 individuals in the UK Biobank. *Nature Genetics, 54*(3), 240–250. doi:10.103841588-021-01011-w PMID:35177841

Kannan, S., Dongare, P. A., Garg, R., & Harsoor, S. S. (2019). Describing and displaying numerical and categorical data. *Airway, 2*(2), 64. doi:10.4103/ARWY.ARWY_24_19

Karimov, E. (2020). Linked Lists. *Data Structures and Algorithms in Swift: Implement Stacks, Queues, Dictionaries, and Lists in Your Apps*, 41-54.

Khandare, A., Agarwal, N., Bodhankar, A., Kulkarni, A., & Mane, I. (2023). Analysis of Python Libraries for Artificial Intelligence. In Intelligent Computing and Networking. *Proceedings of IC-ICN, 2022,* 157–177.

Khriji, S., Chéour, R., & Kanoun, O. (2022). Dynamic Voltage and Frequency Scaling and Duty-Cycling for Ultra Low-Power Wireless Sensor Nodes. *Electronics (Basel), 11*(24), 4071. doi:10.3390/electronics11244071

Kim, D. S., Tran-Dang, H., Kim, D. S., & Tran-Dang, H. (2019). Mac protocols for energy-efficient wireless sensor networks. *Industrial Sensors and Controls in Communication Networks: From Wired Technologies to Cloud Computing and the Internet of Things,* 141-159.

Kiran, S. V., Kaur, I., Thangaraj, K., Saveetha, V., Kingsy Grace, R., & Arulkumar, N. (2021). Machine Learning with Data Science-Enabled Lung Cancer Diagnosis and Classification Using Computed Tomography Images. *International Journal of Image and Graphics.*

Klarin, D., Lynch, J., Aragam, K., Chaffin, M., Assimes, T. L., Huang, J., Lee, K. M., Shao, Q., Huffman, J. E., Natarajan, P., Arya, S., Small, A., Sun, Y. V., Vujkovic, M., Freiberg, M. S., Wang, L., Chen, J., Saleheen, D., Lee, J. S., ... Damrauer, S. M. (2019). Genome-wide association study of peripheral artery disease in the Million Veteran Program. *Nature Medicine, 25*(8), 1274–1279. doi:10.103841591-019-0492-5 PMID:31285632

Klasen, V., Bogucka, E. P., Meng, L., & Krisp, J. M. (2023). How we see time–the evolution and current state of visualizations of temporal data. *International Journal of Cartography,* 1-18. 10.1080/23729333.2022.2156316

Kobbaey, T., Xanthidis, D., & Bilquise, G. (2022). Data Structures and Algorithms with Python. In Handbook of Computer Programming with Python (pp. 207-272). Chapman and Hall/CRC. doi:10.1201/9781003139010-6

Kochenderfer, M. J., & Wheeler, T. A. (2019). *Algorithms for optimization.* MIT Press.

Kong, Q., Siauw, T., & Bayen, A. (2020). *Python programming and numerical methods: A guide for engineers and scientists.* Academic Press.

Lafuente, D., Cohen, B., Fiorini, G., García, A. A., Bringas, M., Morzan, E., & Onna, D. (2021). A Gentle introduction to machine learning for chemists: An undergraduate workshop using python notebooks for visualization, data processing, analysis, and modeling. *Journal of Chemical Education, 98*(9), 2892–2898. doi:10.1021/acs.jchemed.1c00142

Larrier, J. H. (2021). A Brief History of Blockchain. *Transforming Scholarly Publishing With Blockchain Technologies and AI,* 85-100.

Learn To Code For IoT With Python Essentials Course. (2022). Networking Academy. https://www.netacad.com/courses/programming/pcap-programming -essentials-python

Li, Z., Li, H., Ralescu, A. L., Dillman, J. R., Parikh, N. A., & He, L. (2023). *A Novel Collaborative Self-Supervised Learning Method for Radiomic Data.* arXiv preprint arXiv:2302.09807.

Liang, H., Yang, S., Li, L., & Gao, J. (2019). Research on routing optimization of WSNs based on improved LEACH protocol. *EURASIP Journal on Wireless Communications and Networking*, *2019*(1), 1–12. doi:10.118613638-019-1509-y

Li, H. H., Du, X. Y., & Tian, X. (2009). A review-based reputation evaluation approach for Web services. *Journal of Computer Science and Technology*, *24*(5), 893–900. doi:10.100711390-009-9280-x

Li, J., Chen, Q., Hu, X., Yuan, P., Cui, L., Tu, L., Cui, J., Huang, J., Jiang, T., Ma, X., Yao, X., Zhou, C., Lu, H., & Xu, J. (2021). Establishment of noninvasive diabetes risk prediction model based on tongue features and machine learning techniques. *International Journal of Medical Informatics*, *149*, 104429. doi:10.1016/j.ijmedinf.2021.104429 PMID:33647600

Liu, P., Zhou, D., & Wu, N. (2007, June). VDBSCAN: varied density based spatial clustering of applications with noise. In *2007 International conference on service systems and service management* (pp. 1-4). IEEE. 10.1109/ICSSSM.2007.4280175

Liu, X., Huang, G., & Mei, H. (2009). Discovering homogeneous web service community in the user-centric web environment. *IEEE Transactions on Services Computing*, *2*(2), 167–181. doi:10.1109/TSC.2009.11

Liu, Y. H. (2020). *Python Machine Learning By Example: Build intelligent systems using Python, TensorFlow 2, PyTorch, and scikit-learn*. Packt Publishing Ltd.

Liu, Z., Li, P., & Zheng, Y. (2009). Clustering to find exemplar terms for keyphrase extraction. *Proc. 2009 Conf. on Empirical Methods in Natural Language Processing*, 257-266. 10.3115/1699510.1699544

Li, X., Zhang, Y., Leung, J., Sun, C., & Zhao, J. (2023). EDAssistant: Supporting Exploratory Data Analysis in Computational Notebooks with In Situ Code Search and Recommendation. *ACM Transactions on Interactive Intelligent Systems*, *13*(1), 1–27. doi:10.1145/3545995

Lo, Y. T. (2023). Bioinformatics for DNA Sequencing Data Analysis. In Authentication of Chinese Medicinal Materials by DNA Technology: Techniques and Applications (pp. 89-125). Academic Press.

Lutz, M. (2013). *Learning Python: Powerful object-oriented programming*. O'Reilly Media, Inc.

Mahran, S., & Mahar, K. (2008). Using grid for accelerating density-based clustering. CIT 2008 IEEE international conference. doi:10.1109/CIT.2008.4594646

Maiti, M., Vyklyuk, Y., & Vuković, D. (2020). Cryptocurrencies chaotic co-movement forecasting with neural networks. *Internet Technology Letters*, *3*(3), e157.

Malik, M., Kaushik, A., & Khatana, R. (2022). Classification-Based Prediction Techniques Using ML: A Perspective for Health Care. In *Data Science for Effective Healthcare Systems* (pp. 43-56). Chapman and Hall/CRC.

Martelli, A. (2006). *Python in a Nutshell*. O'Reilly Media, Inc.

Massias, H., Avila, X. S., & Quisquarter, J. J. (1999). Design of a secure timestamping service with minimal trust requirement. In *Symposium on Information theory in the Benelux* (pp. 79-86). Werkgemeenschap voor Informatie-en Communicatietheorie.

McKinney. (2022). *Python for Data Analysis*. O'Reilly Media, Inc.

McKinney, W. (2010, June). Data structures for statistical computing in Python. In *Proceedings of the 9th Python in Science Conference* (Vol. 445, No. 1, pp. 51-56). 10.25080/Majora-92bf1922-00a

McKinney, W. (2012). NumPy Basics:Arrays and Vectorized Computation. In *W. McKinney, Python for Data Analysis*. O'Reilly Media, Inc.

Medjedovic, D., & Tahirovic, E. (2022). *Algorithms and data structures for massive datasets*. Simon and Schuster.

Mehlhorn, K. (2013). *Data structures and algorithms 1: Sorting and searching* (Vol. 1). Springer Science & Business Media.

Mezquita, Y., Alonso, R. S., Casado-Vara, R., Prieto, J., & Corchado, J. M. (2021). A review of k-nn algorithm based on classical and quantum machine learning. In *Distributed Computing and Artificial Intelligence, Special Sessions, 17th International Conference* (pp. 189-198). Springer International Publishing. 10.1007/978-3-030-53829-3_20

Millman, K. J., & Aivazis, M. (2011). Python for scientists and engineers. *Computing in Science & Engineering*, *13*(2), 9–12. doi:10.1109/MCSE.2011.36

Mishra, A., & Soni, S. (2023, March). Summarization of Unstructured Medical Data for Accurate Medical Prognosis—A Learning Approach. In *Advances in Cognitive Science and Communications: Selected Articles from the 5th International Conference on Communications and Cyber-Physical Engineering (ICCCE 2022), Hyderabad, India* (pp. 825-838). Singapore: Springer Nature Singapore.

Mohan, P., Neelakandan, S., Mardani, A., Maurya, S., Arulkumar, N., & Thangaraj, K. (2023). Eagle Strategy Arithmetic Optimisation Algorithm with Optimal Deep Convolutional Forest Based FinTech Application for Hyper-automation. *Enterprise Information Systems*. doi:10.108 0/17517575.2023.2188123

Mohapatra, S., Ahmed, N., & Alencar, P. (2019, December). KryptoOracle: A real-time cryptocurrency price prediction platform using twitter sentiments. *2019 IEEE international conference on big data*, 5544–5551.

Molin, S., & Jee, K. (2021). *Hands-On Data Analysis with Pandas: A Python data science handbook for data collection, wrangling, analysis, and visualization*. Packt Publishing Ltd.

Moruzzi, G. (2020). Python basics and the interactive mode. *Essential python for the physicist*, 1-39.

Moussaid, A., Zrira, N., Benmiloud, I., Farahat, Z., Karmoun, Y., Benzidia, Y., . . . Ngote, N. (2023, February). On the Implementation of a Post-Pandemic Deep Learning Algorithm Based on a Hybrid CT-Scan/X-ray Images Classification Applied to Pneumonia Categories. In Healthcare (Vol. 11, No. 5, p. 662). MDPI.

Mukhiya, S. K., & Ahmed, U. (2020). *Hands-On Exploratory Data Analysis with Python: Perform EDA techniques to understand, summarize, and investigate your data.* Packt Publishing Ltd.

Mulani, S. (2022). *Python Advanced.* Retrieved from Vectors in Python: https://www.digitalocean.com/community/tutorials/vectors-in-python

Najma, M., & Sekar, G. (2023, February). Novel CNN Approach (YOLO v5) to Detect Plant Diseases and Estimation of Nutritional Facts for Raw and Cooked Foods. In *Proceedings of Third International Conference on Sustainable Expert Systems: ICSES 2022* (pp. 305-329). Singapore: Springer Nature Singapore. 10.1007/978-981-19-7874-6_23

Nakamoto, S. (2008). Bitcoin: A peer-to-peer electronic cash system. *Decentralized Business Review, 21260.*

Navghare, N., Kedar, P., Sangamkar, P., & Mahajan, M. (2020). Python and OpenCV in automation of live Surveillance. In *Machine Learning and Information Processing* (pp. 235–243). Springer. doi:10.1007/978-981-15-1884-3_22

Neelakandan, S., Rene Beulah, J., Prathiba, L., Murthy, G. L. N., Fantin Irudaya Raj, E., & Arulkumar, N. (2022). Blockchain with deep learning-enabled secure healthcare data transmission and diagnostic model. *International Journal of Modeling, Simulation, and Scientific Computing, 13*(04), 2241006. doi:10.1142/S1793962322410069

NumPy Developers. (2008-2022). Retrieved from Numpy User Guide: https://numpy.org/doc/stable/user/whatisnumpy.html

Oliphant, T. E. (2006). *Guide to NumPy.* Academic Press.

Oliphant, T. E. (2007). Python for scientific computing. *Computing in Science & Engineering, 9*(3), 10–20. doi:10.1109/MCSE.2007.58

Opidi, A. (2019, October 8). *How to Create Your Own Cryptocurrency Using Python.* freeCodeCamp.org. https://www.freecodecamp.org/news/create-cryptocurrency-using-python/

Othman, J. (2023). Data structure uniqueness in Python programming language. *Enhancing Innovations in E-Learning for Future Preparation,* 68.

Parimala M, Lopez D, Senthilkumar N, (2011). A survey on density based clustring algorithms for mining large spatial databases. *Int J Adv Sci Technol.,* 31-59.

Patel, M. (2018). *Data Structure and Algorithm With C.* Educreation Publishing.

Perret, B., Chierchia, G., Cousty, J., Guimaraes, S. J. F., Kenmochi, Y., & Najman, L. (2019). Higra: Hierarchical graph analysis. *SoftwareX*, *10*, 100335. doi:10.1016/j.softx.2019.100335

Piatkowski, J. (2020). The Conditional Multiway Mapped Tree: Modeling and Analysis of Hierarchical Data Dependencies. *IEEE Access : Practical Innovations, Open Solutions*, *8*, 74083–74092. doi:10.1109/ACCESS.2020.2988358

Popescu, G. V., & Bîră, C. (2022, June). Python-Based Programming Framework for a Heterogeneous MapReduce Architecture. In *2022 14th International Conference on Communications (COMM)* (pp. 1-6). IEEE. 10.1109/COMM54429.2022.9817183

Rajaraman, A., & Ullman, J. D. (2012). *Mining of massive datasets*. Cambridge University Press.

Ram, A., Jalal, S., & Kumar, M. (2013). A density based algorithm for discovering density varied clusters in large spatial databases. *IJCA*, *3*(6), 1–4.

Rather, M. A., Agarwal, D., Bhat, T. A., Khan, I. A., Zafar, I., Kumar, S., Amin, A., Sundaray, J. K., & Qadri, T. (2023). Bioinformatics approaches and big data analytics opportunities in improving fisheries and aquaculture. *International Journal of Biological Macromolecules*, *233*, 123549. doi:10.1016/j.ijbiomac.2023.123549 PMID:36740117

Roopitha, C. H., & Pai, V. (2020, January). Survey On Media Access Control Protocols In Wireless Sensor Network. In *2020 Fourth International Conference on Inventive Systems and Control (ICISC)* (pp. 163-168). IEEE. 10.1109/ICISC47916.2020.9171085

S, R. A. (2023, March 31). *What is Blockchain Technology? How Does Blockchain Work?* [Updated]. Simplilearn.com. https://www.simplilearn.com/tutorials/blockchain-tutorial/blockchain-technology

Saabith, A. S., Fareez, M. M. M., & Vinothraj, T. (2019). Python current trend applications-an overview. *International Journal of Advance Engineering and Research Development*, *6*(10).

Salihu, A., Hoti, M., & Hoti, A. (2022, December). A Review of Performance and Complexity on Sorting Algorithms. In *2022 International Conference on Computing, Networking, Telecommunications & Engineering Sciences Applications (CoNTESA)* (pp. 45-50). IEEE. 10.1109/CoNTESA57046.2022.10011382

Sansano, E., Montoliu, R., & Belmonte Fernandez, O. (2020). A study of deep neural networks for human activity recognition. *Computational Intelligence*, *36*(3), 1113–1139. doi:10.1111/coin.12318

Saravanan, S., Lavanya, M., Srinivas, C. M. V., Arunadevi, M., & Arulkumar, N. (n.d.). Secure IoT Protocol for Implementing Classified Electroencephalogram (EEG) Signals in the Field of Smart Healthcare. In Cyber Security Applications for Industry 4.0 (pp. 111-129). Chapman and Hall/CRC.

Sarwar, S., Sirhindi, R., Aslam, L., Mustafa, G., Yousaf, M. M., & Jaffry, S. W. U. Q. (2020). Reinforcement learning based adaptive duty cycling in LR-WPANs. *IEEE Access : Practical Innovations, Open Solutions*, *8*, 161157–161174. doi:10.1109/ACCESS.2020.3021016

Schwarz, J. S., Chapman, C., & Feit, E. M. (2020). *An Overview of Python. Python for Marketing Research and Analytics*. Springer. doi:10.1007/978-3-030-49720-0

Shamim, G., & Rihan, M. (2023). Exploratory Data Analytics and PCA-Based Dimensionality Reduction for Improvement in Smart Meter Data Clustering. *Journal of the Institution of Electronics and Telecommunication Engineers*, 1–10. doi:10.1080/03772063.2023.2218317

Sharma, S., & Guleria, K. (2023). A Deep Learning based model for the Detection of Pneumonia from Chest X-Ray Images using VGG-16 and Neural Networks. *Procedia Computer Science*, *218*, 357–366. doi:10.1016/j.procs.2023.01.018

Sher, D. B. (2004). A simple implementation of a queue with a circularly linked list. *SIGCSE Bulletin*, *36*(3), 274–274. doi:10.1145/1026487.1008112

Shrivas, M. K., Hiran, K. K., Bhansali, A., & Doshi, R. (2022). *Advancements in Quantum Blockchain With Real-Time Applications*. IGI Global.

Soni, G., & Selvaradjou, K. (2020). Performance evaluation of wireless sensor network MAC protocols with early sleep problem. *International Journal of Communication Networks and Distributed Systems*, *25*(2), 123–144. doi:10.1504/IJCNDS.2020.108875

Souravlas, S., Anastasiadou, S., & Katsavounis, S. (2021). A survey on the recent advances of deep community detection. *Applied Sciences (Basel, Switzerland)*, *11*(16), 7179. doi:10.3390/app11167179

Stančin, I., & Jović, A. (2019, May). An overview and comparison of free Python libraries for data mining and big data analysis. In *2019 42nd International convention on information and communication technology, electronics and microelectronics (MIPRO)* (pp. 977-982). IEEE. 10.23919/MIPRO.2019.8757088

Stefan van der Walt, S. C. (2021). The NumPy Array: A Structure for Efficient Numerical Computation. *IEEE, 13*(2), 22-30.

Streib, J. T., Soma, T., Streib, J. T., & Soma, T. (2017). Stacks and Queues Using References. *Guide to Data Structures: A Concise Introduction Using Java*, 173-198.

Subasi, A. (2020). *Practical machine learning for data analysis using python*. Academic Press.

Su, Y., Lu, X., Zhao, Y., Huang, L., & Du, X. (2019). Cooperative communications with relay selection based on deep reinforcement learning in wireless sensor networks. *IEEE Sensors Journal*, *19*(20), 9561–9569. doi:10.1109/JSEN.2019.2925719

Thiagarajan, R. (2020). Energy consumption and network connectivity based on Novel-LEACH-POS protocol networks. *Computer Communications*, *149*, 90–98. doi:10.1016/j.comcom.2019.10.006

Üçoluk, G., Kalkan, S., Üçoluk, G., & Kalkan, S. (2012). Organizing Data. *Introduction to Programming Concepts with Case Studies in Python*, 165-194.

Unpingco, J. (2021). *Python Programming for Data Analysis*. Springer. doi:10.1007/978-3-030-68952-0

Upadhye, S., Neelakandan, S., Thangaraj, K., Babu, D. V., Arulkumar, N., & Qureshi, K. (2023). Modeling of Real Time Traffic Flow Monitoring System Using Deep Learning and Unmanned Aerial Vehicles. *Journal of Mobile Multimedia*, 477-496.

Wiener, R. (2022). Queues and Lists. In *Generic Data Structures and Algorithms in Go: An Applied Approach Using Concurrency, Genericity and Heuristics* (pp. 187–236). Apress. doi:10.1007/978-1-4842-8191-8_6

Wu, X., Zhu, X., & Wu, G. Q. (2014). Data mining with big data. *IEEE Transactions on Knowledge and Data Engineering*, *26*(1), 97–107. doi:10.1109/TKDE.2013.109

Yalçın, O. G. (2021). Complementary Libraries to TensorFlow 2.x. *Applied Neural Networks with TensorFlow 2: API Oriented Deep Learning with Python*, 81-94.

Yang, Y., & Li, X. (2020, October). Design and Implementation of Sliding Window with Circular Linked List for Dynamic Data Flow. In *Proceedings of the 4th International Conference on Computer Science and Application Engineering* (pp. 1-5). 10.1145/3424978.3425152

Yogeshwaran, S., Kaur, M. J., & Maheshwari, P. (2019, April). Project based learning: predicting bitcoin prices using deep learning. In *2019 IEEE Global Engineering Education Conference (EDUCON)* (pp. 1449-1454). IEEE.

Z. (2023, February 22). *Top 10 Useful Python Packages to Pull Cryptocurrency Data Seamlessly*. Analytics Insight. https://www.analyticsinsight.net/top-10-useful-python-packages-to-pull-cryptocurrency-data-seamlessly/

Zeng, W., Shang, M. S., Zhang, Q. M., Lü, L., & Zhou, T. (2010). Can Dissimilar Users Contribute to Accuracy and Diversity of Personalized Recommendation. *International Journal of Modern Physics C*, *21*(10), 1217–1227. doi:10.1142/S0129183110015786

Zhang, H. L., Han, B. T., Xu, J. C., & Feng, Y. (2013). Preparation of the public bus schedule based on fcfs. In *Proceedings of 20th International Conference on Industrial Engineering and Engineering Management: Theory and Apply of Industrial Engineering* (pp. 1021-1029). Springer Berlin Heidelberg. 10.1007/978-3-642-40063-6_100

Zheng, Z., Zhu, J., & Lyu, M. R. (2013). Service-generated Big Data and Big Data-as-a-Service: An Overview. *Proc. IEEE BigData*, 403-410. 10.1109/BigData.Congress.2013.60

Zhou, H. Y., Lu, C., Chen, C., Yang, S., & Yu, Y. (2023). A Unified Visual Information Preservation Framework for Self-supervised Pre-training in Medical Image Analysis. *IEEE Transactions on Pattern Analysis and Machine Intelligence*, 1–16. doi:10.1109/TPAMI.2023.3234002 PMID:37018263

About the Contributors

Mohammad Gouse Galety received his PhD in Computer Science in 2012. His research interests span both computer science and information science. Dr Mohammad Gouse Galety (co-) authorizes more than 50 journal papers and publications in international conference proceedings indexed by Springer, Scopus, two patents, and five books. Since 1999, he has served in different national and international organizations like Sree Vidyanikethan Degree College, Tirupati, India; Emeralds Degree College, Tirupati, India; Brindavan College of Engineering, Bangalore, India; Kuwait Educational Center, Kuwait; Ambo University, Ambo, Ethiopia, Debre Berhan University, Debre Berhan, Ethiopia, Lebanese French University, Erbil, Iraq and Catholic University in Erbil, Erbil, Iraq. He is a professor in the Computer Science Department at Samarkand International University of Technology, Samarkand, Uzbekistan. In addition, he teaches several computer sciences and information technology/science engineering to undergraduate and postgraduate students. His research interests cover several aspects of computer science, mainly web mining, IoT, and Networks. He is a Fellow of the IEEE. As of 2020, Google Scholar reports over 250 citations to his work.

Arul Kumar Natarajan is currently working as an Assistant Professor at Christ (Deemed to be University), Bangalore, INDIA. He received a Ph.D. degree in Computer Science from Bharathidasan University, India, in 2019. His research areas are Computer Networks, Cyber Security, and the Internet of Things (IoT). He published more than 30 research papers in both journals and conferences. He published 4 patents in physics, communication, and computer science. He has chaired many technical sessions and delivered more than 15 invited talks at the national and international levels. He has completed over 33 certifications from IBM, Google, Amazon, etc. He passed the CCNA: Routing and Switching Exam in 2017. Additionally, he also passed the Networking Fundamentals in the year 2017 exam from Microsoft.

A. V. Sriharsha completed his B.Tech from AU, M.Tech from Sathyabama University, and Ph.D. from SV University and SCSVMV University. He holds Honorary Diploma in Computer Programming and Applications moderated by National Computing Center, United Kingdom. He is a member and designated as a chartered engineer by the Institution of Engineers India, Calcutta. Member of ISOC, "The Internet Society", Life Member in IAENG. He has been in IT, IT-enabled services, and Education for about 25+ years. Have 7 years of industrial experience on strategic servers and 19 years of teaching and research. Around 40+ articles of research have been published in journals and conferences of national and international repute where some of them are indexed in Scopus and ESCI. His research interests are data science, privacy-preserving data mining, differential privacy and machine learning, big data, software architectures, and robotics. Freelance programming and consulting for industrial applications, web service frameworks, and cyber security solutions are the regular track of his occupation while building research models adaptable for industry and academia. His academic profile fairs with funded projects and seminar grants from AICTE, ISRO, etc.. He has 3 (three) patents filed, 1 (one) design patent in the amendment, and 1 (one) copyright to his credits.

* * *

Keerthana Devi A. is pursuing MSc in Data Science at Coimbatore Institute of Technology, Coimbatore.

Tesfaye Fufa graduated from Jima University with a Bachelor's Degree in Information Technology in July 2012 and received a Master of Science in Software Engineering from Adama Science and Technology University. Previously, he worked from 2013–2020 as a lecturer at Debre Berhan University, Ethiopia. He is currently working as an Associate Researcher II, Satellite Operator and Development at the Space Science and Geospatial Institute. His research interests include artificial intelligence, network security, cloud computing, big data, image processing, and data science. He has written more than four journal papers.

Pradeepa Ganesan holds her MCA degree in 2003 from Madurai Kamaraj University, Tamilnadu, India, and her M.Phil degree in 2006 from Bharathidasan University, Tamilnadu, India. She has 18 years of teaching experience. Her research interests include cybersecurity, machine learning, and deep learning.

Agrata Gupta is currently working as a Data Science Research scholar at Christ (Deemed to be University), Bengaluru, India. She completed her master's degree in Data Analytics from Christ (Deemed to be University), Bengaluru, India, in 2022 and her bachelor's degree in Statistics (Hons.) from the University of Delhi, India, in 2020. Her research areas are Blockchain technology, Cryptocurrency and Security.

She has completed nine certifications in the field of Statistics and Data Science from different IITs and from other institutions. She also works as a Financial Analyst in a Las Vegas-based software development company, AXEL.

Sunitha Gurram is currently working as Professor at School of Computing, Mohan Babu University, Tirupati, India. Her research interests include Data Mining, Spatio-Temporal Analytics, Machine Learning and Artificial Intelligence. She has 13 patents and 6 books published to her credit. She has published around 70 papers in reputed journals and conferences. She has been serving as reviewer for several journals; and has served on the program committees and co-chaired for various international conferences.

Garamu Iticha graduated from Jima University with a Bachelor's Degree in Information Technology in July 2012 and received a Master of Science in Software Engineering from Adama Science and Technology University. He is currently a lecturer at Debre Markos University, Ethiopia. His research interests include artificial intelligence, cloud computing, networking, and data science. He has written more than two journal papers.

Justin Rajasekaran M. is a Lecturer in the Department of Information Technology at University of Technology and Applied Sciences, Shinas, Sultanate of Oman where he has been since 2011. His research interests span both computer networking and software engineering and quality assurance. Much of his work has been on improving the understanding, design, and performance of computer application systems. He also involved in developing course curriculum in the area of Data Science and Artificial Intelligence.

Sujithra M. is currently working as an Assistant Professor, Department of Computing -Data Science at Coimbatore Institute of Technology, Coimbatore, India. Dr.M.Sujithra received the MCA degree from Bharathiyar University and the BSC degree in Computer Science from Bharathiyar University and also received the Ph.D. degree in computer science from Avinashilingam University, India. She has published more than 85 Research articles in International Journals/Conference proceedings .Moreover, she has published 3 books, few book chapters and 1 patent under a reputed publishers. Her research interests include the cloud computing, Data Security, Mobile Application Development, Machine Learning and Data Analytics and Visualization.

Rajasrkaran Selvaraju has 22+ years of teaching and research experience in the fields of Computer Science and Information Technology. Presently, he is working at the University of Technology and Applied Sciences - Ibri in the Sultanate of Oman. He has acted as a resource person for various international conferences, webinars and workshops. Also, serving as a reviewer for many reputed international journals and conferences. His area of interest is not limited to Data Science, Artificial Intelligence and Machine Learning, Internet of Things and Software Engineering.

Mastan Vali Shaik has 20+ years of teaching and research experience in the fields of Computer Science and Information Technology. Presently, he is working at the University of Technology and Applied Sciences - Ibri in the Sultanate of Oman. He has acted as a resource person for various international conferences, webinars and workshops. Also, serving as a reviewer for many reputed international journals and conferences. His area of interest is not limited to Data Science, Artificial Intelligence and Machine Learning, Internet of Things and Software Engineering.

Olimjon Yalgashev works at Samarkand International University of Technology at Department of Computer Science. He received his doctorate in France, at the Technological University of Belfort-Montbéliard. He is the author of many international and local scientific publications.

Index

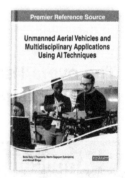

  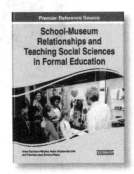 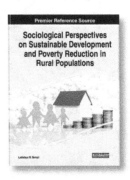